Ajax for Web Application Developers

Ajax for Web Application Developers

Kris Hadlock

DEVELOPER'S
LIBRARY

Sams Publishing, 800 East 96th Street, Indianapolis, Indiana 46240 USA

❖

This book is dedicated to my wife, Lisa, who inadvertently introduced me to the world of web design and development and who also stood by me through endless hours of neglect while I wrote this book. I also dedicate this book to my late grandparents, who selflessly got me where I am today by helping me through school.

❖

Contents at a Glance

V: Interaction

VI: Touches

Table of Contents

About the Author

Kris Hadlock has been a contract web developer and designer since 1996. He is a featured columnist and writer for InformIT and numerous web design magazines. He is also the founder of Studio Sedition, a web application development firm, and is the cofounder of 33Inc, the company responsible for DashboardHQ. He maintains a blog called *Designing with Code*, which focuses on web application development from a design perspective and often features useful code snippets to help enhance web applications. You can find all of the above and more about Kris on his website at www.krishadlock.com.

Acknowledgments

I want to thank Robert Hoekman, Jr., my 33Inc partner who introduced me to tech writing and passionately preaches interaction design and just good common sense. I also gratefully thank Nikki McDonald, my InformIT editor, for introducing me to Sams Publishing.

We Want to Hear from You!

As the reader of this book, *you* are our most important critic and commentator. We value your opinion and want to know what we're doing right, what we could do better, what areas you'd like to see us publish in, and any other words of wisdom you're willing to pass our way.

You can email or write me directly to let me know what you did or didn't like about this book—as well as what we can do to make our books stronger.

Please note that I cannot help you with technical problems related to the topic of this book, and that due to the high volume of mail I receive, I might not be able to reply to every message.

When you write, please be sure to include this book's title and author as well as your name and phone or email address. I will carefully review your comments and share them with the author and editors who worked on the book.

Email: webdev@samspublishing.com

Mail: Mark Taber
           Associate Publisher
           Sams Publishing
           800 East 96th Street
           Indianapolis, IN 46240 USA

Reader Services

Visit our website and register this book at www.samspublishing.com/register for convenient access to any updates, downloads, or errata that might be available for this book.

Introduction

Certainly, something must have attracted you to this book. Maybe you are a web developer who wants to learn how to better integrate Ajax into your work. Maybe you want a handy reference to keep by your desk as you create tomorrow's newest technology with Ajax. Well, whatever the case, we're glad you made it.

This book covers just about everything about Ajax and how to integrate it with your web applications. This book is meant for web professionals with intermediate to advanced experience looking to learn new techniques and bring their web applications to the next level.

The first part, "Getting Started," is all about the basics of Ajax. It includes information on how to make requests in Chapter 2, how to receive responses as both XML and JSON in Chapter 3 and how to handle the rendering of the data using CSS and XHTML in Chapter 4. Part II, "Creating and Using the JavaScript Engine," covers how to create an Ajax engine with JavaScript. In order to get some background on object-oriented JavaScript we will start by learning how to create objects with JavaScript in Chapter 5. Once we understand how to create objects we will then focus on creating the engine in Chapter 6. With the knowledge of how to create the engine we will see how it can be used in a real world web application in Chapter 7. Chapter 8 will focus on all of the debugging methods that are available for JavaScript and how to use them to make your life easier. With a better understanding of the Ajax engine we will see how to extend it by adding additional JavaScript objects in Chapter 9.

Part III, "Creating Reusable Components," covers how to create numerous Ajax-enabled components for rendering the response data that is received from the server. The different components that are covered are an accordion, a tree view, a client-side validator, and a data grid. Part IV, "Ajax Patterns," starts with Chapter 14 where we will cover using the Singleton pattern with specific JavaScript objects and using them in our Ajax-enabled web applications. Chapter 15 is an explanation of how to use the Model View Controller pattern to structure our JavaScript objects. The Observer pattern is then covered in Chapter 16 where we will cover how to create an object to cover error management. The Data Reflection and Multi-User patterns are covered in Chapter 17 in order to provide an understanding of how to create interactive web applications that allow people to share web spaces and see each other's updates as they occur. Chapters 18 and 19 are both chapters that will cover different ways or best practices for interactions and usability in our web applications. Part VI, "Server-Side Interaction," will cover the use of various languages to connect with server-side technologies and even the database. The last part of the book, "Finishing Touches," is as it says, an explanation of how to add some finishing touches to your Ajax-enabled web applications, such as security and some best practices.

An Introduction to the Book Samples

As I mentioned earlier, the goal of this book is to teach you how to create reusable Ajax applications with object-oriented JavaScript. Instead of creating individual samples with no context, I have decided to create individual samples that are usable on their own and as a part of larger web applications as a whole. Therefore, we will learn how to create an Ajax engine, components, and connections to databases as individual chapter samples, but we will also combine these individual pieces into a larger application that will be continually built throughout the book. The final application will consist of all the individual pieces tied together by Ajax to create an internal web mail application that can be used in any user-based application, such as a community-based web application, for example.

The samples that are used in each chapter and ultimately for the final application can be found at samspublishing.com. Within each chapter, the samples that correlate to the final application will be denoted with listing headings that identify each code snippet. Not only will you learn how to create and use your own reusable Ajax components, but you also will learn how to utilize their reusability by connecting them to any future Ajax applications that you build.

Getting Started

1

Introduction to Ajax

Thanks for picking up a copy of my book. My goal for this book is not only to explore the technologies that define Ajax and how they come together to create powerful client-side interactions, but also to teach you how to create practical examples that can be reused in any other Ajax-enabled web application. These examples will be completely object oriented for the scalability and flexibility that is required in enterprise-level applications. This book consists of chapters that will guide you through individual Ajax examples, such as how to create a reusable Ajax engine, how to create Ajax-enabled components, and my personal favorite, how to connect to server-side languages with Ajax. Ajax requires supporting technologies such as XML (Extensible Markup Language) and JSON (JavaScript Object Notation) for the data-interchange and JavaScript and CSS (Cascading Style Sheets) for the data rendering and display; therefore we will be focusing on these technologies before we dive into the more complex world of Ajax. With the knowledge of front-end and back-end integration, you will learn how each example can be combined into a functional application; after all, Ajax does require knowledge of both since they become so tightly integrated. We will also cover common programming patterns that can be applied to Ajax to make development much quicker and cleaner. From there we will learn some best practices for securing our Ajax applications and creating intuitive user interactions, as well as message handling and other client-side data displays.

Ajax is an acronym for Asynchronous JavaScript and XML, and at its heart is the `XMLHTTPRequest` object, which is part of the XML DOM (Document Object Model). Since it is such a critical part of Ajax, let's take a brief look at the XML DOM to see how it fits in with the subjects that we will be covering.

The XML DOM

The XML Document Object Model defines a standard way for accessing and manipulating XML documents. The DOM enables JavaScript to completely access XML or XHTML documents by providing access to the elements which define the structure. The accessibility is possible through a set of intrinsic JavaScript objects that focus on DOM manipulation. This model is something that we will be using throughout the rest of this book because it is required to parse the responses that we receive from the server side when we create an `XMLHTTPRequest` (XHR). As mentioned earlier, the XHR is the core of the Ajax model and without it the model would not exist. This is the piece of the Ajax puzzle that has created the recent buzz because it allows HTTP requests to be made to the server without refreshing the browser.

Though there has been a lot of recent hype surrounding Ajax, it has existed for quite some time. Microsoft originally released the XHR object in 1999 with Windows IE 5 as an ActiveX object available through the use of JavaScript and VBScript. It is now supported by Mozilla, Firefox, Safari, Opera, and Netscape by using a native JavaScript object. This native JavaScript object will also be supported with the release of Windows Internet Explorer (IE) 7. Although the technologies have been in existence and used by some developers in the past, it has only recently gained large popularity. The cause of its recent popularity is largely based on the support that is offered by browsers because not many browsers had the support necessary for powerful DHTML, XHTML, CSS, and XMLHTTPRequests until more recent versions. Now it is possible to create such interactions with successful cross-browser and cross-platform results. The adoption of better support for these technologies has brought Ajax to the forefront and it is once again an exciting time to be a web developer. Small, independent operations are regularly emerging with applications that rival the desktop by providing powerful functionality while immensely improving the user experience.

Measuring the Benefits

Ajax is a powerful collection of languages that, when brought together, create extremely intuitive user interfaces and client-side interactions. Although this is true, there are many developers who get so excited by the hype surrounding it that they simply throw the code into their applications without measuring the benefits of using it beforehand. Not every web application has a need for Ajax, but there are many parts of an application that can be enhanced by utilizing its benefits. In this book, we will cover usability patterns that will handle feedback, server-side form validation before we even submit the form, and Ajax-enabled components that can enhance sections of our web applications without overdoing it. Ajax is also great to use if you would like to make a server-side connection and possibly a database interaction without refreshing the browser. This is what makes Ajax so powerful because it allows us to interact with the server, receive HTTP status codes, save data to a database, and determine what to present to the user without ever refreshing the page. This request/response pattern can continually persist as a desktop application does, but Ajax-enabled web applications are, well, on the Web—accessible by anyone with a connection, without any downloads or shipping costs for delivering large fancy boxes. The Web is the new desktop, and we are on the verge of a major software shift that we can actively participate in as the pioneers of on-demand information.

Ajax can be a valuable connection between the interface and back-end logic, allowing the back end to be robust and powerful with a simple yet intuitive interface that provides on-demand feedback to users. It also provides ways to exchange data with server-side languages and store it in databases without disconnecting the user from the application like standard applications do when refreshing the browser window. After reading this book, you will have the information needed to create fully functional Ajax applications.

2

The Request

Now that you have some background on Ajax and a brief overview of what we will set out to accomplish with the sample project, you are ready to assemble the request. This chapter will introduce the inner workings of the request and provide you with the knowledge to not only create the request object, but to also understand how to approach different request models.

An In-Depth Look at XMLHttpRequest

The XHR (`XMLHttpRequest`) object is the core of the Ajax engine. It is the object that enables a page to get data from (using the `GET` method) or post data to (using the `POST` method) the server as a background request, which means that it does not refresh the browser during this process. As we covered in Chapter 1, "Introduction to Ajax," the hype surrounding Ajax has been based on this object and the fact that the interaction model it creates is more intuitive than a standard HTTP (Hypertext Transport Protocol) request. This is because changes happen on demand when the user makes them, and allow web applications to feel more like desktop applications. The XHR eliminates the need to wait on the server to respond with a new page for each request and allows users to continue to interact with the page while the requests are made in the background. This is a key factor in maintaining an intuitive user experience: Users should never be aware of the process; rather, they should be focused on the task at hand, which is using your service. The on-demand nature of the XHR is extremely beneficial when dealing with web applications where users are trying to accomplish tasks because the standard HTTP request is better suited for presentation-type websites.

Aside from the background data processing, the `GET` and `POST` methods of the XHR object work the same as a standard HTTP request. Using either the `POST` or the `GET` method allows you to make a request for data from the server and receive a response in any standardized format. The most common formats in which to receive a response are XML, JSON (JavaScript Object Notation), and text. We will cover all formats in detail in Chapter 3, "The Response." `POST` is specifically useful when sending data that is larger than 512 bytes (an amount that the `GET` method cannot handle). After a response is received, the application can be populated with new data from the server by using the DOM with DHTML, which is a combination of XHTML, JavaScript, and CSS.

All Ajax requests start with a client-side interaction that is typically managed by JavaScript. JavaScript creates the XHR object and makes an HTTP request to the server. What happens from here can take on many different forms. Let's take a look at three of the most common request models and their processes.

A Standard XHR

If you were to break down an Ajax request to its bare functionality, this is what you would be left with. In this scenario, a static XML, JSON, or text file residing on the same domain is requested by the XHR object through the GET method. It is then returned by the server to be handled by the client-side code that requested it. Take a look at Figure 2.1 to see the flow of a standard Ajax model.

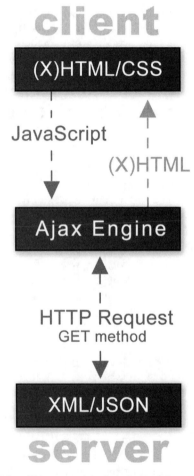

Figure 2.1   This request is the simplest form of the Ajax request/response model, involving only a static XML, JSON, or text file residing on the same domain.

This type of request can be beneficial if a web-savvy client or a developer is updating the requested file on the server, which is typically not the case, especially with large-scale applications. If this model is not going to meet your needs, the next approach has what this model is missing most: a database.

A Database-Enabled XHR

Learning how to create a database-enabled XHR is like making your first database interaction. It opens a whole new world of possibilities and is not as complicated as you would think; it is trivial compared to the complex functionality that you can achieve with database-integrated Ajax. To use this model, we would start with a request to a server-side language. The server-side language would query the database, based on what was requested, via custom methods that we would write to handle specific database interactions. After the data has been received by the server-side language, it can be returned to the XHR that originally requested it as XML, JSON, or text and handled by the client-side code. This request allows users to retrieve custom data based on the requests that they make. See Figure 2.2 to get a better understanding of the flow in a database-enabled XHR.

Although this request model is quite a bit more powerful than a standard request, you might want even more control. The next model will provide you with the ability to post data to the database and receive data based on the request, or simply receive a Boolean for a successful database `INSERT`, all without refreshing the page.

Sending Data to a Database-Enabled XHR

Sending data to the database starts with an XHR `GET` or `POST` to a server-side language/engine. After the server receives the request, it parses the XML or simple key/value pair sent by the XHR and updates the database accordingly. This request model updates the database based on user interaction, without ever refreshing the browser. This is a great way to replicate the Save button in a desktop application. We will use this model in the sample by saving sent emails to the database to allow the user to retrieve it at a later time. Figure 2.3 shows the flow of this request type with optional response data, which we will cover in Chapter 3.

Sending data to a database-enabled XHR provides the most power out of the request models mentioned in this chapter. Essentially, it provides us with full database control through the XHR. There are many different situations in which you will want to post data to the server with the XHR. For example, you might want to password-protect your XHR by sending a password to the server, and then authenticate it before querying the database. Or, you might want to insert or update records in a database, or select records based on the request.

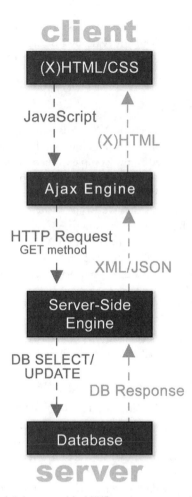

Figure 2.2   A database-enabled XHR opens up a world of possibilities
and will take your Ajax applications to a whole new level.

Server-side interaction with Ajax allows us to create on-demand database updates, just as
a desktop application would save our progress. There is so much to cover on the server
side of a request, which is why I dedicated an entire section of the book to this very
topic in Part V, "Server-Side Interaction." But first, it is important that there be a solid
understanding of the object and its capabilities before diving into complex code.

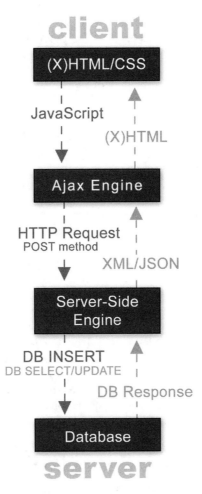

Figure 2.3   A database-enabled XHR **POST** allows you to combine the
XHR with complete database access.

Creating the Object

With a better understanding of the XHR and different request models, we can now
focus on creating the object. Creating the request object is trivial in comparison to the
power that is unleashed when applying it to a project.

To create the request object, you must check to see if the browser uses the XHR or
the ActiveX object. The primary difference between the objects is the browsers that use
them. Windows Internet Explorer (IE) 5 and above use the ActiveX object, whereas
Mozilla, Firefox, Netscape, Opera, and Safari use the native JavaScript XHR object. The

second difference is the way in which we create each object: Windows IE requires the name of the object to be passed as a parameter to the ActiveX constructor, whereas the other browsers provide us with the native JavaScript object, which only we need to instantiate:

```
function makeRequest(url)
{
    if(window.XMLHttpRequest)
    {
        request = new XMLHttpRequest();
    }
    else if(window.ActiveXObject)
    {
        request = new ActiveXObject("Msxml2.XMLHTTP");
    }

    sendRequest(url);
}
```

As you can see from the code sample, the object creation is really a very simple task. We create a method named `makeRequest` to handle—you guessed it—making the request and to decipher what type of object the browser uses by creating a condition that checks for the native XHR object. If this object is not available, we check for the `ActiveXObject`. After the correct object type has been identified for the current browser, the correct object is instantiated and a request object is created. This object can now be used to access all the properties and methods listed in Tables 2.1 and 2.2, which are available to the XHR object.

Table 2.1   **A List of XHR Properties and Corresponding Definitions**

Properties	Definitions
`onreadystatechange`	An event handler that fires when the state of the request object changes.
`readyState`	Returns number values that indicate the current state of the object. These values are listed in Table 2.3.
`responseText`	String version of the response from the server.
`responseXML`	DOM-compatible document object of the response from the server.
`status`	Status code of the response from the server.
`statusText`	A status message returned as a string.

Table 2.2   **A List of XHR Methods and Corresponding Definitions**

Methods	Definitions
`Abort()`	Cancels the current HTTP request.
`getAllResponseHeaders()`	Retrieves the values of all the HTTP headers.
`getResponseHeader("label")`	Retrieves the value of a specified HTTP header from the response body.
`Open("method", "URL"[, asyncFlag [, "userName"[, "password"]]])`	Initializes an MSXML2.XMLHTTP or Microsoft.XMLHTTP request, and specifies the method, URL, and authentication information for the request.
`Send(content)`	Sends an HTTP request to the server and receives a response.
`SetRequestHeader("label", "value")`	Specifies the value of an HTTP header based on the label.

These two tables might look like they have only a small number of options, but as you will find in the following chapters, they pack a lot of power when used with back-end code, a database, and a dynamic front end.

Asynchronous Data Transfers

If you are new to data transfers and you are not exactly sure what the term *asynchronous data transfers* actually means, don't worry—you are probably unaware of the fact that you already understand them and have used them while developing in other languages. This type of transaction is most typical of programming languages, and is a very important part of the XHR and, ultimately, all enterprise Ajax applications. This section will demystify asynchronous data transfers before we begin to dive into coding the object-oriented Ajax engine.

Asynchronous data transfers are a type of two-way communication that occurs with a time delay, allowing data to respond on its own time, when it is available. In other words, you can make a request to the server, continue to process other data, and receive a response at the server's leisure, thus making web applications very flexible. Asynchronous is the default nature of the request/response model of the XHR in an Ajax engine. This means that the request/response data is not transferring at predetermined or regular set intervals. For example, you can make an HTTP request to a server and continue to process other client-side interactions while waiting for the response in the background. This can all be happening while the user is working on other tasks or performing other interactions—completely unaware of the data processing in the background. This means that you can make calls to a server-side language to retrieve data from a database, and return that data as XML, JSON, or text. You can also send data to a server-side language to be stored in a database, or you can simply load a static XML, JSON, or text file to dynamically populate pages of your website without refreshing the page or interrupting user interaction on the front end.

In order to process this request, we must first call two XHR methods: `open` and `send`. The `open` method of the XHR object takes three parameters. The first is a string that represents the method in which the request is to be sent. This method value can be `GET`, `POST`, or `PUT`. The second parameter is the URL that is being requested in the form of a string, which can be XML, JSON, a text file, or a server-side language that returns any of these formats. The last parameter, which happens to be the one that we are focusing on, is a Boolean that has a default value of `true` for asynchronous and `false` for synchronous. The `send` method follows `open` and is the actual method that sends the HTTP request and receives a response in the format that you specify. This method takes one string parameter, which can be XML or a simple key/value pair to be sent as a `POST`. Here is an example of the `open` and `send` methods as they would be used in a simple Ajax request:

```
request.open("method", "URL", true);
request.send(null);
```

Asynchronous data transfers can prove to be complicated to manage in large-scale situations, but they are far more scalable and usable than synchronous data transfers. In order to serve complex audiences with varying skills and experience, developers need to create complex applications that can handle many tasks. Asynchronous interactions can supply this audience with the possibilities of multitasking and completing tasks efficiently, without the hassle of waiting for server responses. Synchronous transactions wait for a response to one request before another can be made. In a robust web application, this type of transaction could easily freeze up the page while the server is processing the requests in a queue, one after the other. Ultimately, this would be unusable and could easily turn users away.

The Ready State

After the XHR object has been created and the request has been made, we need a way to know when the response has been received. This is where the `onreadystatechange` event handler is used. The `onreadystatechange` event handler fires when the state of the request object changes and allows us to set a callback method to be triggered. After this callback method is triggered, it is up to us to handle the response. The custom callback method named `onResponse`, shown in Listing 2.1, will be covered in Chapter 3, where we will cover all aspects of an Ajax response.

Listing 2.1   **Sending a Request**

```
function sendRequest(url)
{
    request.onreadystatechange = onResponse;
    request.open("GET", url, true);
    request.send(null);
}
```

Listing 2.2 is a custom method named `checkReadyState` that checks the ready state of the XHR object and handles each state in a separate branch based on the number that the current state equals. This custom method will be called from the `onResponse` method to determine the ready state of the XHR before it handles parsing the response object.

Listing 2.2   **Determining the `readyState` Value**

```
function checkReadyState(obj, id)
{
    switch(obj.readyState)
    {
        case 0:
            document.getElementById(id).innerHTML = "Sending Request...";
            break;
        case 1:
            document.getElementById(id).innerHTML = "Loading Response...";
            break;
        case 2:
            document.getElementById(id).innerHTML = "Response Loaded...";
            break;
        case 3:
            document.getElementById(id).innerHTML = "Response Ready...";
            break;
        case 4:
            document.getElementById(id).innerHTML = "";
            return (obj.status == 200);
            break;
        default:
            document.getElementById(id).innerHTML = "An unexpected error has
            occurred.";
    }}
```

Notice that there are two parameters in this method. The first parameter; named `obj`, is the XHR object that made the request and is now being used to check the `readyState` status of the response from the server. The different numbers that are returned in relation to the `readyState` are listed in Table 2.3 with a definition for each.

Table 2.3   **A List of the readyState Values, with Translations and Definitions for Each**

readyState Values	Translations	Definitions
0	Uninitialized	The object is not initialized with data.
1	Loading	The object is loading its data.
2	Loaded	The object has finished loading its data.
3	Interactive	The user can interact with the object even though it is not fully loaded.
4	Complete	The object is completely initialized.

The second parameter, named `id`, is the ID of an HTML element that can be located in the client-side XHTML. This ID is located by using JavaScript's `document.getElementById` method to find the specified element by id in the current page using the DOM. After this element is located, the `innerHTML` property for the element is set to a custom message that we choose to display in relation to each ready state. This is an excellent way to provide feedback to the user regarding the status of a request. As you can see from Listing 2.2, we are adding a text message that essentially represents a loading message that is specific to each state of the request to present a frame of reference to the user. After the `readyState` reaches a value of 4, this means that it has completed loading. When it has completed loading, the `checkReadyState` method returns whether the status of the response is equal to 200. An HTTP status of 200 means that the request has succeeded and that it is ready to be handled. This is one of many HTTP status codes that can be received and should be properly handled by the Ajax engine. The next section covers more status codes and supplies examples of typical uses for both HTTP status codes and headers.

HTTP Status Codes and Headers

The request status of the Ajax object is equivalent to the HTTP status of the file that is being requested. HTTP status codes represent the response from the server based on the status of the file that is being requested. There are five categories of status codes available for the HTTP request and the XHR:

- Informational: 1xx
- Successful: 2xx
- Redirection: 3xx
- Client Error: 4xx
- Server Error: 5xx

When a status code is received through the Web, it is represented as a number, such as when you try to go to a website and get a 404 error. This is not an arbitrary number; it is representative of the file status and in this case represents the "File Not Found" response. All status codes must be handled appropriately by the server and, ultimately, the requesting Ajax engine. When making a request with the XHR object, these status codes need to be handled by the script that is receiving the response. This means that the developer is responsible for providing feedback to the user based on the response and should do so to make a more usable web application. Typically, if there is a successful response, new data is rendered on the client side as XHTML; otherwise, a message of some sort can be displayed to inform the user that the transaction was not successful and what went wrong. Error handling is not the most exciting thing to code, but it is essential to creating a usable application and can give you skills that you would not gain in other coding situations. We will learn more about error handling in Part II, "Creating and Using the JavaScript Engine," where we will create a custom object to handle all the available HTTP status codes, and respond with useful messages for debugging and ultimately providing users with feedback. To learn more about HTTP status codes, a full list of definitions can be found on the W3C (World Wide Web Consortium) website at http://www.w3.org/Protocols/rfc2616/rfc2616-sec10.html.

The XHR object can also get or set HTTP headers on the server. Headers can be used to retrieve specific data about a requested file or information regarding specific server attributes. An example of how this data can be useful is in determining how to parse a requested file based on the content-type header. For instance, if the content type is text/XML, we know that we can parse it using the XML DOM and create appropriate methods for handling different types of content. There are many other determinations that can be made based on HTTP headers.

There are three native header methods in the XHR object: `setRequestHeader`, `getResponseHeader`, and `getAllResponseHeaders`. The `setRequestHeader` method enables you to set a header's value by specifying the header by label and passing a value. The syntax for this method is

```
request.setRequestHeader("label", "value");
```

By setting the request header, you are adding, deleting, overriding, or replacing the default value of the HTTP request header on the server during that particular request. If a header is not well formed, it is not used and an error occurs, which stops the header from being set.

In addition to setting headers, the XHR enables you to retrieve headers during the response as well. There are two methods that can be used to retrieve headers: `getResponseHeader` and `getAllResponseHeaders`. The `getResponseHeader` method takes a header label as the parameter, which is used to get specific data from that header. Here is a sample of each method:

```
request.getResponseHeader("label");
request.getAllResponseHeaders();
```

The `getAllResponseHeaders` method returns all the headers from the response, which varies depending on the server that is responding. Figure 2.4 shows a sample of all the response headers available for an XML file on the Windows server where my website is currently running.

Figure 2.4   A list of available HTTP headers that can be retrieved by the `getAllResponseHeaders` method.

This was just an introduction to how useful headers can be in your web applications. There are hundreds of uses that you will find that are out of the scope of this book. To learn more about HTTP headers, a full list can be found on the W3C website at http://www.w3.org/Protocols/rfc2616/rfc2616-sec14.html.

3

The Response

In Chapter 2, "The Request," we started to discuss the response when we covered the ready state and status codes of the XHR. This chapter will go beyond this state of the request and focus on two specific data-interchange formats in which the response can be received. An Ajax response can come in various formats; the most common include JSON and the most widely accepted, XML. Each format can be useful depending on the results you are trying to achieve. However, deciding on a single format for your application can be useful as a convention for future management, especially if you are building a large-scale application. For example, if you decide to use XML as the response in one situation, it would be much easier to continue to count on that format as the response when making all other requests. This might differ from one application to the next but, if possible, it is an important theory to keep in mind. It is also good to keep in mind the scalability of the technology that you choose, especially if you are planning on creating a scalable application in which you expect exponential growth. Let's get started by taking an in-depth look at XML, the syntax, how to parse it, and how to use it in your next application.

XML

XML (Extensible Markup Language) is a popular choice for XHRs, simply because it is the standard intermediate language that all programming languages are able to share. It is also supported both on the server side and client side, which makes it the most flexible solution. XML is essentially a custom tag-based structure that you, the developer, define. XML's tag-based structure is similar to that of HTML, except that HTML has predefined tags that represent its structure, such as the head, the body, tables, and so on. The following is an extremely simple example of an HTML table, which could easily be translated or used as XHTML:

```
<table><tr><td></td></tr></table>
```

XML can be passed between the front end and the back end for easy communication of multiple languages. Having this common language between the front end and the back end is extremely powerful. It enables us to create direct connections from the GUI to a server-side language and, ultimately, if desired, a database. Communicating with XML between the GUI and the front end allows for complete separation of the two application layers. Separation of the GUI and the back-end logic is extremely important because it enables us to have a completely decoupled application in which GUI developers can work on the front end, while the back-end developers work on the back end. This might seem like common sense, but it is an approach lacking approach in many companies. It keeps specific parts of the application separated for easier management, and allows teams or individual developers to focus on the layer that is in need of growth. Not only is this approach ideal for teams of developers, it is also important for any individual developer who might be working on every part of the application. With this structure, an individual developer can focus on specific layers of the application without interfering or having to make changes to the adjacent layers.

XML formatting is trivial, but there are important principles to consider when planning a solution. Imagine having to format email data into a structure that could be requested through an Ajax engine and displayed with client-side JavaScript objects. This is a structure that we will be creating for the sample in this book. When architecting this structure, we want to keep in mind that we may use it in multiple objects or locations of the application and should therefore keep it as abstract as possible. We will start by defining the main elements that will create this structure.

Elements

XML is composed of custom tags called *elements*, which are defined in the architecture phase of a web application. They can represent any name, value, or data type that will be used in your application. When creating an XML structure, you become the architect of your application, deciding what data you will need to display certain items on the screen, or what response should happen based on a user's interaction.

It is important to keep our structures as abstract as possible by not naming items specific to the target application, but there are often unique situations that prevent us from being as abstract as we need to be. In these cases, it is not beneficial to spend the extra time to make our XML structure abstract because it might not even be necessary to reuse the XML data in multiple areas of the application. With that said, it is possible to be abstract with our email XML sample and it will be reused in other aspects of the application. The following is a usable XML format, but not an extremely scalable or reusable option:

```
<categories>
    <From/>
    <Subject/>
    <Date/>
</categories>
```

In order to keep these categories abstracted, we will change the names of the elements to **category** (see Listing 3.1).

Listing 3.1   **An Abstract List of Categories (.xml)**

```
<categories>
    <category>From</category>
    <category>Subject</category>
    <category>Date</category>
</categories>
```

This option provides the flexibility that allows us to add additional categories with ease. There are many reasons that this option is more scalable; an important one to remember is the fact that we can add a new category without having to change the structure of our XML data. This is why it is so flexible and a more scalable option than the previous example. Also, if we create object-oriented objects to display the data, we do not need to add additional parsing and display code to handle the new elements. This is why it is so important to architect the solution with abstract structures that can be scalable and easily ported to other applications or objects. For instance, imagine that you need to display the same list of categories in two different ways, such as in a data grid and an email preview. This same set of elements can be used in both objects, which eliminates any redundancies in code from our application.

Although elements are what make XML, there is a limit to what can be achieved with elements alone. Let's take a look at attributes and how they help us add additional information to our XML data.

Attributes

XML attributes are additional properties that can be added to your elements to provide more information specific to the structure. From the email sample, let's focus on an email element. An email has many attributes, such as an action that is triggered when the email is selected, and an icon association, such as a sealed or opened envelope, based on the read status of the email. In order to represent our emails in the XML, we will create a group of items that can eventually become a collection of objects or an array when they are parsed on the client side. This is where we will add our action and icon attributes. Attributes are easy additions to elements. Take a look at Listing 3.2 to get an idea of how we will add the action and icon attributes to an XML element.

Listing 3.2   **An Abstract List of Items (email.xml)**

```
<items action="alert('Grace Hopper');" icon="img/mail.gif">
    <item><![CDATA[Grace Hopper]]></item>
    <item><![CDATA[<b>BUG Found</b>]]></item>
    <item>2006-03-31 09:27:26</item>
</items>
```

There are some issues that are very important to be aware of when using attributes, especially in large applications where making a mistake in the architecture stage can create havoc when scaling. One of the biggest issues with attributes is not having the ability to add multiple values in one attribute. This could create an issue if you later decide that you need to have more than one instance of a specific detail that was already defined as an attribute, leaving you or your fellow developers having to make changes in multiple locations where there are references to the attributes.

Another important issue, and one that we will discuss a solution for in the next section, is adding HTML to your XML. HTML cannot be added to attributes because it will create an invalid structure. The only way to add HTML to an XML structure is within an element. It is much safer to add an element than an attribute because if you realize that you made a mistake and forgot to format the element properly to contain HTML, you can always reformat it later to accept HTML without breaking any code that might be referencing it. In order to add HTML to elements so that it is readable by the programming language that is parsing it and does not break the validation of the XML, we need to add CDATA tags to the element tags.

CDATA

CDATA makes XML—and, ultimately, the web applications that use it—extremely powerful by allowing us to add HTML to elements. The HTML can then be used to display formatted data directly into a DOM element in our Ajax application front end. When XML is parsed by the programming language that we are using, the value between the element tags is also parsed. The following example shows a group of <item> elements that are nested in an </items> element:

```
<items action="alert('Grace Hopper');" icon="img/mail.gif">
    <item>Grace Hopper</item>
    <item>BUG Found</item>
    <item>2006-03-31 09:27:26</item>
</items>
```

These nested elements need to be parsed into subelements by the parser in order to be interpreted by the programming language as child nodes, for example. This means that nesting HTML tags inside of XML elements will not work because the parser will see these elements as nested or child elements of the parent element rather than HTML tags, which will make the XML invalid, causing parsing errors or unexpected results. The following XML will parse with the HTML bold tag (</b>) as an XML element because the parser will see the bold tags as nested XML tags rather than HTML:

```
<item><b>BUG Found</b></item>
```

In order to add HTML to the XML element, we are required to use CDATA. XML parsers do not parse the data immediately following these tags, leaving us with a valid XML structure and ultimately the HTML format that we would like to display in the page. The following code shows valid XML with HTML tags nested in an element using CDATA:

```
<item> <![CDATA[<b>BUG Found</b>]]></item>
```

When this data is parsed by the client-side scripting language, which in our case will be JavaScript, the HTML will render as is between the tags. For example, the text value of `BUG Found` will display as bold text to the user in the GUI if we write the data to the document. The data can be written to the document by simply targeting an HTML tag using the DOM and appending the value with JavaScript's intrinsic `innerHTML` property, or we could simply use `document.write();` to write the value directly to the location in which we place this line of code. Let's take a deeper look at parsing the response.

Parsing XML

When planning the format and tag names that you will be using in your XML, it is important to keep a number of things in mind. For instance, it is usually beneficial to have unique names for elements that are at different depths in your file. This will eliminate parsing issues when using JavaScript's intrinsic `getElementsByTagName` method. Using this method will return an array of all the elements by the name that you specify without looking at the depth in which they reside. One issue that this could cause is that groups of values from different depths that do not belong together can be combined into one array that does not delineate the correct location of the data, causing a parsing nightmare for you or your fellow developers. There are ways to parse data that use nested tags with duplicate names, such as targeting with the `childNodes` property, but this can become difficult and lengthen the development process. You could also create an object that has methods for parsing specific items by name at specific depths, such as XPath does in other languages, or use attributes to distinguish different nodes with the same name. But for our purposes, we will simply define our structure in a way that we do not have to worry about such issues.

There are fairly standard ways of parsing XML with different languages, but parsing XML with JavaScript is a bit different. As I have mentioned, JavaScript has an intrinsic method named `getElementsByTagName`, which can target a group of elements directly by name and allow us access to them so that we can easily parse element or attribute values. This method will either return a single element or a group of elements by the tag name specified as the parameter, as in the following example:

```
response.getElementsByTagName('items');
```

When the method finds a group of elements, it will return an array of `childNodes` that you will need to parse to receive their inner `nodeValues`. To use this method in your parsing, it is important to target the XHR object correctly after the response has been made. Let's take a look at Listing 3.3 for the completed XML sample that we will use as a parsing example.

Listing 3.3   **The Final Email XML File** (email.xml)

```
<?xml version="1.0" encoding="iso-8859-1"?>
<data>
    <categories>
        <category>From</category>
        <category>Subject</category>
        <category>Date</category>
    </categories>
    <row>
        <items action="alert('Grace Hopper');" icon="img/mail.gif">
            <item><![CDATA[Grace Hopper]]></item>
            <item><![CDATA[<b>BUG Found</b>]]></item>
            <item>2006-03-31 09:27:26</item>
        </items>
    </row>
    <row>
        <items action="alert('Pi Sheng');" icon="img/mail.gif">
            <item><![CDATA[Pi Sheng]]></item>
            <item><![CDATA[Movable type]]></item>
            <item>2006-01-15 12:32:45</item>
        </items>
    </row>
</data>
```

In order to sample our parsing methods, we will need to create an HTML file that will have two hyperlinks: one that will request an XML file as a response, and another that will request a JSON response. Listing 3.4 shows the index HTML file that will contain the requesting hyperlinks.

Listing 3.4   **The Index File for XML and JSON Request Samples** (index.html)

```
<html>
<head>
<title>The Response</title>
<script type="text/javascript" src="javascript/ajax.js"></script>
</head>

<body>
<a href="javascript:makeRequest('services/email.xml', onXMLResponse);">xml</a>
   
<a href="javascript:makeRequest('services/email.js', onJSONResponse);">json</a>
<br/><hr noshade="noshade">
<div id="loading"></div>
<div id="body"></div>
</body>

</html>
```

As you can see, this file simply has two hyperlinks that, when clicked, make a request through the `makeRequest` method that we created in Chapter 2. The only difference with the method is that I have now added a variable callback method. This allows us to pass a callback method of our choice, which provides us with the opportunity to parse the response as we would like, based on the specific request being made. We also have two `div` tags in place to display different data. One `div` tag has an `id` value of `loading` and the other of `body`. The `loading div` is used for the loading message that is returned while checking the ready state. The `body div` is used to display the actual data after we parse the response. This data can be formatted any way we choose—it can be displayed as anything from a simple list of data to an entire GUI that is formatted with XHTML and contains interaction data. To begin parsing the XML response, we must first add the callback method that we specified in the request. We will add a method named `onXMLResponse` to the `ajax.js` that we are importing in the index, check the ready state, and target the XML data with a property of the XHR called `responseXML` (see Listing 3.5).

Listing 3.5   Creating a Response Method and Checking the Ready State (`ajax.js`)

```
function onXMLResponse()
{
    if(checkReadyState(request, 'loading') == true)
    {
        var response = request.responseXML.documentElement;
        //Parse here
    }
}
```

By checking the ready state, we are accomplishing two things. First, we are checking the status of the request to decipher whether it has completed loading and is ready to be parsed. Second, we are passing a `div id` to display the ready state messages with its `innerHTML` property. There are two properties listed in Table 2.1 that can be used to target data with the XHR—one is `responseText` and the other is `responseXML`. The `responseText` property returns a string version of the response from the server, and the `responseXML` property returns a DOM-compatible document object of the response from the server. In this case, we will use the `responseXML` property because we need a DOM-compatible object for the XML response so that we can target specific items in the file. After we have this code written, we can begin to parse values from the elements. We will start by parsing the category values from the XML file and adding them to the `body div` via the `innerHTML` property as shown in Listing 3.6.

Listing 3.6   Retrieving the Category Values from the XML (`ajax.js`)

```javascript
// Categories
document.getElementById("body").innerHTML = "------------<br/>";
document.getElementById("body").innerHTML += "<b>Categories</b><br/>";
document.getElementById("body").innerHTML += "------------<br/>";

var categories = response.getElementsByTagName('category');
for(var i=0; i<categories.length; i++)
{
    document.getElementById("body").innerHTML +=
      ➥response.getElementsByTagName('category')[i].firstChild.data +"</br>";
}
```

In order to target each of the categories, we need to use the `getElementsByTagName` method and pass `category` as the parameter. This will provide us with an array of `categories` that we can iterate and add one by one to the `body div`. As we add the `categories` to the document, we are targeting the data within each of the tags in order to display the actual value of each element.

After we have the `categories` displayed, we can move on to the `item` tags from the XML. We will parse these slightly different by targeting the parents, which are the `row` tags, and receiving an array of rows. Then we will iterate through the rows to target the `action` and `icon` attributes within the `items` tags through JavaScript's intrinsic `getAttribute` method. After we are finished writing the attribute values to the `div`, we can target the individual items within each row. We will do this by nesting two `for` loops within the `for` loop that we are using for the rows, leaving us with a three-layer loop. One loop will be used to iterate the `items` tag and the other to iterate the node values within the individual `item` tags as shown in Listing 3.7.

Listing 3.7   Retrieving the Item Values from the XML (`ajax.js`)

```javascript
// Items
document.getElementById("body").innerHTML += "------------<br/>";
document.getElementById("body").innerHTML += "<b>Items</b><br/>";
document.getElementById("body").innerHTML += "------------<br/>";

var row = response.getElementsByTagName('row');
for(var i=0; i<row.length; i++)
{
    var action = response.getElementsByTagName('items')[i].getAttribute('action');
    var icon = response.getElementsByTagName('items')[i].getAttribute('icon');

    document.getElementById("body").innerHTML += action +"<br/>"+ icon +"</br>";

    var items = response.getElementsByTagName('items')[i].childNodes;
    for(var j=0; j<items.length; j++)
    {
        for(var k=0; k<items[j].childNodes.length; k++)
```

Listing 3.7   **Continued**

```
    {
        document.getElementById("body").innerHTML +=
items[j].childNodes[k].nodeValue +"</br>";
    }
  }
  document.getElementById("body").innerHTML += "------------<br/>";
}
```

Parsing requested XML is fairly simple if you know what format to expect as the response from the server. If we did not know what to expect in the previous example of the response, we could have started by using the `responseText` property to display the XML structure as a string and decipher what tags we needed to target.

```
function onXMLResponse()
{
    if(checkReadyState(request, 'loading') == true)
    {
        var response = request.responseText;
        alert(response);
    }
}
```

This would have provided us with the entire XML structure in an alert prompt. At that point, we would be able to take a look at the structure and figure out what we wanted to parse with the `responseXML` property.

As you can see, XML can basically accomplish any type of data structure—it is essentially up to the objects that read the XML to do something useful with it. Let's take a look at how JSON compares and what the benefits are when formatting a response.

JSON

JSON, or JavaScript Object Notation, is a data-interchange format that is becoming more widely accepted as a viable format for Ajax applications. It is essentially an associative array or a hash table, depending on the programming language with which you are most familiar. This means that names or labels are associated with values in an array structure or comma-delimited list. This format rivals XML as a data format used in Ajax applications because of its lightweight syntax and the adoption of JavaScript as a standard client-side scripting language. JSON parsing is also supported natively with JavaScript's `eval` method, which makes it extremely simple to parse when using it in your Ajax applications. The downfall is that the parsing can be quite slow due to the use of the `eval` method and, even more important, using this method can be very insecure. The bright side is that this does not mean that JSON is out of the running as an Ajax data-interchange format contender. It simply means that you need to be smarter when choosing it as your data format. This can be done by adding encrypted passwords to your requests for example, which we will cover in Chapter 23, "Securing Your Application."

Now that we have a little bit of background on JSON, let's take a look at the syntax in which to structure it.

The Syntax

The JSON syntax is very simple and arguably a bit sleeker than XML. XML can get quite heavy when there is a lot of data, which is due to the redundancy of elements, making JSON a great alternative. JSON is not a standard data-interchange format, but there are many parsers available that make it a viable option. There is just about every type of JSON parser available on http://www.json.org, and if you cannot find a parser for a language in which you are interested in using, you can easily write one because the syntax is not very difficult to parse.

The JSON syntax is very intuitive when you look at it from an object-oriented angle. The structure of a JSON file is representative of a JavaScript object in the way that one file can consist of multiple objects, arrays, strings, numbers, and Booleans. Table 3.1 displays a list of data types formatted as JSON.

Table 3.1   **JSON Representations of Each Data Type**

Data Types	JSON Representations
String	`"icon": "img/mail.gif"`
Number	`"mynumber": 100`
Boolean	`"myboolean": true`
Array	`"items":`

```
[
  {
      "action": "alert('Grace Hopper');",
      "icon": "img/mail.gif",
      "item": ["Grace Hopper", "<b>BUG Found</b>",
  "2006-03-31 09:27:26"]
  },
  {
      "action": "alert('Pi Sheng');",
      "icon": "img/mail.gif",
      "item": ["Pi Sheng", "Movable type", "2006-
  01-15 12:32:45"]
  }
]
```

Table 3.1   **Continued**

Data Types	JSON Representations

Object	`"categories":`
	`{`
	`    "category": ["From", "Subject", "Date"]`
	`}`

All JSON data types are represented by a name or label as a string value followed by a colon. The values are what differ from one type to another. The simple types are self-explanatory—a string value is represented as a string, a number is represented as a number, and a Boolean is represented as a value of `true` or `false`. The more complicated data types are arrays and objects. An array is represented as a comma-delimited list, which is contained within square brackets. A JSON object contains properties of any data type, within curly braces, such as a class would be formatted in other languages; the difference here is that we do not give a name to the main structure.

Using JSON

After you understand the syntax of JSON, formatting it is fairly simple. Comparing JSON with an XML format is interesting when working with large amounts of data because the JSON format ultimately becomes a much smaller data structure. In this section, we will convert the samples from the XML section and compare the two different formats to see the differences in terms of size and readability. After we draw the comparisons, we will cover parsing the JSON data structures in the next section. I have converted the XML file from the last section into a JSON data structure in Listing 3.8.

Listing 3.8   **The Completed JSON Sample Format** (`email.js`)

```
{
    "data":
    {
        "categories":
        {
            "category": ["From", "Subject", "Date"]
        },

        "row":
        {
            "items":
            [
                    {
                    "action": "alert('Grace Hopper');",
                    "icon": "img/mail.gif",
```

Listing 3.8   **Continued**

```
                        "item": ["Grace Hopper", "<b>BUG Found</b>", "2006-03-31
                        09:27:26"]
            },
            {
                "action": "alert('Pi Sheng');",
                "icon": "img/mail.gif",
                "item": ["Pi Sheng", "Movable type", "2006-01-15 12:32:45"]
            }
        ]
    }
}
}
```

As you can see, it is much slimmer than the XML version because of the lack of redundancy in tag names, which is the nature of the XML structure. Keep in mind that this file can be a lot more compact—I have simply chosen to display it in a way that is more readable. The JSON data structure is approximately 200 characters smaller with a total character count of 316, whereas the XML data format has 519 characters, which is quite a difference. As the data in your application grows, it can cause a bandwidth issue, but as I mentioned earlier, the client-side parsing can be slower with JSON. What it ultimately comes down to is what format is more usable in your application, or what is easier to parse and write for you.

Parsing JSON

Parsing JSON as a response from an XHR differs from parsing all other data-interchange formats that can be used with Ajax. Unlike using the `responseXML` property, which is used for XML, we need to use the `responseText` property. Using this property with plain text or straight XHTML is trivial because we would use solely it as the value of the response, as in the following example:

```
document.write(request.responseText);
```

Using this property with JSON is also trivial; it is just different based on the fact that we need to evaluate the `responseText` in order for it to be readable for parsing. By evaluating the response, we are essentially creating a JavaScript object from the data, which can then be used on the client side as the display data in the GUI. In order to parse the data, we will begin by creating the callback method, checking the ready state of the request, and evaluating the `responseText` (see Listing 3.9).

Listing 3.9   **Creating a Response Object** (`ajax.js`)

```
function onJSONResponse()
{
    if(checkReadyState(request, 'loading') == true)
    {
        eval("var response = ("+request.responseText+")");
    }
}
```

As we covered in the XML section of this chapter, the `checkReadyState` method is used for two different purposes—checking that the response has been completely loaded, and displaying a loading message to the user in any HTML element that is specified as the parameter. After the response has been completely loaded, we will begin parsing by evaluating the `responseText` from the XHR and creating an object named `response` as a result. This object can then be used to target any values that were added to the object during the evaluation or data parsing. Let's start by targeting the categories from the data and appending them to the `body div` that is in our index HTML file (see Listing 3.10).

Listing 3.10   **Parsing JSON Categories** (`ajax.js`)

```
// Categories
document.getElementById("body").innerHTML = "-----------<br/>";
document.getElementById("body").innerHTML += "<b>Categories</b><br/>";
document.getElementById("body").innerHTML += "-----------<br/>";

for(var i in response.data.categories.category)
{
    document.getElementById("body").innerHTML +=
     ➥ response.data.categories.category[i] +"<br/>";
}
```

As you can see, it is very easy to target the data after it is parsed into a JavaScript object. Property values are accessible by simply using dot syntax to target them by the proper path. In Listing 3.10, we are targeting the categories, which are arrays based on the fact that there were multiple values in the `category` property. In order to target this category array, we use the dot syntax to literally write the path to that specific property in the response object.

Now that we have the categories parsed and displayed in the `body div`, we will target the items. In order to target the items, we will need to nest two `for` loops as we did in the XML example, but parsing the actual values will be slightly different for the actual items and their attributes. See Listing 3.11 to get an idea of how we parse this data.

Listing 3.11   **Parsing JSON Items (`ajax.js`)**

```
// Items
document.getElementById("body").innerHTML += "------------<br/>";
document.getElementById("body").innerHTML += "<b>Items</b><br/>";
document.getElementById("body").innerHTML += "------------<br/>";

for(var i in response.data.row.items)
{
    for(var j in response.data.row.items[i])
    {
        document.getElementById("body").innerHTML += response.data.row.items[i][j]
        ➥+"<br/>";
    }
    document.getElementById("body").innerHTML += "------------<br/>";
}
```

As I mentioned, the item attributes are targeted much differently than they were with the XML parsing. We can simply do a `for...in` loop to target all the property values within a specific object. In this case, we are using this method of data retrieval to access the values of the item attributes and the item arrays.

Using JSON as a response format can be even more powerful by specifying event handlers within the data format to represent specific object types that can be rendered to the document. We will not go into this level of detail, but it is important knowledge to be aware of because it might be very beneficial to your future applications. I will leave you with an example of how to approach structuring this data:

```
"items": [
    {"value": "Read e-mail", "onclick": "displayEmailDetail()"}
]
```

Now that we have a detailed understanding of how to handle an Ajax response, we can focus on formatting it and creating GUI with CSS or XHTML.

4

Rendering the Response with XHTML and CSS

Now that we have covered how to request data with the XHR object and parse the response, we are ready to render and display the data in a browser. There are many ways to handle displaying the data that we receive from an XHR response; in this chapter, we will be focusing on using XHTML and CSS. XHTML and CSS will render our data and keep it easy to manipulate through JavaScript via DOM. This solution is the perfect answer to rendering Ajax data and creating easy-to-manipulate HTML elements.

XHTML

One of the beauties of Ajax-enabled web applications is their simplicity. This can also be seen as a downfall: Search engines cannot locate content that is dynamically added to the page because it does not appear in the source code. This should definitely be a concern in certain situations but, when building a web application, you are not always looking for high-ranking search results within the application itself. Rather, you are typically looking at ranking the home page or other such pages that are not on the inside of the application. Most web applications, such as the sample we are building in this book, do not require search engine rankings. Most of the time, these applications contain personal and secure information, and so it naturally becomes easier for us to keep the source code hidden.

If you are used to creating nested table layouts in your HTML, it might be a strange transition when you begin using `div` tags. Although it might be odd at first, you will find that `div` tags are extremely easy to use, the browser can render them faster, and they require a lot less source code than unruly nested tables. The best part is that they are much easier to manipulate when using DHTML coupled with Ajax data requests, and your styles and content are much more separated, which makes updates far easier. I look at `div` tags as containers for storing data. These containers provide ways of referencing them through the `id` and `name` attributes so that we can target them to manipulate their contents, their position or, for that matter, any of their associated styles.

We can easily identify what elements we need to create by taking a look at the response we are receiving. As you might remember from Chapter 3, "The Response," the XML and JSON files we created consisted of different items that would appear in an email. In this section, we will be creating HTML elements in which to display the data from these files. The first set of data that these files contained was categories. Each of these categories will ultimately be the section header for the items in the item collections. Therefore, we will need to create a grid-like structure to represent this data and format it into identifiable sections of corresponding data. When we are able to identify the contents of our page and separate it into distinct sections, we will then be able to create HTML elements to contain and structure the data.

In Chapter 3, we created two methods in the `ajax.js` file—one called `onXMLResponse` and the other called `onJSONResponse`. These methods rendered the response by pushing the data to the `body div` in our index HTML page. In this section, we are going to rewrite these methods to create `div` elements that will encapsulate this data, and then we will append them to the `body div`. This will allow us to later associate styles with elements via CSS. First, we will strip all the unnecessary code we added to visually separate the categories and the items because the styles will do this for us in a much more subtle way. For now, we will simply add a placeholder `div` element for an icon header, plus numerous others `div` elements in which we will assign an `id` value of `header` and populate with the data from each of the categories from both the XML and JSON responses. Later in the book we will learn how to create HTML elements dynamically via the DOM, but for now we will keep it simple and add content to previously created `div` elements.

XML

```
var response = request.responseXML.documentElement;

document.getElementById("body").innerHTML = "<div id='icon'></div>";
var categories = response.getElementsByTagName('category');
for(var i=0; i<categories.length; i++)
{
    document.getElementById("body").innerHTML +=
    ➥"<div id='header'> "+ response.getElementsByTagName('category')
    ➥[i].firstChild.data +"</div>";
}
```

JSON

```
eval("var response = ("+request.responseText+")");

document.getElementById("body").innerHTML = "<div id='icon'></div>";
for(var i in response.data.categories.category)
{
    document.getElementById("body").innerHTML += "<div id='header'> "+
    ➥response.data.categories.category[i] +"<div/>";
}
```

As you can see, we are simply encapsulating the icon and category data into these `div` tags. These `div` tags will later be stylized with CSS and separated from the item data that we will associate with these categories. In other words, we will basically be creating a grid of corresponding data from the response. Now that we have the header `div` elements created, we will add `div` elements to the item data and associate the action and icon for each. Each item `div` tag will simply get an `id` value of `item`. The action will be associated with each of the item `div` tags by simply adding an `onclick` event to each and appending the action variable. When adding the icons, we do not want to add them to each `div`; rather, we only want to add them as the first item in each group of items. The following code represents the addition of the `div` tags to the item code for both the XML and JSON response.

XML

```
for(var i=0; i<row.length; i++)
{
    var action = response.getElementsByTagName('items')[i].getAttribute('action');
    var icon = response.getElementsByTagName('items')[i].getAttribute('icon');
    var items = response.getElementsByTagName('items')[i].childNodes;
    document.getElementById("body").innerHTML += "<div id='icon'><img src='"+
    ➥ icon +"'/></div>";
    for(var j=0; j<items.length; j++)
    {
        for(var k=0; k<items[j].childNodes.length; k++)
        {
            document.getElementById("body").innerHTML += "<div id='item'
                ➥onclick=\""+ action +"\"> "+ items[j].childNodes[k].nodeValue
                ➥+"</div>";
        }
    }
}
```

JSON

```
for(var i in response.data.row.items)
{
    document.getElementById("body").innerHTML += "<div id='icon'><img src='"+
    ➥response.data.row.items[i].icon +"'/></div>";

    for(var j in response.data.row.items[i].item)
    {
        document.getElementById("body").innerHTML += "<div id='item' onclick=\""+
            ➥response.data.row.items[i].action +"\">"+
            ➥response.data.row.items[i].item[j] +"</div>";
    }
}
```

Now that we have the XHTML writing to the page, it is time to add the styles that will render the final layout. We will do this by associating CSS with the elements.

CSS

Using XHTML with CSS to render Ajax response data adds layers of separation to our code, which allows us to update specific areas of the application without ever touching others. Now that we know how to render the data as XHTML by adding it to `div` elements with JavaScript, we can begin to add design to the page. We will do this by creating CSS classes that will define individual element styles and, ultimately, the entire page layout. The first step in using CSS in our HTML page is importing the CSS files that will define the styles for the page elements. Let's first create a new file and name it `layout.css`. Building on the examples in Chapter 2, "The Request," and Chapter 3, we will add the following code to the head of our index HTML file in order to import the CSS:

```
<link href="css/layout.css" rel="stylesheet" type="text/css" />
```

Because we have already identified and populated the HTML elements in our page, we know what elements we will need to create styles for. Before we create the styles, we must visualize how we want the page layout to look. If it does not come easy to mentally visualize a page layout, we could create wire frames or mockups in a graphics editor. Either way, after we have a concept we can begin to arrange the elements through CSS. The look we are going for with this example is a grid of mail data, with section headers and data that pertains to the sections displayed underneath the headers in sets of rows. Figure 4.1 shows the final layout of the data within this grid structure.

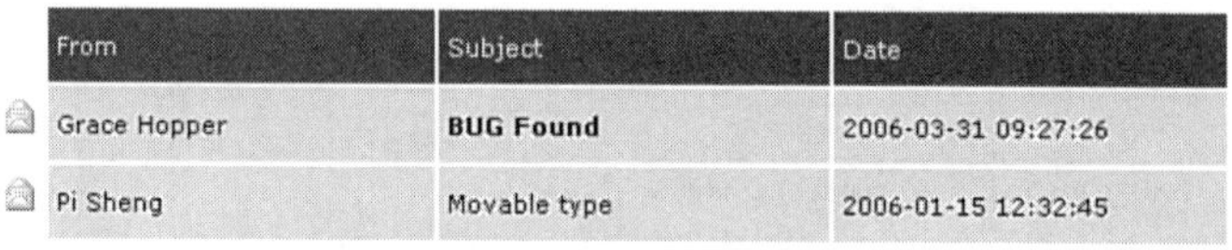

From	Subject	Date
Grace Hopper	**BUG Found**	2006-03-31 09:27:26
Pi Sheng	Movable type	2006-01-15 12:32:45

Figure 4.1   The final grid layout for response data after CSS has been applied to the HTML elements.

In our new CSS file, we will create four classes: `body`, `header`, `item`, and `icon`. These are the four elements we have already added to the page through our response methods in the `ajax.js` file from the previous section. Starting with the `body` div, which was added to the page by default, we will create a class with a `width` of 570px. This `width` will compensate for the `margin` we will add around each of the items in the grid, but we will talk more about this after we have completed adding the `header` and `item` classes. The following is the code that creates the `body` class:

```
#body
{
    width: 570px;
}
```

Next, we will create a class for the **header div** element. Looking back at the XML and JSON files we are requesting, we can see there are three headers and three items. These headers and items should sit next to each other to form rows of data. To accomplish this, we must start by adding a **float** attribute with a value of **left**. This will left-align each **header** and **item** tag next to each other to form a row of data. Each new row will start when we have reached the container's width limit, which we defined in the **body** class. We have also added a pointer cursor to distinguish each item as clickable. Following is the code that each of the headers and items is assigned:

```
#header
{
    float: left;
    width: 180px;
    padding: 10px 0px 10px 0px;
    background-color: #666;
    color: #fff;
    margin: 1px;
}

#item
{
    float: left;
    width: 180px;
    padding: 10px 0px 10px 0px;
    background-color: #eaeaea;
    color: #333;
    margin: 1px;
    cursor: pointer;
}
```

The width we have set for the **body** accommodates the width and the margin of the three items that will display in each row, plus the width and margin of the icons. If we wanted to display more items in a row, we would simply adjust the width of the container, taking the margin and other spacing of the elements into consideration. Figure 4.2 reveals an inside look at the different elements that appear in the grid.

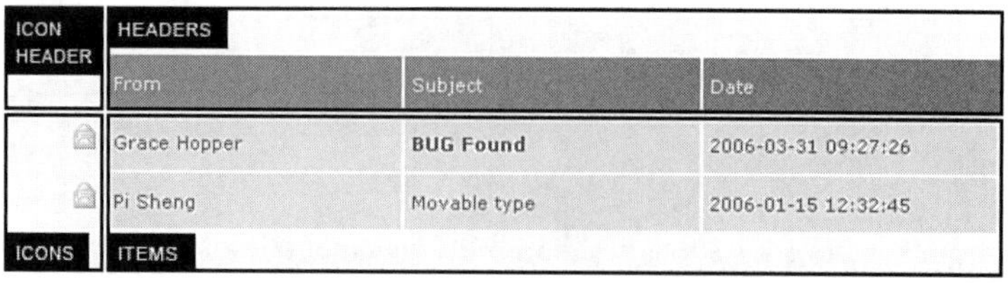

Figure 4.2   An inside look at the HTML elements that define the grid.

As you can see, we have stylized the headers and items a bit with background colors, font colors, and a pointer cursor for each item to make it obvious that they are clickable. There are millions of ways to customize these elements; my suggestion is to have fun experimenting.

The last element we have to create a class for is the `icon` element. The icon will be very small, so it should not take up the same `width` as a typical `item`, which is the reason we have created a separate class for icons. The `icon` element will be used as both a placeholder for the space that is required for each icon in the header and the actual icon that will be placed to the left of the items. It floats left as all the elements in the grid have to do in order to create the rows. It also has other common properties, such as a `width`, `padding`, font `color`, and `margin`.

```
#icon
{
    float: left;
    width: 20px;
    padding: 5px 0px 5px 0px;
    color: #333;
    margin: 1px;
}
```

Now that we have the knowledge to request data, receive a response, and stylize a page of dynamic data with CSS and XHTML, we can take it up a notch by creating a cleaner process and encapsulating code into objects and an Ajax engine. The next chapter will explain how to create an object-oriented Ajax engine with JavaScript, how to debug our requests and responses, and how to extend the engine by creating additional objects that streamline the process of creating Ajax-enabled web applications.

II

Creating and Using the JavaScript Engine

5

Object-Oriented JavaScript

Object-oriented JavaScript is essential when building large-scale Ajax applications. This approach to programming lends reusability, scalability, and flexibility to our applications. Object-oriented approaches provide a blueprint for object reusability, which ultimately tends to minimize the amount and duplication of code in our applications. Minimizing the amount and duplication of code not only helps us build an application faster, but it also makes updates and management a simple chore for developers. When approaching your application in an object-oriented way, there is some planning that is involved to make sure that your objects are reusable now and, in the mapped future, to lend scalability for any additions and/or updates to the application. Creating these objects may sometimes seem like overkill if a developer thinks she can just knock out an application in a short amount of time, which is frequently the case. However, by beginning to approach all of our applications in this way, we will be conditioned to think of applications in a new light—from more of an engineer's perspective—and we will automatically begin to approach and build them in a better way. This allows us to use our objects in other applications and reuse code in ways that will speed up our development time immensely.

This chapter may not be the most glamorous, and you may be wondering why you would need to understand object-oriented programming (OOP) concepts with JavaScript in order to create Ajax applications. The use of JavaScript objects in your Ajax applications makes it very simple to manipulate data and create graphical user interface (GUI) elements that can be ported from one application to the next. This allows you to put more time into the planning, engineering, and development of the site or, hopefully, even the development of new Ajax components, rather than rewriting the same code in each of your applications or, as they say, "reinventing the wheel." With that said, understanding the creation of these different object types is essential to creating custom objects, components, and even libraries of our own.

Unlike other programming or scripting languages, there are many ways to create objects with JavaScript. Although this book will primarily use prototypes as the object-oriented approach of choice, we will also cover object constructors in this chapter. Object constructors are valid and useful ways to create objects and translate rather seamlessly into our sample application. You can use this approach in the book sample or in your future Ajax applications—the choice is yours.

Object-Oriented Approaches

As I have already mentioned, there are many different ways to approach object-oriented programming with JavaScript. You can create objects or pseudo-objects with any of the following:

- Object constructors
- Prototypes
- The new operator
- Literal notation
- Associative arrays
- JScript.NET

Each of these methods for creating objects or pseudo-objects in JavaScript is valid, yet some are more flexible than others. This does not mean that these methods are not useful—there are definitely situations where a particular method would be better than all the other approaches. Let's take a brief look at each of these approaches and what situations they would be useful in.

> **Note**
>
> Since this chapter will be focusing in-depth on object constructors and prototypes, we will not cover these two methods in this section.

Using the new Operator

Using the new operator is probably one of the simplest approaches to creating objects in JavaScript because, of course, it is the native way of doing so. In order to create an object using JavaScript's native new operator, we simply choose a name for our object and set it equal to a new Object.

```
var employee = new Object();
employee.id = 001;
employee.firstName = "Kris";
employee.lastName = "Hadlock";

employee.getFullName = function()
{
    return this.firstName + " " + this.lastName;
}
```

In this sample, we are defining a custom object named employee with id, firstName, and lastName properties, and a method called getFullName, which returns a concatenated version of the firstName and lastName properties. This solution is acceptable and can work in many solutions, especially if you do not plan on creating multiple instances of the object. Its limit is that it is unable to create multiple instances of the same object—for instance, we would not be able to create more than one employee with this method.

Literal Notation

Literal notation is a more complex way of defining objects with JavaScript and is supported in JavaScript 1.2 and above. This approach is a sort of shorthand way of creating objects, which makes them easy to build but a bit hard to read because of the unique syntax that they require. Here is a sample of creating the same object (with the literal notation approach) we created with the new operator.

```
employee = {
        id : 001;
        firstName : "Kris";
        lastName : "Hadlock";
        getFullName : function()
        {
            return this.firstName + " " + this.lastName;
        }
}

alert(employee.getFullName); // Results: Kris Hadlock
```

As you can see, this approach is easy to create, but could be rather hard to manage if we were to add a lot of methods and properties. Don't get me wrong, though—this is a viable solution, and I wouldn't necessarily recommend against it. It's just that I personally prefer to use a more familiar syntax.

Associative Arrays

Associative arrays are defined as any other array is defined, but strings are inserted in place of numbers as indexes. This solution allows us to call an item in an array by name rather than by an index number, which obviously makes it easier to target specific items. This can be useful when trying to replicate a hash map of sorts, which is not a native data type in JavaScript. Here is a sample of the syntax for this option.

```
var employee = new Array();
employees["firstName"] = "Kris";
employees["lastName"] = "Hadlock";
```

As you can see, this option may make it easier to target specific items, but again, imagine having to create multiple employees. Here is an example of how unruly this could become.

```
var employee = new Array();
employees[001]["firstName"] = "Kris";
employees[001]["lastName"] = "Hadlock";

employees[002]["firstName"] = "John";
employees[002]["lastName"] = "Doe";
```

This solution can become a real mess if you are working with a lot of data and having to remember all of the paths to certain items in the array. With that said, using this method to create a custom hash map object could be very useful, but I'll leave that part up to you.

JScript.NET

JScript.NET enables us to create full-fledged .NET applications—as if we were using a language such as C# or VB.NET—by compiling our code into Intermediate Language (IL). One of the great things about this method is that it allows us to use strict data typing and access modifiers, such as private and public properties, which I know seems very alien when thinking of JavaScript. The strict data typing allows for better code readability and much easier debugging methods.

Here is an example of the syntax that you would use to create a JScript.NET object.

```
<script language="JScript" runat="server">

public class employee (_id, _firstName, _lastName) {

    private id : String  = _id;
    private firstName : String = _firstName;
    private lastName : String = _lastName;
    private getFullName : Function = function(e)
    {
        return this.firstName + " " + this.lastName;
    }
}

</script>
```

For developers with an OOP background, this approach could be easier to grasp. However, the syntax for the data typing is a bit strange, and the fact that you need to use and install the .NET Framework could be limiting in terms of development—it really just depends on your situation.

Now that we have a little bit of background on other ways to create an object with JavaScript, we will cover the two approaches that I believe have the most flexibility for what we are trying to accomplish. These next two approaches allow for the creation of multiple objects because of the reusability they lend to JavaScript. Let's take a look.

Object Constructors

Object constructors are a great way to structure objects so that they are reusable, without having to create or redefine a completely new object when there is a slight difference from one to another. This method of object creation allows us to reuse one object by applying different property values to it and creating multiple instances from that same object blueprint.

Instances

Creating instances, or instantiating an object, is simply the act of taking an object definition and creating multiple objects that model its definition. These separate instances can have different property and method parameter values, which makes one unique from another. An object definition is essentially a blueprint that a developer uses to create multiple instances of an object. When an object is instantiated, it intrinsically contains all of the properties and methods that the object defines. Therefore, if we had an `employee` object with a `name` property, we could create multiple instances and give each employee a different name. This section will explain how to use the object constructor approach for creating multiple instances of objects to gain maximum reusability in our web applications.

Object constructors are simply a regular JavaScript function in which we encapsulate properties and methods. It is instantiated by use of the native JavaScript `new` operator. This method is very similar to the Literal Notation method, but the syntax conforms more to a common programming model. We start by creating a simple function in which we provide an object name. In the following example, we are creating an `employee` object constructor.

```
function employee(_id, _firstName, _lastName)
{
}
```

As you can see, this is a standard JavaScript function, that takes three parameters: an `_id`, a `_firstName`, and a `_lastName`. This function becomes our access point to the object—in other words, if you are familiar with OOP, it is our constructor function. We will use the name of our function as our object name. If you are familiar with building classes with other programming languages, think of this approach as a way of creating a class without defining the object as a class, or creating a class with a function instead of a class declaration. We still have our constructor, properties, and methods; we simply do not have the class declaration encapsulating the object's details. With our constructor in place, we can begin to instantiate the object. This is where we begin to see the reusability.

```
var kh001 = new employee(001, "Kris", "Hadlock");
var jd002 = new employee(002, "John", "Doe");
```

These examples show how simple it is to create multiple instances of an object using this approach. The exciting part about this is that we can continue to use this object for any employee that we need to add, and if we need to add a method or property, it is not going to have any effect on the other `employee` objects. They will simply ignore these items unless they are updated.

In order to make these objects more flexible, we are allowing parameters to be passed to the object constructor. These parameters will be used to define different properties within the objects to make one object different from another. For instance, we may want to create a new employee with our `employee` object and need to provide a new first and last name for each. In the previous example, we are passing a first and last name as our parameters, which will be used as properties in our class. Let's take a look at how we take these values and set them to object properties.

Properties

Taking the parameter from the object constructor and turning it into a local object property is extremely simple. First, we need a value as the parameter, which we are already receiving. Next, we must create local properties within the object that we will use to set to the value of these parameters.

```
function employee(_id, _firstName, _lastName)
{
    this.id = _id;
    this.firstName = _firstName;
    this.lastName = _lastName;
}
```

This method is receiving an `_id`, a `_firstName`, and a `_lastName` parameter, which we are using to set to local properties in the object. These parameters allow us to distinguish one employee from the others, and provide us with a reference to retrieve specific details about each employee. Local object properties can be used at any later point. For example, we could reference these `employee` objects with another object and then get the first and last names. These `employee` objects would retain that information, regardless of how many employees were created.

These properties can be set and referenced solely, or we could use methods within the object to handle this detail. Using methods in our object constructors helps us to combine common functionality into one reference. Let's now take a look at how to add a method to an object constructor and understand how it is beneficial to the scalability of our application.

Methods

Objects are so powerful because of the data they store and the methods they contain, which can be called to perform specific functions. These methods can be used to set new values for object properties or retrieve a value from object properties. They also can be used to perform complex algorithms, call other methods, create other objects, and any other custom functionality that you or your clients need. Here is an example of the `employee` object with a method called `getFullName`.

```
function employee(_id, _firstName, _lastName)
{
    this.id = _id;
    this.firstName = _firstName;
    this.lastName = _lastName;

    this.getFullName = function()
    {
        return this.firstName + " " + this.lastName;
    }
}
```

This method returns two concatenated properties, which form an employee's full name. This is just the beginning of what we can accomplish with an object like this. For example, we can create methods for retrieving or setting an employee's job title because this is something that could change if an employee gets a promotion. These are simple methods to add, yet they provide a lot of power to someone who has the ability to change an employee's job title. Here is an example.

```
function employee(_id, _firstName, _lastName, _jobTitle)
{
    this.id = _id;
    this.firstName = _firstName;
    this.lastName = _lastName;
    this.jobTitle = _jobTitle;

    this.getFullName = function()
    {
```

```
            return this.firstName + " " + this.lastName;
        }

        this.setJobTitle = function(_jobTitle)
        {
            this.jobTitle = _jobTitle;
        }

        this.getJobTitle = function()
        {
            return this.jobTitle;
        }
}
```

These methods require us to add a new property called jobTitle. This property can be set through the constructor function or set with our new setJobTitle method. After we set the value, we can also retrieve it with the getJobTitle method. These methods are the equivalent of getter and setter methods for JavaScript because they allow other objects to get or set values of specific properties of an object. We could also make a property a read-only property by allowing only a getter and not a setter.

A more complicated example is an employee's sick days. This requires us to create an array of sick days for each employee object. Let's say that we need a way to retrieve a list of sick days that is formatted into an HTML list. Here is an example of how we would accomplish this functionality.

```
var sickDays = new Array("1-12", "1-13", "1-14");
var kh = new Employee(001, "Kris", "Hadlock", "GUI Developer", sickDays);

function employee(_id, _firstName, _lastName, _jobTitle, _sickDays)
{
    this.sickDays = _sickDays;
    this.id = _id;
    this.firstName = _firstName;
    this.lastName = _lastName;
    this.jobTitle = _jobTitle;

    this.getFullName = function()
    {
        return this.firstName + " " + this.lastName;
    }

    this.setJobTitle = function(_jobTitle)
    {
        this.jobTitle = _jobTitle;
    }
```

```
this.getJobTitle = function()
{
    return this.jobTitle;
}

this.getSickDayList = function()
{
    var sickDayList = "<ul>";
    for(var i=0; i<this.sickDays.length; i++)
    {
        sickDayList += "<li>"+ this.sickDays[i] +"</li>";
    }
    sickDayList += "</ul>";
    return sickDayList;
}
}
```

Creating unique methods such as this is a main source of power when creating instances of objects. This is because each of the object's instances will contain this functionality and can call on it at any point in time.

Prototypes

The prototype object was introduced in JavaScript 1.1 as an intrinsic object that simplifies the addition of custom properties and methods to existing objects. When we begin to create objects and prototypes, we are getting into the real nuts and bolts of JavaScript and will be able to create some powerful functionality. An example of how the prototype object works is fairly simple: If it is asked for a method or property that it does not contain, it checks the prototype of the class that created it. It will continue to follow this chain of looking at the parent objects if it does not find the property or method that was called. As a last resort, it will find the `Object.prototype` (which is the object that creates all objects), but most likely it will call the method in a custom object if it is scoped correctly. The following are three layers that exist in all prototype objects:

- `Object.prototype`
- `Class.prototype`
- Instance

These next three layers represent the layers that exist in each of the employee instances:

- `Object.prototype`
- `employee.prototype`
- kh

These layers represent object inheritance, which simply means that the kh instance inherits all the properties and methods from the employee and Object objects, and the employee object inherits all the properties and methods from the Object object. This will become more apparent as we learn more about how to use the prototype object and really tackle some complex objects in Part III, "Creating Reusable Components," where we create reusable objects to handle data structuring in Ajax-enabled components.

JavaScript is more powerful than some people give it credit, as you will learn throughout this book. It can be used to create entire dynamic applications, components, and even interact with the server and database as we will see when we implement the server side with Ajax in Part V, "Server-Side Interaction." Prototypes are one of the methods that I chose for creating reusable objects in the samples throughout this book. The other method is a variation on the new operator, which actually creates a pattern that we will be covering in Chapter 14, "Singleton Pattern." There we will actually want to only have one instance of an object. The prototype method for creating objects allows us to easily append properties and methods to objects that we are creating for the first time and extend existing objects to include additional custom functionality. Another reason why this object creation method is so powerful is because we can create multiple instances, making the objects more scalable and reusable. Let's take a look at how these objects are instantiated and how they can be so powerful.

Instances

In order to create instances of a prototype-based object, we must first create a constructor function. The constructor function is the access point to all objects and therefore is the first item that is created in the object. A constructor function can receive unlimited parameters to specify certain attribute or property values. These values are what set one object apart from the next, and is another reason why objects are such a powerful force in programming. Here is an example of a constructor function for an object named employee, as we have created in the previous sections. Again, this object takes three parameters, which specify the unique ID of the employee and his first and last names. The first and last names are simply not enough to set apart one employee from another, especially if two people have the same name; hence, the id parameter.

```
function employee(_id, _firstName, _lastName)
{
    // Set properties
}
```

As you can see, creating a constructor function for a prototype object is trivial, yet it is one of the most important pieces of the object.

Creating Properties

Adding properties to our object is extremely simple. In this case, we need to first define parameters in the constructor as we did with the other objects. This allows us to pass values to the properties and set them when an instance of the object is created. After the object is created and the parameters are retrieved by the object's constructor function, we create the properties and set their values. In the following example, we set the `id`, `firstName`, and `lastName` of each employee object that is created.

```
function employee(_id, _firstName, _lastName)
{
    this.id = _id;
    this.firstName = _firstName;
    this.lastName = _lastName;
}
```

As I said earlier, these properties are extremely easy to create and set within an object. The object's properties are scoped to the object by using the **this** keyword. It is good practice to use this syntax because it is easier to distinguish a local **method** property from an **object** property when one is using the **this** keyword and the other is not.

Thus far, the object is not any different from an object constructor, but this will now change. If we had an instance of an **employee** object and wanted to add an email address property, we could use the following code:

```
var kh = new employee(001, "Kris", "Hadlock");
kh.emailAddress = "my@email.com";
```

This code would not be usable by other instances of the object. For example, if we were to create another employee, she would not have an email address property. In order to add this new property to the employee object—which all of the employee instances can see and use—we will need to use the prototype. Here is an example of using the prototype to extend our **employee** object by adding an email address property.

```
var kh = new employee(001, "Kris", "Hadlock");
employee.prototype.emailAddress = "";
kh.emailAddress = "my@email.com";
```

This is not the best solution for creating a new property with the prototype, but it is an example of how we would add this property and have it be accessible to all other instances. Typically, a property would be encapsulated in a method, such as a getter or setter, if not in the constructor. The only reason why we would want to add a property this way is if we needed to extend the object for some reason. The reason why this solution is not the best is because it can become much harder to maintain your code if developers are randomly extending the object in different locations. Keeping the methods and properties centralized in one JavaScript file keeps the management extremely easy, and allows us to reference the file from multiple locations and know that we are receiving the same code from each.

Overriding and Overwriting Properties

We also can override and overwrite properties in a prototype object. For example, we may set a default value for the email address.

```
var kh = new employee(001, "Kris", "Hadlock");
employee.prototype.emailAddress = "shared@email.com";
kh.emailAddress = "my@email.com";
var jd = new employee(002, "John", "Doe");
```

Overriding a property value simply changes the value for the instance that you are setting it with. So, now the kh employee has a new email address, but the jd employee has the email address that was set with the prototype.

Overwriting an object property is completely different. If we were to change the email address for the kh employee after we had already set it, we would be overwriting the original value. Here is an example:

```
var kh = new employee(001, "Kris", "Hadlock");
employee.prototype.emailAddress = "";
kh.emailAddress = "my@email.com";
kh.emailAddress = "new@email.com";
```

Property Protection

Property protection keeps an object's local properties from being changed by any other instance of that object. In other words, if an instance changed the value of one of its properties, the value would not change in the object from which it is inheriting. For example, let's say that you inherited blond hair from your parents. If your hair color was to darken throughout your childhood, this would not mean that your parents' hair color would change. Here is an example of a value that would change in the instance, not the object.

```
function employee( ){}
employee.prototype.totalVacationDays = 10;
```

```
var kh = new employee( );
kh.totalVacationDays --;
kh.totalVacationDays --;
kh.totalVacationDays --;
```

The reason why this instance is decrementing its own property and not the object's local property is because all the other instances of the object would reflect these changed properties as well. In the example, we are using the total vacation days that an employee has left. Imagine if modifying that property modified every other employee's properties or vacation days—management would have a lot of angry employees on its hands! This is why property protection is so important and the nature of the way these object properties function. Object properties are essential to the makeup of an object, but they can only get us so far. This is why methods are such a powerful addition to object structures. Let's see how we would add methods to our prototype objects.

Methods

Creating a method within a prototype object is a bit different from creating a typical object method. In order to create a method, we need to call the object by name and add the prototype object followed by the method name. Here is an example of the `getFullName` method that we have been using throughout this chapter using a prototype-based method.

```
employee.prototype.getFullName = function()
{
    return this.firstName + " " + this.lastName;
}
```

This method becomes an `employee` method that can be referenced by every instance that is created from this definition. Each object instance will have its own values for the properties that are being returned; therefore, it will return its custom values if the method is called. For example, if I were to create an `employee` object and pass it a first name of `John` and a last name of `Doe`, calling the `getFullName` method would return a string representation of `John Doe`.

Extending Objects with Prototyped Methods

Using prototype objects also enables us to extend an existing object, whether it is an intrinsic JavaScript object or a custom one. Let's take the `String` object as an example. Say that we would like to add a method to all strings that allow us to turn one into an array of letters by calling a method from that string. In order to accomplish this, we would use a prototype.

```
function stringToArray()
{
    var arr = new Array();
    for (i=0; i<this.length; i++)
    {
        arr.push(this[i]);
    }
    return arr;
}

String.prototype.convertToArray = stringToArray;

var s = "Test String";
document.write(s.convertToArray());
```

Any string variable that we create in the application that contains this code will now have the capability to intrinsically call the **convertToArray** method and receive an array of the characters in that string. When you are adding code to native JavaScript objects, you know that you have reached a moment of achievement. Now it is time to create additional functionality that handles common Ajax data manipulation. This is just the beginning of what we can and will accomplish with prototype objects. As I mentioned at the beginning of this chapter, we will be using this object creation method to create custom Ajax-enabled components, which will be reusable in any project, in Part III. These prototype-based objects are extremely flexible and can be scaled to any situation. This is why I have chosen prototypes as the primary method of creating objects for the samples in this book. Utilizing these object creation methods will allow us to create very dynamic and interactive web applications with Ajax.

6

Creating the Engine

In Chapter 2, "The Request," we created a few functions to create an XHR, and handle receiving and displaying a response. This solution works fine in many cases, especially for simple Ajax-based web pages, but it is not the best solution for large web applications. In order to manage multiple requests and delegate responses to specific requesting objects, we will create an Ajax engine. This engine will consist of two objects: `Ajax` and `AjaxUpdater`. The `AjaxUpdater` will manage all requests and delegate them to the `Ajax` object. The `Ajax` object will receive the requests from the `AjaxUpdater` and instantiate an XHR object. After the XHR object has been instantiated and the requesting object receives a response, the requestor can then call two more methods within the `Ajax` object. The first method checks the ready state of the request and the second returns the request object in its completed form. We will cover these methods in more detail throughout this chapter. Let's start by creating the Ajax wrapper, which we will later be able to reuse to manage large Ajax applications.

Creating a Custom Ajax Wrapper

The Ajax wrapper that we will be creating is simply called `Ajax`, and is an object that follows the Singleton pattern, which we will cover in detail in Chapter 14, "Singleton Pattern." This object will handle all requests to the server through the XHR as a single object that will always be reliable and never change states—hence the Singleton pattern. This way, any object that needs to make a request will do so through the same object, keeping the requests structured and organized. In order to create this object, we first need to simply construct it as in Listing 6.1.

Listing 6.1   **Constructing the `Ajax` Object (`Ajax.js`)**

```
Ajax = {};
```

After the object is constructed, we can create all the methods we will need to call in order to make requests, check the ready state, and receive a response object for parsing and either displaying or manipulating the data on the client side. We will start by covering how to create a method to handle making our XHR requests.

Making Requests

One of the most important functionalities of our `Ajax` object is making XHRs. In order to make this process more streamlined and easier to manage, we will be creating a method named `makeRequest`. This method will take three parameters: The first is a method in which to make the request, which will consist of either a POST or a GET method. The second parameter is the URL in which to make the request; this URL also will include our query string for passing data to the server when we make a request. The last parameter is the callback method, which we will want to invoke to handle the response when the ready state is completed. Listing 6.2 shows the entire method for handling this functionality.

Listing 6.2   **Streamlining the Process of Making XHRs (`Ajax.js`)**

```
Ajax.makeRequest = function(method, url, callbackMethod)
{
    this.request = (window.XMLHttpRequest)? new XMLHttpRequest(): new
       ➥ActiveXObject("MSXML2.XMLHTTP");
    this.request.onreadystatechange = callbackMethod;
    this.request.open(method, url, true);
    this.request.send(url);
}
```

This method should look very familiar because it contains all the same functionality that we used to create an XHR object and send that data to the server in Chapter 2. The difference with this method is that it wraps all this functionality into an easy-to-manage object that we can access from anywhere in a large application. We start by deciphering which XHR object to instantiate based on the browser type. After we instantiate the appropriate XHR object, we set the **onreadystatechange** event to the callback method that was provided as the third parameter of this method. This means that the callback method you provide to this method will be fired when the XHR has been received, and is ready to be parsed for displaying or manipulating data on the client side of the application. The last two methods are the **open** and **send** methods of the XHR object. The **open** method initializes the request, and specifies the method in which to make the request, the URL to make the request to, plus a query string, if one applies, and a Boolean for asynchronous versus synchronous. We set the Boolean to **true** by default because we do not want to make synchronous requests; they will freeze your application until the response has been received from the request. If you are making numerous requests in a large application, this will render your application unusable. The last method, the **send** method, will be used to actually send the HTTP request to the server and wait to receive the response. This method takes the same URL as the **open** method, plus any key/value pairs that may exist in a query string.

After this method instantiates the XHR object and makes the request based on the information that we provide it, a response will be received in the callback method that we set. The callback method will need to check what is called the *ready state* of the

XHR object and either parse the object after the ready state is completed or handle any HTTP status code errors that may be returned from the server. In order to check the ready state of the XHR object, we will be creating a method that does this for us called `checkReadyState`, which will become part of the `Ajax` object.

The Ready State

As we covered in Chapter 2, the ready state of the object tells us when a response has been received from the server and is available to be parsed by JavaScript through the Document Object Model (DOM). The `readyStateChange` event handler fires when the state of the request object changes and allows us to set a callback method to be triggered as we did in the `makeRequest` method. After this callback method is triggered, it is up to us to handle the response with our callback method. In order to do this, we will call the `checkReadyState` method to get the `readyState` and eventually the HTTP status of the response. This method takes one parameter, which is an ID of an HTML element that will display a loading message during this process. This message can be changed to a custom message of our choice for each state of the request. Listing 6.3 shows the complete method with the loading message states and the returned HTTP status of the XHR object after the ready state has completed.

Listing 6.3   **Checking the Ready State of the XHR (`Ajax.js`)**

```
Ajax.checkReadyState = function(_id)
{
    switch(this.request.readyState)
    {
        case 1:
            document.getElementById(_id).innerHTML = 'Loading ...';
            break;
        case 2:
            document.getElementById(_id).innerHTML = 'Loading ...';
            break;
        case 3:
            document.getElementById(_id).innerHTML = 'Loading ...';
            break;
        case 4:
            AjaxUpdater.isUpdating = false;
            document.getElementById(_id).innerHTML = '';
            return this.request.status;
    }
}
```

This method is very similar to the method that we created in Chapter 2, but it is now encapsulated into the `Ajax` object to lend structure and organization to our code base. For each state of the `readyState`, we set a custom loading message to the `innerHTML` property of the HTML element that we passed the ID for as a parameter. This message can become anything you would like to change it to. Each state can actually have its own loading message passed as a parameter to the method to give the requesting object more power over what messages display. For instance, say that we have a request to update an inbox of an email application. We could show states specific to this request, such as `Retrieving new mail`, for example. Remember that after this object has been created, it can be manipulated to handle any custom functionality you need to handle—this is the beauty of creating an object-oriented code base for our applications.

After the `readyState` has reached a state of `4`, the XHR object is complete and ready for use. At this point, one of two things can happen: The HTTP status can be successful, or it can return an informational, redirection, client, or server error code. Based on the code that is returned, we will decide how to handle the client side. We will cover this in much more depth in Chapter 9, "Extending the Engine," when we create a custom object to extend the `Ajax` object and handle all the HTTP status codes available. One thing I am sure you noticed is that we are setting an `AjaxUpdater` object's `isUpdating` property to `false`. I'm sure you are wondering what this object is and why we are setting this property. This object will be created in the next section of this chapter and will be used to handle all Ajax requests. It will be used as one degree of separation between the client-side objects and the engine, and will keep our code base much more organized and secure. But before we cover this object, we will see how to get the response object after the `readyState` is completed.

The Response

This last method, called `getResponse`, is extremely simple because it only deciphers what type of response property needs to be returned to the requesting object. Take a look at Listing 6.4 to see how we are handling this functionality.

Listing 6.4   **Getting the Appropriate Response Object (`Ajax.js`)**

```
Ajax.getResponse = function()
{
    if(this.request.getResponseHeader('Content-Type').indexOf('xml') != -1)
    {
        return this.request.responseXML.documentElement;
    }
    else
    {
        return this.request.responseText;
    }
}
```

In order to get the response from the `Ajax` object, we simply call this method from our callback method after the `readyState` is complete, and it will return the appropriate response property. It returns the appropriate response property based on the response header that is returned with the response from the server. If the `Content-Type` response header has an index of the string `xml` in it, we know that the response is in the form of

XML and should therefore be returned to the callback method as a DOM-compatible document object of the response from the server. Otherwise, this method returns the `responseText` property, which is a string version of the response from the server.

Now that we have a custom object to control and manage all of our `Ajax` requests, we can add one more layer of abstraction to the code to make our requests more manageable and secure.

Creating an Ajax Updater

In order to keep our `Ajax` object in the background and add a layer of abstraction to our engine, we will create an object called `AjaxUpdater`. This object is another that follows the Singleton pattern to keep it accessible from all scopes of the application for easy XHR management and control. The object is very simple and consists of only a few methods—one of which could be the only one that is ever used. The other is optional, or a backup for handling optional functionality. Let's start by constructing the object.

Constructing the Object

We will construct this object as we did with the `Ajax` object. The difference with this object is that we will be initializing the property we used in the `Ajax` object that we briefly discussed in the last section. This Boolean property is called `isUpdating` and is set to `false` by default (see Listing 6.5). This is due to the fact that we are not currently updating any Ajax requests because this property will be used to decipher if a request is in progress at any point in our application.

Listing 6.5   **Constructing the `AjaxUpdater` and Initializing Properties (`AjaxUpdater.js`)**

```
AjaxUpdater = {};

AjaxUpdater.initialize = function()
{
    AjaxUpdater.isUpdating = false;
}
AjaxUpdater.initialize();
```

After we construct the object, we immediately initialize its properties for use by the rest of the methods in the object.

Updating the Request Object

In an Ajax application, the most widely used method will most likely be the one that handles XHRs. This is the method that will handle all these requests and interact directly with the `Ajax` object. This method takes three parameters: a method in which we will be making the request, such as a `POST` or a `GET`; what I am calling the "service parameter," which is essentially the URL with optional key/value pairs for sending data to the server through the request; and last, an optional callback method. The callback method is optional in this method because we will have a default or catch-all method, called `onResponse`, to handle any response if a callback method is not passed to this method. After the callback method has been deciphered, we make the request through the `Ajax` object and set the `isUpdating` property to `true` (see Listing 6.6).

Listing 6.6   **Handling XHRs** (`AjaxUpdater.js`)

```
AjaxUpdater.Update = function(method , service, callback)
{
    if(callback == undefined |¦| callback == "") { callback =
      ➥AjaxUpdater.onResponse; }
    Ajax.makeRequest(method, service, callback);
    AjaxUpdater.isUpdating = true;
}
```

This method is a fairly simple way to manage all the XHRs made through our application. The power of using this abstraction layer is that we could add more custom code to control other aspects of the request before the request is made and without affecting the actual Ajax engine in the future. This keeps our Ajax engine intact so that we never have to worry about any of the logic changing in the future.

The Response

The last method in the `AjaxUpdater` object is the catch-all method called `getResponse` I mentioned in the last section. This method simply gets all responses for the XHRs that do not set a callback method when they make a request (see Listing 6.7).

Listing 6.7   **Handling Responses** (`AjaxUpdater.js`)

```
AjaxUpdater.onResponse = function()
{
    if(Ajax.checkReadyState('loading') == 200)
    {
        AjaxUpdater.isUpdating = false;
    }
}
```

The method first checks the ready state as we covered in the `Ajax` object and sends the loading message to an HTML element with an `id` value of `'loading'`. After the `readyState` is complete and successful, it simply sets its `isUpdating` property to a value of `false` as a precaution, just in case the `Ajax` object has not done so already.

Now that we have a reusable engine for our Ajax requests, we can move forward with building the fun stuff, like Ajax components, database-enabled requests and, best of all, an entire Ajax-enabled application. But first, let's move on to the next chapter, where we will find out how to put this engine to use.

7

Using the Engine

Now that we have an Ajax engine created, let's take a look at how to use it. This chapter will focus on how to make an XHR through the `AjaxUpdater`, and how to access properties and call various methods within the `Ajax` object. After we have completed this chapter, you will know how to put the engine to work in any Ajax application, no matter how big or how small. This engine provides great flexibility because it abstracts all of an application's XHRs, keeps them consistent and, ultimately, makes them easier to manage. We will start with the basics by getting the files loaded in a sample application.

Getting Started

Before we are even able to use the Ajax engine that we constructed in the previous chapter, we will have to import all the JavaScript files that are associated with the engine. We currently have created a total of two objects that are necessary for the engine to run, but by the end of this part of the book, we will have a total of four that are necessary because we will be extending the engine with a `Utility` object and an `HTTP` object in Chapter 9, "Extending the Engine." To make things easier to remember, the following code will include all four objects that the engine will ultimately need to import in order to run properly. Here is how the four import statements should look in an application's head:

```
<script type="text/javascript" src="javascript/Utilities.js"></script>
<script type="text/javascript" src="javascript/model/AjaxUpdater.js"></script>
<script type="text/javascript" src="javascript/model/HTTP.js"></script>
<script type="text/javascript" src="javascript/model/Ajax.js"></script>
```

As you can see, importing the JavaScript objects is trivial, but it is the first required step in using the engine and therefore noteworthy. After these objects have been imported, we can make requests, access properties, and get the status of specific requests at any time. Let's move forward by learning how to make our first request through the Ajax engine.

Making a Request

In order to make requests, we will always use the `AjaxUpdater` as our access point. This object provides a layer of separation in our code to keep our XHRs easier to manage and consistent across the application. In this section, we will use this object to make our first engine request and get an idea of why this layer of abstraction is necessary. When we make a request through the `AjaxUpdater`, we will use a method called `Update`. The `Update` method takes three parameters: a method, a service, and an optional callback method. If a callback method is not specified, a default callback will be set in the `AjaxUpdater` object, which will reset a Boolean called `isUpdating` to `false`. This Boolean is set to `true` each time a request is made and set to `false` within the `Ajax` object when a response has been received. This is a useful property for checking whether the object is in the process of making a request, and could ultimately be used as a way to add items to a request queue. In addition to the import code from the previous section, we will add code to make a request for the XML file called `email.xml` from Chapter 3, "The Response." Again, we will make the request through the `Update` method in the `AjaxUpdater` object via the `GET` method, with a callback method named `onResponse`, which we will create in the next section.

```
<script type="text/javascript">
function initialize()
{
    AjaxUpdater.Update("GET", "services/sample.xml", onResponse);
}
</script>
</head>

<body onload="javascript:initialize();">
<div id="loading"></div>
<div id="body"></div>

</body>
</html>
```

In order to make sure all of our objects have been imported completely, we need to add our `Update` request to a method that is fired when the body of the document loads. After the body loads, it will fire the `Update` method, which, as you can see, passes the parameters that were previously mentioned. Another important part of the request is providing feedback to the user regarding the progress of the request. In order to display the progress, we have a `div` element with an `id` of `loading`. When we receive a response from the `Ajax` object, we will display a loading message in the element as we did in the first part of the book. After we receive the response from the engine, we will need a place to add it to the page. This place will be the `div` element, which we gave an id of body. As I am sure you noticed, the concepts in this chapter are all the same as in the first part of the book. The only difference in this second part of the book is that we now have a clean way of executing these tasks, which will make large-scale development much easier to manage and keep our applications much more scalable. Let's move forward by creating the onResponse method I mentioned earlier. This object will contain our first method call to the Ajax object.

Engine Methods and Properties

When we create the callback method for the request, we will need to check the ready state of the response in order to know that it is completed and ready to be parsed. In order to check the ready state with our engine, we will call our first Ajax method named checkReadyState. Following is a snippet of our onResponse method, which will make this call:

```
function onResponse()
{
    if(Ajax.checkReadyState('loading') == "OK")
    {
        // Parse response here
    }
}
```

After the ready state of the response is complete, we can parse the data as we did in Chapter 3. In order to parse the data, the Ajax object has another method named getResponse. This method will provide the correct data format based on the header response from the server. In other words, you do not have to worry about it—it all happens for you, which is a reason why this object makes life easier. Therefore, if there is a response and its content type is XML, this method will return the responseXML with the first documentElement so that the data is immediately ready to be parsed. If the data is not XML, the method will return the reponseText value, which can be used in any way you see fit. Following is a quick example of how simple it is to use this method in our onResponse callback:

```
function onResponse()
{
    if(Ajax.checkReadyState('loading') == "OK")
    {
            var categories = Ajax.getResponse().getElementsByTagName
            ('category');
            for(var i=0; i<categories.length; i++)
        {
            document.getElementById("body").innerHTML +=
```

```
➥Ajax.getResponse().getElementsByTagName('category')[i]
  ➥.firstChild.data +"</br>";
        }
    }
}
```

This sample code will get all the category nodes from the XML and iterate through them in order to populate the **body** element's **innerHTML** property, resulting in a list of categories on the page. Since JavaScript does not have any data typing or member visibility, it is obviously not a requirement to use this method to receive a response because it is only a way to make things easier during development. If you simply want to view the response as a string, you can call the request property in the **Ajax** object directly and use it to access the **responseText** and/or **responseXML** property.

This chapter is an example of how the engine simplifies our requests by eliminating a lot of the overhead and allowing us to focus on other aspects of the application. The next two chapters will explain how easy it is to debug with the engine in place and how flexible the engine is by allowing us endless ways of extending and scaling it.

8

Debugging

For years now, debugging JavaScript has not been the easiest thing to accomplish because there has been a lack of tools and a lack of native ways of doing so. Of course, there has always been the simple, yet trusty, alert debugging, shown in Figure 8.1, and the more sophisticated alert debugging approaches involving the `onerror` event.

Figure 8.1   Trusty alert debugging.

This chapter will briefly cover the more sophisticated methods of alert debugging that can be achieved with the `onerror` event and `responseText` property from the XHR object. With that in mind, the main focus of this chapter will be to discuss a few tools that will help us debug our Ajax applications with extreme ease and leave us wondering how we ever developed without them. These tools are the Internet Explorer (IE) Developer Toolbar, Safari Enhancer, and my personal favorite, FireBug. This chapter will also feature screenshots from the final application, which we will debug with the various approaches that we will be discussing throughout this chapter. Let's get started by covering JavaScript's own `onerror` event.

The JavaScript onerror Event

JavaScript has quite a few built-in events that handle various situations. One that can help quite a bit when debugging our web applications is the `onerror` event. Using the `onerror` event allows us to capture all the JavaScript errors that happen during runtime. This event returns three parameters that can be manipulated in any custom callback function that we define. The three parameters are the error message that was received, the URL of the file with the issue, and the line number in the file that is causing the error. For the most part, this event is useful but it can be quite vague at times, making sense only to someone who is intimately familiar with the code that is throwing the error.

In order to set up the `onerror` event, we must create a callback method to which the event will point. This callback method accepts the three parameters I mentioned previously.

```
function errorHandler(message, url, line)
{
    // Add custom error handling
    // return a true or false value;
}
onerror = errorHandler;
```

The `errorHandler` method should return `true` or `false`, depending on whether we want to display the browser's standard error message. If we return `true`, the browser does not display its standard error message and vice versa. Obviously, using `false` would be somewhat redundant, unless we wanted to handle the error message in two ways. In order to display our own custom error-handling message, we could do something similar to the following example:

```
<html>
<head>
<script type="text/javascript">

function errorHandler(message, url, line)
{
    var errorMessage = "Error: "+ message +"\n";
    errorMessage += "URL: "+ url +"\n";
    errorMessage += "Line Number: "+ line +"\n";
    alert(errorMessage);
    return true;
}
onerror = errorHandler;

function invokeError()
{
    allllert("Hello World!");
}
</script>
</head>
```

```
<body>
    <input type="button" value="View Error" onclick="invokeError();" />
</body>

</html>
```

This example provides a button to invoke an error because the `alert` function within the `invokeError` method is not written properly. After the error occurs, the `onerror` event will fire the callback method and pass it the three parameters regarding the error. The callback method that we create, called `errorHandler`, will concatenate a string version of the error and present an alert to the user. In Chapter 16, "The Observer Pattern," we will create a more sophisticated version of this method that will send an email to us (as the developers) with a hyperlink to the file that contains the error. For the time being, we can see that this method of error handling can be useful for debugging because it can present us with a bit more detail than some of the built-in error handling that browsers provide. Of course, when we begin to discuss installing extensions, this will all change, but this method is still a viable solution to debugging our applications.

responseText

Before we discuss the extensions that we can use for debugging our applications, we will cover one more form of alert debugging. For a quick and dirty look at the response received from an XHR, we could use the `responseText` property. This property is a part of the XHR object and returns a string version of any response received from the server. This includes XML, plain text, JSON, and so on. It can be helpful when used with alert debugging to get an idea of the document structure with which you are interacting. After the structure is known, it is easy to plan an approach for targeting specific items in the response. When working with XML, we can see the structure of the nodes and how they are encapsulated with their parents and ancestors, and so on.

After this is working, we can use the `responseXML` property to actually target the correct data that we need to receive for display or confirmation of data retrieval.

IE Developer Toolbar

The IE Developer Toolbar is quite helpful when debugging web applications in Internet Explorer, especially because the built-in JavaScript error console is incredibly vague and unhelpful. In this chapter, we will discover how this tool provides us with the power to disable the cache, navigate the DOM, and view class and `id` information within the browser. Before we learn how to use each of these features, we will first need to install the plug-in.

Installing the Plug-in

The IE Developer Toolbar can be downloaded from http://www.microsoft.com/ downloads. After you have downloaded and installed the toolbar, it is quite simple to get started. Go to the View menu and select Toolbars, Developer Toolbar. This will provide us with the toolbar at the top of IE. After we have the toolbar set up, we can either click View DOM, or go to the View menu and select Explorer Bar, IE DOM Explorer from the drop-down. These options provide us with the DOM Explorer, which we can use for a number of debugging purposes, all of which we will talk about now.

Disabling the Cache

One of the most helpful debugging features is the option to disable the cache, which I am sure will make your day if you have been testing applications in IE for any length of time. IE's cache has always been hard to test around, and the process of clearing it takes too many clicks, a long wait time, and is not very reliable. This option can be set by selecting the Disable option from the toolbar and choosing Cache from the various options within the drop-down menu. With this option set, we will never have to clear the cache again, but one thing to keep in mind is that we must reset this option every time we restart IE because it does not save the setting.

Navigating the DOM

Another useful feature in the toolbar is the ability to navigate the DOM. The DOM Explorer allows us to view all the tags within a web application, by simply choosing the View DOM button from the toolbar. We will see a tree view on the left side of the DOM Explorer, which represents the structure of the document that is currently active within the browser. We can then navigate the DOM by selecting the plus/minus symbols next to each tag. As we choose different items in the structure, we will get an obnoxious, flashing blue border around the tag that we are selecting in the display. This obnoxious border is actually pretty helpful because it helps us find elements in the page by navigating the HTML. Another feature in the DOM Explorer view is that each time an element is selected, it shows the attributes and the styles for the tags by name with their current values. Take a look at Figure 8.2 to get an idea of what the DOM Explorer looks like.

When viewing the entire DOM in most applications, it can get quite convoluted and near impossible to locate elements. This is why the Find Element option is so useful. This option can be found by choosing Find from the DOM Explorer and selecting Find Element from the drop-down menu. Once open, we can search for any element in the page, the options are Element, Class, Id, and Name. Figure 8.3 shows an example of the Find Element option in action.

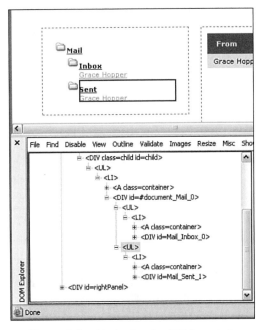

Figure 8.2   Navigating the DOM can help discover issues that arise during runtime.

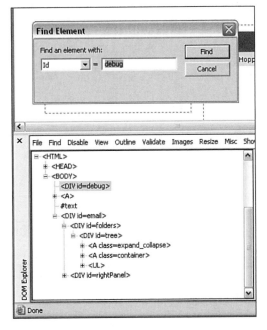

Figure 8.3   Finding specific elements in the DOM doesn't have to be hard.

The tree view is one of three panels that appear in the DOM Explorer; the other two are a node attributes panel and a styles detail panel. The node attributes panel displays attribute information about each node. It also enables us to add or subtract attributes as an additional debugging feature. The styles panel contains the style details about each HTML tag in the tree view. While navigating the tree view, each tag that we choose will display its style details in the style panel. Take a look at Figure 8.4 to see both of these panels in action.

Viewing Class and ID Information

This feature of the toolbar is simple: It provides us with the ability to view class and ID information. This is a great way to gather information about a web application. If we are having trouble discovering where specific elements are nested within a page, we can use this feature.

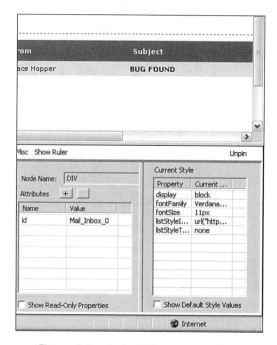

Figure 8.4   Node attributes and styles.

Safari Enhancer

If you happen to use a Mac and want to debug your JavaScript applications, the Safari Enhancer is a great tool. The Safari Enhancer does exactly what the name implies: It is a great addition to the browser and helps debug JavaScript issues where as no other tool, that I have come across, does.

Installing Safari Enhancer

If we are using a new Mac, Safari comes pre-installed on the system. Therefore, to install the Safari Enhancer we must simply visit http://www.celestialfrontiers.com/safari_enhancer.php and click on the latest releases download link. Once the installer is downloaded we can install by simply double-clicking the installer and following the prompts. When the installation has completed we can open the Safari Enhancer and set a preference in order to debug our applications. The preference which you will want to check is the Activate Debugging Menu option as seen in Figure 8.5. This figure also shows the Deactivate Cache option as being checked. It is up to you if you would like to set this option, I prefer to know that I am dealing with fresh data when I develop.

This will add a new menu item to Safari called Debug. Under this menu will be a list of debugging options, such as Show DOM Tree, Show Render Tree, Show View Tree, and many more. My favorite happens to be the JavaScript console and it happens to be the most relevant to our situation.

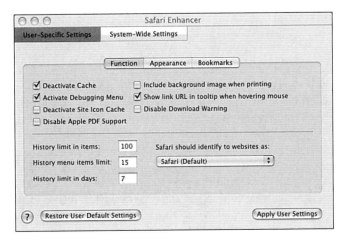

Figure 8.5   Activating the Debugging menu in Safari.

The JavaScript Console

The JavaScript console works much like other consoles that are available in other browsers. The difference with this console is that it obviously is attached to Safari and therefore provides us with issues specific to this browser that other browsers consoles may not pick up. Since all browsers handle code differently it is essential to test in them all if you want to have a universally compatible application. Figure 8.6 shows the JavaScript console as it appears with logged errors.

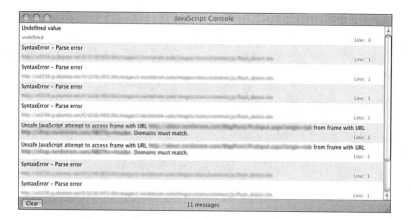

Figure 8.6   Logged errors in the JavaScript console.

FireBug

I definitely saved the best for last with this extension. FireBug is one of the premier debugging tools for Ajax, JavaScript, CSS, and XHTML applications. It supports error and warning descriptions for JavaScript and CSS. This tool not only provides extremely accurate feedback about errors—such as what went wrong, what line it happened on, and what file it happened in—it also opens the file within the Debugger tab and highlights the line of code that is throwing the error. Now that is accuracy! But it gets even better: Not only does it provide the error, it allows us to set breakpoints in the code from the Debugger panel and rerun the page to stop the page when that line of code is reached. I never dreamed of such things with JavaScript! Most relevant to our Ajax applications is the fact that it also allows us to spy on XHRs and returns just enough detail about them to eliminate the need for the `responseText` in an alert approach.

Installing FireBug

In order to install the extension, we first need to have the Firefox browser, which can be downloaded from http://www.mozilla.com/firefox/. After we have the browser installed, we can get the FireBug extension at http://www.joehewitt.com/software/firebug/. Joe Hewitt has built a very minimal and easy-to-use debugging tool that can accomplish a lot of debugging techniques. In order to use the extension after it is installed, we need to either click on the check mark on the bottom-right corner of the browser window or go to Tools, FireBug and choose an option from the extension's list. Figure 8.7 shows a screenshot of the options we get after the extension has been opened.

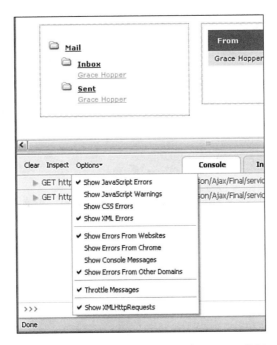

Figure 8.7   These are the options that are available
for displaying errors, warnings, and XHRs.

The Command Line

The command line enables us to write arguments against the page with JavaScript and receive responses, which would typically display in an alert (that is, if we were alert debugging). This step eliminates the need to go back and forth between our development tool of choice, check out the file from the server, and write the code we want to test, by either adding it to an alert or writing it to the document, and then re-upload the file and test. These four steps are eliminated with a simple command line, which is built in to the bottom of the tool. Take a look at Figure 8.8 for a screenshot of the command line in action.

The command line enables us to do much more than write simple strings to the console. Writing a reference to an object creates a hyperlink in the FireBug console. When we click an object hyperlink in the console, we are taken to the Inspector, which displays the selected object in the appropriate tab. For example, the sample application has a `div` element named `email` in the index, which contains all the components in the application. If we wanted to test the object hyperlinking, we could type `document.getElementById('email');` into the command line and view the results. Figure 8.9 shows an example of the hyperlink that appears in the console when we write this code.

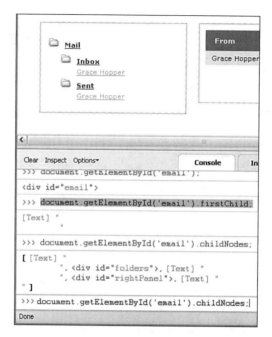

Figure 8.8   The command-line input and results provide a quick way to test JavaScript.

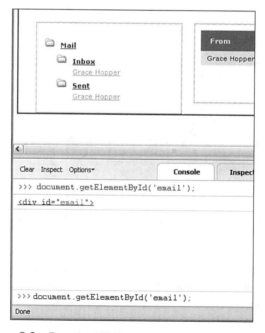

Figure 8.9   Targeting HTML elements via the command-line.

Table 8.1 shows a list of built-in functions that can be invoked from the command line. These functions are useful shorthand approaches to receiving command-line responses.

Table 8.1　**FireBug's Built-in Command-Line Functions**

Functions	Definitions
`$("id")`	Represents the following function: `document.getElementById()`.
`$$("css")`	Returns an array of elements that match a CSS selector.
`$x("xpath")`	Returns an array of elements that match an XPath selector.
`$0`	Variable containing the most recently inspected object.
`$1`	Variable containing the next most recently inspected object.
`$n(5)`	Returns the nth most recently inspected object.
`inspect(object)`	Displays the specified object in the Inspector.
`dir(object)`	Returns an array of property names from an object.
`clear()`	Clears the console.

Logging Messages in the Console

The `console.log` method is a sophisticated replacement for alert debugging. This method takes two parameters: The first is anything that you want to display in the console, and the second is an optional parameter that selects a tab in the Inspector based on the value specified. This would be the perfect solution to displaying the `responseText` that we were debugging earlier in the chapter. Using the `console.log` method is very simple:

```
console.log(param, 'optional tab');
```

This obviously does not work in other browsers because FireBug does not have compatible versions, so when deploying the live version of an application that uses them, make sure that we remove them.

The `basic logging` method is not just an alert-debugging replacement. As we learned with the command line, writing a reference to an object creates a hyperlink in the FireBug console. When we click an object hyperlink in the console, we are taken to the Inspector, which displays the selected object in the appropriate tab. This also applies to passing an object reference as a parameter to the `console.log` method. This suddenly makes the `console.log` method a lot more powerful and sets it far above other debugging methods. As if that wasn't enough there are also different levels of logging messages according to severity.

Levels of Logging

In order to log errors, warnings, debug messages or other random information we can use the different levels of logging that exist in FireBug. They not only visually separate different types of messages in the console, they also provide a link in the console to the exact line number in the source code where they reside. This can be extremely useful during development phases by eliminating excessive debugging time. In order to use these different methods in your JavaScript you would write them as follows:

```
console.debug("message" [,objects]);
console.info("message" [,objects]);
console.warn("message" [,objects]);
console.error("message" [,objects]);
```

Inspecting Elements

FireBug provides the capability to inspect elements within a page called Instant Inspecting. I believe this is the most useful approach to debugging that I have come across. Instant Inspecting can be accessed by either going to Tools, FireBug, Inspect Element or by clicking the check mark at the bottom-right corner of the browser and choosing the Inspect button from the top-left menu, next to the Clear button. After we have activated the Inspector, we can hover the mouse over the page to inspect the elements within the page. As we hover over them, we see the structure of our page and how certain items relate to others. Figure 8.10 shows the Inspector in action as it highlights the tag in the code for the element that is currently being hovered over.

Another unbelievably helpful feature the Inspector includes is live editing. Live editing enables us to click on a tag attribute value, such as a `div id` value, and change it within the editor to test the new behavior. This is another great timesaver that eliminates quite a bit of steps from the traditional debugging approach. Figure 8.11 shows an example of live editing with a `div id` from the sample application.

Inspecting events is another feature that FireBug offers, which can be used by selecting the Inspector tab and then the Events tab from the bottom of the window, and then clicking the Inspect button. After we have activated the Inspector, we can hover over the application to receive all the events within the page. As we can see in Figure 8.12, all the events—from a simple `mousemove` to a `DOMActivate`—are displayed within the Inspector.

At first glance, it is obvious that the event inspecting can become fairly messy, especially with all the `mousemove` events. Luckily, there is a feature that allows you to filter the events you want to inspect. The search box that is located in the top-right corner of FireBug is used for this solution. Just type in the event you want to see, such as **mouseover**, and it will automatically filter out all other events—very handy.

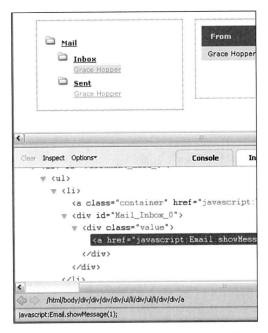

Figure 8.10   Instant Inspecting provides a different
perspective on web applications.

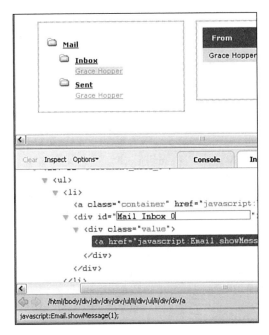

Figure 8.11   Live editing enables us to edit tag
attributes during runtime to test functionality.

Figure 8.12   Inspecting events provides vital information during runtime.

Spying on Ajax

XHRs can be watched (or spied on) with a built-in XHR event listener in FireBug. This tool provides us with the Post or Get tab, the Response tab, and the Headers tab from a request's response. To activate the XHR spy, we must choose the Show XMLHttpRequests option from the Options drop-down in FireBug. Once activated, it will display all XHRs that are made within a web application. By default, it shows the requested URL and the method that was used to make the request. When one is selected it expands, leaving us with three options: Post or Get (based on the type of request), Response, and Headers. By clicking each of the tabs, we can view the data that was used for each. The Post or Get tab shows us the request that was made, whereas the Response tab shows the response from the server, such as XML, JSON, and so on. The Headers tab displays the headers from the server that were received with the response. No more writing alerts on the request headers! The Post or Get tab can be useful if we want to see the URL that is being requested and the parameters that are being sent in the query string. Figure 8.13 shows a request with a couple of parameters as a query string.

In this case, the Response tab shows the XML that is being returned from the server. See Figure 8.14 to get an idea of how this looks.

As Figure 8.15 shows, the Headers tab displays the headers that were sent by the server where the sample is residing.

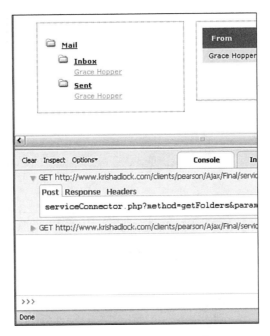

Figure 8.13   Viewing an XHR.

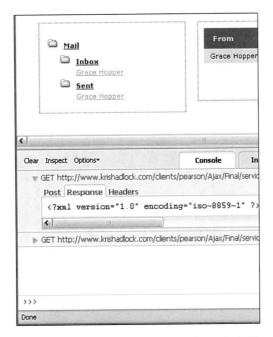

Figure 8.14   Viewing the response from the XHR.

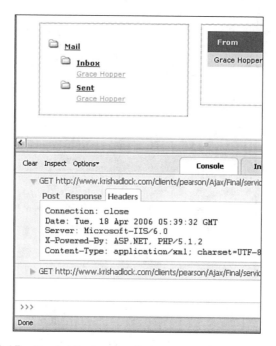

Figure 8.15   Viewing the headers that were sent by the server with the
response to the XHR.

9

Extending the Engine

Using an object-oriented design for the Ajax engine provided us with the flexibility to extend or incorporate the code into any web application. The engine that we have created can accomplish any type of request. To make this engine extremely powerful, we can create additional objects that extend the engine's functionality and provide us with ways of handling common situations when developing our Ajax applications.

This chapter will focus on extending the Ajax engine with two completely different types of objects. The first object that we will create is a `Utilities` object, which will handle all of the common front-end functionalities, such as creating HTML elements, simplifying common JavaScript functions, and providing our applications with reusable GUI-focused methods. The second object is an HTTP object, which will handle all the possible status codes that may be returned with the Ajax response. Although the `Utilities` object is completely focused on front-end code, this object has the dual purpose of providing both the front end and back end with appropriate status code responses as strings.

Creating a Utilities Object

The samples that we build throughout the rest of this book will rely heavily on specific DOM-related methods. These methods will simplify common JavaScript functions, create any HTML element that we need, and be reused to avoid the duplication of common code throughout our applications.

Before we create any methods, we must first instantiate the `Utilities` object as follows:

```
Utilities = {};
```

This object is based on the Singleton pattern, which we will discuss in Chapter 14, "Singleton Pattern." Creating methods in this object is simple: First use the name of the object, followed by the name of the method. Take a look at the following example:

```
Utilities.createElement = function() {}
```

The methods that currently exist in the `Utilities` object are extremely reusable and will be used heavily throughout the rest of the book samples. We will start by adding two methods: one that includes JavaScript files named `includeJS` (see Listing 9.1), and another named `includeCSS`, which includes CSS files (see Listing 9.2). Each method includes the corresponding array of files in any document by accepting an array of file paths.

Listing 9.1   **Including JavaScript Files (`Utilities.js`)**

```
Utilities.includeJS = function(filepaths)
{
    for(var i=0; i<filepaths.length; i++)
    {
        document.write('<script type="text/javascript"
          ➥src="'+filepaths[i]+'"></script>');
    }
}
```

Listing 9.2   **Including CSS Files (`Utilities.js`)**

```
Utilities.includeCSS = function(filepaths)
{
    for(var i=0; i<filepaths.length; i++)
    {
        document.
      write('<link href="'+filepaths[i]+'" rel="stylesheet" type="text/css" />');
    }
}
```

These methods are simple but they save a lot of typing, or copying and pasting, and make our HTML page more manageable. They also save time and prevent errors if a change needs to be made to the `include` statement because we will have to make the change only in the method rather than in multiple tags that would reside in the HTML file. The following is an example of how we could use these methods in a web page:

```
var cssFiles = new Array("pathto/css/file.css", "pathto/another/css/file.css");
➥Utilities.includeCSS(cssFiles);
```

```
var jsFiles = new Array("pathto/javascript/file.js",
    "pathto/another/javascript/file.js ");
Utilities.includeJS(jsFiles);
```

The next method, named `getElement`, is even simpler than the previous two. This method returns an element by ID by accepting a string parameter and using JavaScript's intrinsic `getElementById` method. Ultimately, this method is just a shorthand version of the intrinsic method and allows us to make changes to the method only if we need to do so in the future.

```
Utilities.getElement = function(i) { return document.getElementById(i); }
```

Debugging is one of the largest complaints when it comes to JavaScript aside from the debugger tools that I mentioned in Chapter 8, "Debugging." This next method has saved me a lot of grief and will hopefully do the same for you. It is conveniently named `debug` and takes any value as a parameter and writes it to a debug tag that you must specify anywhere in your HTML (see Listing 9.3), specifically during development and testing. This method also gives us an example of how to use the `getElement` method, which we just covered.

Listing 9.3   **Debugging with the `Utilities` Object** (`Utilities.js`)

```
Utilities.debug = function(val)
{
    this.getElement('debug').innerHTML += val +"</br>";
}
<!-- A Sample Debug Element -->
<div id="debug""></div>
```

In Chapter 18, "Interaction Patterns," we will learn about interaction patterns and GUI-related code that can be used in your Ajax applications. The next method, named `toggle` (see Listing 9.4), is one that will get a lot of use in chapters to come. This method takes an ID of a DOM element and checks to see whether the element's display style is equal to an empty string or to the string value of `'none'`. If it is empty, it sets it to `'none'`; if it is `'none'`, it sets it to an empty string. This code toggles the visibility of any DOM element by ID at anytime, from any object.

Listing 9.4   **Toggle Element Visibility** (`Utilities.js`)

```
Utilities.toggle = function(id)
{
    this.getElement(id)
        ➥.style.display = (this.getElement(id).
        ➥style.display == '') ? 'none' : '';
}
```

The next method that we will examine is one that creates a DOM element that can later be written to the document body. I have conveniently named this method `createElement` (see Listing 9.5). The `createElement` method takes two parameters: a string that represents the HTML element type that you want to create, and an object.

Listing 9.5   **Creating Elements with the `Utilities` Object (`Utilities.js`)**

```
Utilities.createElement = function(e, obj)
{
    var element = document.createElement(e);
    for(prop in obj)
    {
        element[prop] = obj[prop];
    }
    return element;
}
```

The `createElement` method dynamically creates elements that can be used to display data in the page. It can create any HTML element—a few examples are `div`, `span`, `img`, `a`, `li`, and so on—based on the string that is passed as the first parameter. What makes this method even more extraordinary is the fact that it can accept properties as JSON and append them along with their values to the element. This method appends properties to DOM elements by iterating through the properties in the JSON parameter and creating properties on the DOM element. The following is an example of how to use this method:

```
var title = Utilities.createElement("div", {id:'title', className:'title',
➡innerHTML:'title'});
```

This method might have created an HTML element, but the `createElement` method cannot write this element to the page on its own. This is why we need to create the next method, named `appendChild` (see Listing 9.6).

Listing 9.6   **Appending Child Elements to the Document (`Utilities.js`)**

```
Utilities.appendChild = function()
{
    if(this.appendChild.arguments.length > 1)
    {
        var a = this.appendChild.arguments[0];
        for(i=1; i<this.appendChild.arguments.length; i++)
        {
            if(arguments[i])
            {
                a.appendChild(this.appendChild.arguments[i]);
            }
        }
    }
```

Listing 9.6   **Continued**

```
        return a;
    }
    else
    {
        return null;
    }
}
```

This method handles appending HTML elements to one another and, ultimately, the current document by appending elements to the document body. It uses JavaScript's intrinsic `arguments` property, which is an array that contains all the input parameters for the current method. This `arguments` array can then be iterated to provide each parameter that was passed to the method. This property allows developers to create methods that can change based on the parameters. The following is an example of how we could write the previously created `title div` to the document body:

```
<html>
<head>
<title>Sample</title>
<script type="text/javascript" src="../javascript/Utilities.js"></script>
<script type="text/javascript">
function init()
{
    var title = Utilities.createElement("div", {id:'title', className:'title',
    ➡innerHTML:'title'});
    Utilities.appendChild(document.body, title);
}
</script>
</head>

<body onload="javascript:init();">

</body>
</html>
```

As you can see, we must wait to create the element and append it to the document until the body of the document has completely loaded. If we do not wait until the document has fully loaded, the element that we are appending to will most likely not exist when this code is executed and will throw an error that cause the code to fail. Therefore it is important to be patient. After it has loaded, we can write the element and append it however we please. Remember, this is a very simple example to show you how to use these methods. It might seem like a lot of overhead just for writing the word `title` to a web page (and it obviously is), but imagine adding a stylesheet to the page to handle formatting the elements that you are writing, or appending other elements to the title element before appending it to the body. The possibilities are endless and can become extremely efficient when we create objects to manage rendering components. All we need to do is pass the newly created element content from an Ajax request that returns dynamic XML based on data in a database. And don't forget, this will all happen without a page refresh.

The next method is named `removeChildren` and it does just that. It takes an element as a parameter, and checks to see if the parameter is null; if so, it returns nothing. If the value is not null, we enter a `while` loop based on the `hasChildNodes` method. This creates a loop while the element has `childNodes`. In this loop we perform a `removeChild` on the element and pass its `firstChild` as the parameter. In the end the element is stripped of all its children and the method has accomplished its goal. Listing 9.7 shows the complete `removeChildren` method.

Listing 9.7   Removing Children from Their Parents (`Utilities.js`)

```
Utilities.removeChildren = function(node)
{
    if(node == null)
    {
        return;
    }

    while(node.hasChildNodes())
    {
        node.removeChild(node.firstChild);
    }
}
```

The next two methods are useful for adding listeners for events based on how the browser happens to handle them, since the browsers cannot seem to get along. The first method will be named `addListener` and the second `removeListener`. Both methods take the same three parameters; an object, an event name, and a listener. The `obj` parameter represents the element in which you want to assign the listener to, such as the document object. The `eventName` parameter represents the event to register the listener to, which could consist of anything from a `mousemove` event to a `click` event. The last parameter listener is the custom method that you want to be called each time the event is fired. This is the actual method doing the listening. The only difference between the two methods is that one adds and one removes listeners. Listing 9.8 shows both methods as they appear in the `Utilities` object.

Listing 9.8   Adding and Removing Listeners (`Utilities.js`)

```
Utilities.addListener = function(obj, eventName, listener)
{
    if (obj.attachEvent)
    {
        obj.attachEvent("on"+eventName, listener);
    }
```

Listing 9.8   **Continued**

```
    else if(obj.addEventListener)
    {
        obj.addEventListener(eventName, listener, false);
    }
    else
    {
        return false;
    }
    return true;
}

Utilities.removeListener = function(obj, eventName, listener)
{
    if(obj.detachEvent)
    {
        obj.detachEvent("on"+eventName, listener);
    }
    else if(obj.removeEventListener)
    {
        obj.removeEventListener(eventName, listener, false);
    }
    else
    {
        return false;
    }

    return true;
}
```

Each method checks to see what browser the user is using. If it is IE, we add the `"on"` string to the beginning of the `eventName` when we `attachEvent` of `detachEvent` in order to reference the event name as IE expects it. If the user is in another browser, the method uses the `addEventListener` and `removeEventListener` events and the parameters are passed to these methods as is.

The last method in the `Utilities` object is a visual one. The object is called `changeOpac` and it changes the opacity of an element in any browser by simply passing a number and an element ID to the method. Listing 9.9 shows this method and how it handles changing all the different browser opacities.

Listing 9.9   **Changing the Opacity of an Element (`Utilities.js`)**

```
Utilities.changeOpac = function(opacity, id)
{
    var object = Utils.ge(id).style;
    object.opacity = (opacity / 100);
    object.MozOpacity = (opacity / 100);
```

Listing 9.9   **Continued**

```
    object.KhtmlOpacity = (opacity / 100);
    object.filter = "alpha(opacity=" + opacity + ")";
}
```

Handling Status Codes with an HTTP Object

HTTP status codes have a dual purpose: They are not only useful in the back end for development purposes, but they are also very useful on the front end for providing users with the status of their interactions.

As we briefly covered in Chapter 2, "The Request," the request status of the Ajax object is equivalent to the HTTP status of the file that is being requested. HTTP status codes represent the response from the server based on the status of the file that is being requested. The codes are broken up into five categories, which cover all the possible responses that a server could return to an HTTP request. The HTTP status code categories are listed next; the xx after each number represents other digits which exist in each category and are used to specify a type of error.

- Informational: 1xx
- Successful: 2xx
- Redirection: 3xx
- Client Error: 4xx
- Server Error: 5xx

In order to handle these status codes and provide meaningful user feedback, we will create an **HTTP** object. The object that we will be creating will take the request status from the Ajax object, which will be a number from 1 to 4. It will then return the status code that corresponds with that number value as a string that will contain an explanation of what occurred on the server side. Providing this level of detail is essential when creating web applications because a user should always understand what is happening and what, if anything, went wrong. The **HTTP** object is fairly simple, but it is quite large because of the level of detail it covers. The following is a condensed version of the object and the methods it contains:

```
HTTP = {};

HTTP.status = function(_status){}

HTTP.getInformationalStatus = function(_status){}

HTTP.getSuccessfulStatus = function(_status){}

HTTP.getRedirectionStatus = function(_status){}
```

```
HTTP.getClientErrorStatus = function(_status){}

HTTP.getServerErrorStatus = function(_status){}
```

The **HTTP** object has been separated into different methods for each response category. To make this object more usable, there is a **status** method that is used as the access point to the object. All status calls are filtered through this method to the corresponding category to which they belong. Each method takes the status that is passed as a parameter and returns a string response that we, as the developers, choose to respond with. As you will see, the current object has default responses, which represent the literal status code titles, but these can and should ultimately be changed to responses that are more informative and user friendly. Let's take a look at the status method in Listing 9.10 to get an idea of how this method handles delegating the status number value to the corresponding method category.

Listing 9.10   **Delegating HTTP Status Codes to the Correct Methods (HTTP.js)**

```
HTTP.status = function(_status)
{
    var s = _status.toString().split("");
    switch(s[0])
    {
        case "1":
            return this.getInformationalStatus(_status);
            break;
        case "2":
            return this.getSuccessfulStatus(_status);
            break;
        case "3":
            return this.getRedirectionStatus(_status);
            break;
        case "4":
            return this.getClientErrorStatus(_status);
            break;
        case "5":
            return this.getServerErrorStatus(_status);
            break;
        default:
            return "An unexpected error has occurred.";
    }
}
```

The status code categories are split into different numbers. When the status method receives the _status parameter, it takes the first number from the parameter and locates the corresponding method based on its category number. For example, if the object received a 404 status code value, it would use the first number in the code, which would be the number 4, to locate the appropriate method category and delegate it to that method. In order to use the first number in the status code, we need to convert the number to a string and split it into an array of strings. After we have created the array, we can target its first item, which is the item in the 0 position, and perform a switch on it to match it with the corresponding method category.

HTTP Status Code Categories

The five method categories that the HTTP object consists of correspond to the HTTP status code definition categories. Each of the methods in the object takes a **_status** parameter, which is used to return the corresponding message. This section will cover the status codes that are handled by each method, but will not go into detail about each status code definition. As a useful reference, I have also added the URL in each method to the status code definition categories, which are defined in detail on the W3C website. The first method that we will focus on, which can be viewed in Listing 9.11, corresponds to the Informational category.

Listing 9.11   **Handling Informational Status Codes (HTTP.js)**

```
HTTP.getInformationalStatus = function(_status)
{
    // Informational 1xx
    // http://www.w3.org/Protocols/rfc2616/rfc2616-sec10.html#sec10.1
    switch(_status)
    {
        case 100:
            return "Continue";
            break;
        case 101:
            return "Switching Protocols";
            break;
        default:
            return "An unexpected error has occurred.";
    }
}
```

The getInformationalStatus method handles all the informational status codes for the HTTP object. The informational status code category consists of two status codes:

- Continue: 100
- Switching Protocols: 101

The second method, named getSuccessfulStatus (see Listing 9.12), handles all the successful HTTP status codes.

Listing 9.12   **Handling Successful Status Codes (HTTP.js)**

```
HTTP.getSuccessfulStatus = function(_status)
{
    // Successful 2xx
    // http://www.w3.org/Protocols/rfc2616/rfc2616-sec10.html#sec10.2
    switch(_status)
    {
        case 200:
            return "OK";
            break;
        case 201:
            return "Created";
            break;
        case 202:
            return "Accepted";
            break;
        case 203:
            return "Non-Authoritative Information";
            break;
        case 204:
            return "No Content";
            break;
        case 205:
            return "Reset Content";
            break;
        case 206:
            return "Partial Content";
            break;
        default:
            return "An unexpected error has occurred.";
    }
}
```

The successful status code category consists of six status codes:

- OK: 200
- Created: 201
- Accepted: 202
- Non-Authoritative Information: 203
- No Content: 204
- Reset Content: 205
- Partial Content: 206

The third status code method category is the `getRedirectionStatus` (see Listing 9.13) method.

Listing 9.13   **Handling Redirection Status Codes (`HTTP.js`)**

```
HTTP.getRedirectionStatus = function(_status)
{
    // Redirection 3xx
    // http://www.w3.org/Protocols/rfc2616/rfc2616-sec10.html#sec10.3
    switch(_status)
    {
        case 300:
            return "Multiple Choices";
            break;
        case 301:
            return "Moved Permanently";
            break;
        case 302:
            return "Found";
            break;
        case 303:
            return "See Other";
            break;
        case 304:
            return "Not Modified";
            break;
        case 305:
            return "Use Proxy";
            break;
        case 307:
            return "Temporary Redirect";
            break;
        default:
            return "An unexpected error has occurred.";
    }
}
```

The `getRedirectionStatus` method handles all the redirection status codes for the
`HTTP` object. The redirection status code category consists of seven status codes:

- Multiple Choices: 300
- Moved Permanently: 301
- Found: 302
- See Other: 303
- Not Modified: 304
- Use Proxy: 305
- Temporary Redirect: 307

The fourth method for handling status codes is the `getClientErrorStatus` (see
Listing 9.14) method.

Listing 9.14   **Handling Client Error Status Codes** (HTTP.js)

```
HTTP.getClientErrorStatus = function(_status)
{
    // Client Error 4xx
    // http://www.w3.org/Protocols/rfc2616/rfc2616-sec10.html#sec10.4
    switch(_status)
    {
        case 400:
            return "Bad Request";
            break;
        case 401:
            return "Unauthorized";
            break;
        case 402:
            return "Payment Required";
            break;
        case 403:
            return "Forbidden";
            break;
        case 404:
            return "File not found.";
            break;
        case 405:
            return "Method Not Allowed";
            break;
        case 406:
            return "Not Acceptable";
            break;
        case 407:
            return "Proxy Authentication Required";
            break;
        case 408:
            return "Request Timeout";
            break;
        case 409:
            return "Conflict";
            break;
        case 410:
            return "Gone";
            break;
        case 411:
            return "Length Required";
            break;
        case 412:
            return "Precondition Failed";
            break;
```

Listing 9.14   **Continued**

```
        case 413:
            return "Request Entity Too Large";
            break;
        case 414:
            return "Request-URI Too Long";
            break;
        case 415:
            return "Unsupported Media Type";
            break;
        case 416:
            return "Requested Range Not Satisfiable";
            break;
        case 417:
            return "Expectation Failed";
            break;
        default:
            return "An unexpected error has occurred.";
    }
}
```

The `getClientErrorStatus` method handles all the client error status codes for the `HTTP` object. This status category is intended to present statuses based on an error that occurs from an interaction that a client makes. The client error status code category is the largest of the five categories, consisting of seventeen status codes:

- Bad Request: 400
- Unauthorized: 401
- Payment Required: 402
- Forbidden: 403
- File not found: 404
- Method Not Allowed: 405
- Not Acceptable: 406
- Proxy Authentication Required: 407
- Request Timeout: 408
- Conflict: 409
- Gone: 410
- Length Required: 411
- Precondition Failed: 412
- Request Entity Too Large: 413
- Request-URI Too Long: 414

- Unsupported Media Type: 415
- Requested Range Not Satisfiable: 416
- Expectation Failed: 417

The fifth and final status code category method is named **getServerStatus** (see Listing 9.15), which consists of all the server error status codes that could be returned from an HTTP request. The difference between the client and the server status code categories is instead of responding with errors based on client interactions, the server status codes are relative to the server and its inability to perform a request.

Listing 9.15   **Handling Redirection Status Codes (HTTP.js)**

```
HTTP.getServerErrorStatus = function(_status)
{
    // Server Error 5xx
    // http://www.w3.org/Protocols/rfc2616/rfc2616-sec10.html#sec10.5
    switch(_status)
    {
        case 500:
            return "Internal Server Error";
            break;
        case 501:
            return "Not Implemented";
            break;
        case 502:
            return "Bad Gateway";
            break;
        case 503:
            return "Service Unavailable";
            break;
        case 504:
            return "Gateway Timeout";
            break;
        case 505:
            return "HTTP Version Not Supported";
            break;
        default:
            return "An unexpected error has occurred.";
    }
}
```

The server error status code category consists of five status codes:

- Internal Server Error: 500
- Not Implemented: 501
- Bad Gateway: 502

- Service Unavailable: 503
- Gateway Timeout: 504
- HTTP Version Not Supported: 505

As you can see, the `HTTP` object is fairly simple, yet it is fairly large as well due to the fact that it handles every single status code that an HTTP request could possibly return. This object will save a lot of coding time; all that you must do for your applications is provide a custom message or even an action based on the code.

Using the HTTP Object

Adding the `HTTP` object to the Ajax engine is extremely simple after the JavaScript file has been imported into the current document. We will need to call only a single method, which will provide the status feedback as a string. Listing 9.16 shows how to return the status to the Ajax requestor.

Listing 9.16   Returning the HTTP Status As a String (`Ajax.js`)

```
Ajax.checkReadyState = function(_id)
{
    switch(this.request.readyState)
    {
        case 1:
            document.getElementById(_id).innerHTML = 'Loading ...';
            break;
        case 2:
            document.getElementById(_id).innerHTML = 'Loading ...';
            break;
        case 3:
            document.getElementById(_id).innerHTML = 'Loading ...';
            break;
        case 4:
            AjaxUpdater.isUpdating = false;
            document.getElementById(_id).innerHTML = '';
            return HTTP.status(this.request.status);
        default:
            document.
    getElementById(_id).innerHTML = "An
    ➥unexpected error has occurred.";
    }
}
```

Now that we have the HTTP object created, we can begin to return meaningful status codes to requesting objects as feedback to the user or we can use these status codes to provide the user with other options. For instance, let's say that we have an application that is attached to a shopping cart and we receive a `402: Payment Required` response from the server. We could either redirect the user to a payment page or dynamically write a payment form to the page through DHTML. Another possibility could be a `401: Unauthorized` response, which we could handle by redirecting the user to a login page or, again, we could use DHTML to present a form to the user for login/registration without refreshing the page. When the user logs in or registers, we could send the request through Ajax. After we receive a successful response, we could present the user with the original data she was requesting.

There is a huge difference between providing the user with feedback versus providing her with options. When we provide a user with feedback, she does not have any options and is usually left wondering what to do next. If we provide the user with options, we make the process much more intuitive and allow the user to progress on her own without worrying about reading cryptic messages from the server side. In fact, those cryptic messages also take time for developers to write. Rather, developers could be planning their next response to provide the user with a new option. HTTP status codes are just one of the features that make Ajax so powerful, yet they are very seldom a topic of conversation. If you think of the example situations in this context, you can accomplish some fairly complex user interaction scenarios that will dynamically occur based on your users' interactions after your project has been completed. It will become a living application that reacts based on the current users' status and interactions.

III

Creating Reusable Components

10

Accordion

Adding massive amounts of data to one web page is not a recommended design approach because it can be completely disorienting to the user, and might cause him to go to another site. There are always exceptions, though, which is the case when using an accordion component to display data. Using an accordion component enables a single web page to display much more content without disorienting the user in the process. An accordion has multiple panels that can expand and collapse to reveal only the data that a user is interested in viewing without overwhelming him with everything at one time.

In this chapter, we will learn how to create a custom Ajax-enabled accordion component. An Ajax-enabled accordion can lend itself to many unique situations. For example, you can connect the component to live XML data from a database via a server-side language, which can send and receive XML or any other format that you prefer. The accordion component can be the graphical user interface for a custom web mail application that displays threads in different panels. The server can push new data to the component when mail has been updated, deleted, or added to the database, and the accordion can parse it to update, delete, or add new panels to the thread. This is a perfect example of providing access to massive amounts of content without scaring away the users of the application. It is also a great way to organize the content so that the application is ultimately more usable and purposeful.

Getting Started

In order to get started we must do a few things first. We must define an XML structure for the object to accept, which will be scalable and grow with a large application. Once we have defined this data structure we must then create a process for requesting it. This section will focus on both of these assignments in order to get us started toward creating the object.

The XML Architecture

Before we begin, we need to architect an XML structure that will be used to represent an accordion with all its properties. Aside from the XML declaration, which needs to be

added to the top of the file, the first element that we will create will be named
`accordion` to represent the actual object or component. If we were to visualize an
accordion, we would know that it consists of multiple panels, so we will use `panel` as
the first child node name. To identify which panel is expanded by default when the
accordion is rendered, we will add an `expanded` attribute to the `panel` element and
populate it with a Boolean of `true` for expanded. Each panel should also include a
`title` and have `content` that displays when the panel is expanded; therefore, we will
create these elements as child nodes of the panel. If multiple panels are necessary to present content, we can easily duplicate the panel and its enclosed children elements so that
there are numerous panels, one after the other. There is no limit to the amount of panels
that can be added, but the accordion component will render slower as more data is
added. Ultimately, however, a difference is not noticeable until your XML file gets very
large. Take a look at the sample code in Listing 10.1 to get an idea of how to construct
an accordion XML file that will be parsed by our custom component.

Listing 10.1   **The XML Sample for the Accordion (`accordion.xml`)**

```
<?xml version="1.0" encoding="iso-8859-1"?>
<accordion>
    <panel expanded="true">
        <title></title>
        <content></content>
    </panel>
    <panel>
        <title></title>
        <content></content>
    </panel>
</accordion>
```

After the structure has been created, we can add data between the XML node elements.
This data will be used to display in the corresponding parts of the accordion component. Accepting HTML in any node element will make this component much more
flexible and can be very easily achieved by simply adding CDATA tags between the
`content` elements. Here is an example of how easy this is to accomplish:

```
<content><![CDATA[<b>html text goes here</b>]]></content>
```

Adding CDATA tags allows us to use any HTML that we would like to display in any
given panel. We could display everything from complex tables, images, and even other
components. After you have completed creating all of the components in this book, you
can combine them to make additional ways of interacting with data. After we have populated the XML file, we are ready to request it and use its content to render the component.

Requesting the XML

It is now time to set up the request for the XML. We will request the XML that we created in the last section and push it to the parsing method in the component. To make
the request, we will first create an HTML file to hold all the code that will create and
facilitate communication between the component and Ajax. Keep in mind that aside
from building this sample, you will probably not use this component solely as you might
have an existing file that you want to incorporate the component into. With the correct
files and a few tweaks to the placement of the component, you can easily add one to any
page. In the header of the new sample HTML file, add references to the accordion CSS
and all the necessary JavaScript files, as in Listing 10.2. Keep in mind that you will have
to run the files on a server in order for the XHR to work.

Listing 10.2   **The HTML Container for the Project (`accordion.html`)**

```
<!DOCTYPE html PUBLIC "-//W3C//DTD XHTML 1.0
    ➥Transitional//EN" "http://www.w3.org/TR/xhtml1/DTD/
    ➥xhtml1-transitional.dtd">
<html xmlns="http://www.w3.org/1999/xhtml">
<head>
<title>Accordion</title>
<link href="css/accordion.css" rel="stylesheet" type="text/css" />
<script type="text/javascript" src="../javascript/Utilities.js"></script>
<script type="text/javascript" src="../javascript/utils/AjaxUpdater.js"></script>
<script type="text/javascript" src="../javascript/utils/HTTP.js"></script>
<script type="text/javascript" src="../javascript/utils/Ajax.js"></script>
<script type="text/javascript" src="../javascript/components/Panel.js"></script>
<script type="text/javascript"
    ➥src="../javascript/components/Accordion.js"></script>
```

We are including a number of JavaScript files—one of which is the `Utilities` object
that we created in Chapter 14, "Singleton Pattern"—because it will be used to create the
accordion's HTML elements that get rendered on the screen. The other JavaScript files,
`Panel` and `Accordion`, are the objects that we will be focusing on creating throughout
the rest of this chapter. In order to get started, you can create these files in the corresponding JavaScript directory.

After we have the files included, we need to create an `initialize` method (see
Listing 10.3) in the header and add an `Update` call with the `AjaxUpdater` to request
the accordion XML file. This object will make the request to the Ajax object based on
the HTTP method and the query parameters that you pass. The Ajax object will then
make an XHR to the XML file that we are passing and will finally respond to the callback method that you specify. In this case, it is the `display` method for the accordion,
which will parse the XML and render the accordion and its panels. The first parameter is
the HTTP method for the request. The second is the requested file, plus any query
string that you need to append for posting data, which we will be doing more of in Part
V, "Server-Side Interaction," when we begin to interact with server-side languages and

databases. The last parameter is the method that you would like to be used as a callback method for the request.

Listing 10.3   **The XHR Request Code (`accordion.html`)**

```
<script type="text/javascript">
function initialize()
{
    AjaxUpdater.Update("GET", "services/accordion.xml", Accordion.display);
}
</script>
</head>
```

As you can see in Listing 10.3, we need to make sure that all the code is available or fully instantiated. We must simply wait until the page loads before we call the `initialize` method that makes the request. The following shows an example of the `body onload` method:

```
<body onload="javascript:initialize();">
```

I have also added a `loading div` element (see Listing 10.4) to handle the ready state status of the request. This is a good way to present the user with a message regarding the state.

Listing 10.4   **A `div` Element to Display Loading Status (`accordion.html`)**

```
<div id="loading"></div>
</body>
</html>
```

When we have the HTML file ready to go, we can start creating the objects that make up the accordion component. Let's start with the `Accordion` object itself.

Creating the Accordion Object

The first object that needs to be created for the accordion component is the `Accordion` object. The `Accordion` object will handle parsing the XML as well as creating and controlling a variable number of panel objects. Accordions consist of multiple panels that stack on top of each other and expand and collapse to reveal hidden content. We will create a `panel` object that uses the prototype structure we discussed in Chapter 5, "Object-Oriented JavaScript." This will allow us to create multiple `panel` objects. Before we move onto the details of creating the panels, however, we will finish creating the `Accordion` object. Creating the `Accordion` object and initializing the properties is trivial, but there is an important sequence of events that needs to happen—otherwise, the object will not initialize properly. First, we must instantiate the object so that we can use its other methods. In order to trigger the `initialize` method, we must declare the method before we call it. The code snippet in Listing 10.5 shows an example of how we can accomplish this.

Listing 10.5   **Accordion Instantiation and Initialization (`Accordion.js`)**

```
Accordion = {};

Accordion.initialize = function()
{
    panels = new Array();
    expandedPanel = 0;
}
Accordion.initialize();
```

Calling the `initialize` method before declaring it will cause an error because the method does not exist in memory at this point and is not accessible. Notice that we have two properties in the `initialize` method: A new `panels` array is created and the `expandedPanel` number is set to 0. The `panels` array is simply an array of `panel` objects that the `Accordion` object will contain after the panels have been created. These panels will be added to the array in the `display` method and then be accessible to the other methods in the `Accordion` object. The `expandedPanel` number is used to determine which panel is expanded by default when the accordion is rendered. This is the property that will be set when we get the results of the XML file's `expanded` attribute.

To render the accordion, we will create a `display` method. This is the method we are using as the callback function for the Ajax request in the HTML file we created at the beginning of the chapter. The first thing we need to do in the `display` method is to check the ready state of the Ajax object. If the ready state returns `"OK"`, we will continue with the method; if we do not receive `"OK"` as the value, we can add a number of branches to handle the different scenarios. For the example, I simply created a `try-catch` to display a generic message for failed requests.

When we receive a successful message, we need to create an accordion `div` element to act as the parent container for all the panels. When we have our `accordion div` element created, we need to iterate through the panels from the response by targeting the `panel` node element by name in the response XML. After we have an array of panel data from the response, we can use the `length` property of the `panel` array to iterate through the array. While iterating through the `panel` array, we need to get the `title` and `content` data for each panel. We will find the `panel` element with an `expanded` attribute that is set to `true` and use its iteration number to set the `expandedPanel` variable. The `expandedPanel` number will be useful for matching purposes because it will represent the unique ID of each panel object. When we have all the data from the XML targeted to local variables, we can push a new `panel` object into the `panels` array we instantiated in the accordion's `initialize` method. When creating the new `panel` we will pass it the iteration number as a unique ID, along with the title and content strings.

Now that we have the `panel` objects created, we can append the panel HTML elements to the accordion. We will accomplish this by using the `appendChild` method in the `Utilities` object and passing the `accordion div` element and each panel `display` method. The panel `display` method will pass all the HTML elements that are created inside the `panel` object and append them to the accordion. When we have completed iterating through the panels array and have appended them to the accordion, we will be able to append the accordion to the document body. Appending the accordion to the document body will render the accordion in the web page. Take a look at Listing 10.6 to see the `display` method in its entirety.

Listing 10.6   **The Accordion's `display` Method (`Accordion.js`)**

```
Accordion.display = function()
{
    try
    {
        if(Ajax.checkReadyState('loading') == "OK")
        {
            var accordion = Utilities.createElement("div", {id:'accordion'});
            var p = Ajax.getResponse().getElementsByTagName('panel');
            for(var i=0; i<p.length; i++)
            {
                var title = Ajax.getResponse().getElementsByTagName('title')[i].
                    ➥firstChild.data;
                var content =
                    ➥Ajax.getResponse().getElementsByTagName('content')[i].
                    ➥firstChild.data;
                if(p[i].getAttribute('expanded')) { expandedPanel = i; }
                panels.push( new Panel(i, title, content) );

                Utilities.appendChild(accordion, panels[i].display());
            }

            Utilities.appendChild(document.body, accordion);
            Accordion.toggle(expandedPanel);
        }
    }
    catch(err)
    {
        document.write(err);
    }
}
```

As you can see, there is a `toggle` method that I did not mention, which is called at the end of the `display` method. This is the reason we created the `panel` array and the `expandPanel` number variables. When the `toggle` method is called, it iterates through the `panel` array and checks to see whether there is a panel `ID` that matches the ID parameter. When it finds a match, it expands that panel by `ID`; when it does not match, it collapses that panel. The expand/collapse panel methods are in the `panel` object, which we will create in the next section. Listing 10.7 shows the entire code for the accordion's `toggle` method.

Listing 10.7   **The Accordion's `toggle` Method (`Accordion.js`)**

```
Accordion.toggle = function(id)
{
    for(var i=0; i<panels.length; i++)
    {
        if(panels[i].id == id)
        {
            panels[i].expand();
        }
        else
        {
            panels[i].collapse();
        }
    }
}
```

As mentioned, the `toggle` method takes an element ID as a parameter and iterates through the `panels` array. When it discovers a matching ID, it expands that particular panel; otherwise, it collapses it.

Now that we have the `Accordion` object created, we can now focus on creating the panels. Another way to handle the accordion panels' `toggle` method is to allow multiple panels to be open at one time. To do this, you need to create a method that does not collapse other panels that are open. You also need to check whether the current panel that is being clicked is already expanded (if so, it should be closed). This keeps the expand/collapse nature of the panel intact.

Panel Functionality and Data Display

The `panel` object uses the prototype structure to keep it reusable, which essentially allows us to create multiple panel objects. An accordion panel needs a unique ID for reference purposes and can include a title, which is displayed in a panel header, and content that is exposed when a user expands the panel. The `id`, `title`, and `content` values will become properties of the `panel` object and will be visually represented in the accordion. These properties will be accessible during runtime and contained within the panels that created them. In order to create these properties, we will use the values we passed to the new `panel` objects while iterating through them in the accordion `display` method. Listing 10.8 shows how these values were passed to the `panel` object's constructor function and are scoped to the panel.

Listing 10.8   The Panel Object Properties and Constructor (Panel.js)

```
function Panel(id, title, content)
{
    this.id = id;
    this.title = title;
    this.content = content;
}
```

The constructor function is used to instantiate the panel and set the property values of the object. After the panel is instantiated, it can be used to call other methods within itself. In the `Accordion` object, the first method we called was the `display` method. This method creates the `div` elements that are used to display the data that is passed to the object. To create the elements that are necessary to render a panel, we will need to use some of the utility methods that we created in the `Utilities` object in Chapter 10. In order to create the display, we will need to create the following elements: `panel`, `header`, `title`, and `content`. The `panel` element is simply a container for the other elements, whereas the `header` element contains the `title` element and has an `onclick` event that will expand and collapse individual panels. The final two elements are `title` and `content`. They both have an `innerHTML` property that is set to the relative properties that were set in the constructor. After we have created all the necessary elements, we need to append them to the `panel` element. When we complete the `display` method, we return the `panel` element and append it to the document body in the `Accordion` object. Listing 10.9 shows the entire code for creating the elements, appending them, and returning the panel.

Listing 10.9   The Panel's Display Method (Panel.js)

```
Panel.prototype.display = function()
{
    var panel = Utilities.createElement("div");

    var header = Utilities.createElement("div", {
        className: 'header',
        onclick: this.toggle(this.id)
        });

    var title = Utilities.createElement("div", {
        className: 'title',
        innerHTML: this.title
        });

    var content = Utilities.createElement("div", {
        id: 'content_'+ this.id,
        className: 'content',
```

Listing 10.9   **Continued**

```
        innerHTML: this.content
        });

    Utilities.appendChild(panel, Utilities.appendChild(header, title), content);
    return panel;
}
```

As you probably remember when we created the `Accordion` object, the panels display method is called from the accordion's display method as a parameter of the `appendChild` call, along with the parent accordion element. This is how the panels are added to the accordion and then the accordion was added to the document body.

The `toggle` method in Listing 10.10 is used in the `header div` as an `onclick` event. This method is interesting because it returns another method. The method that is returned is triggered during an `onclick` event and ultimately calls the accordion's `toggle` method. The header is also passing the panel ID when the code is executed to be used as a parameter in the accordion's `toggle` method. This is the ID that is used to decipher which panel should be expanded and which panels should be collapsed.

Listing 10.10   **Toggling the Panel State (`Panel.js`)**

```
Panel.prototype.toggle = function(id)
{
    return function()
    {
        Accordion.toggle(id);
    }
}
```

The `collapse` and `expand` methods in Listing 10.11 simply hide and reveal the `content divs` in the panels. They both use the `Utilities getElement` method, which gets the `content` element by name in the document. The `collapse` method sets the `display` style to `none` to hide it, whereas the `expand` method sets the `display` style to an empty string to reveal the `content`'s data.

Listing 10.11   **The Panel's Collapse and Expand Methods (`Panel.js`)**

```
Panel.prototype.collapse = function()
{
    Utilities.getElement('content_'+ this.id).style.display = 'none';
}

Panel.prototype.expand = function()
{
    Utilities.getElement('content_'+ this.id).style.display = '';
}
```

Creating the CSS

The CSS file for the accordion contains the styles for each of the elements within the accordion. As Listing 10.12 shows, the accordion element sets the font-family, font-size, width, and border attributes. These styles are inherited by each of the panels because they are encapsulated within the accordion element.

Listing 10.12   **The Accordion's Styles (accordion.css)**

```
#accordion
{
    font-family: Arial, Helvetica, sans-serif;
    font-size: 12px;
    width: 600px;
    border: #ccc 1px solid;
}
```

The header holds the title for each panel, and has a style shown in Listing 10.13 that contains a border-bottom attribute, which matches the border that surrounds the panels to make it look more incorporated into the accordion. It also has a background-color, a width to set the size of the clickable area, and a pointer cursor to show users that they can click the headers to toggle their state.

Listing 10.13   **The Accordion Header Style (accordion.css)**

```
.header
{
    border-bottom: #ccc 1px solid;
    background-color: #eaeaea;
    width: 600px;
    cursor: pointer;
}
```

The title class in Listing 10.14 simply bolds the font with the font-weight, changes the color of the font, and adds a little padding to keep the title away from the edges of the header that contains it.

Listing 10.14   **The Accordion Title Style (accordion.css)**

```
.title
{
    font-weight: bold;
    color: #333;
    padding: 5px;
}
```

The class for the panel content simply sets the padding to keep the content away from the edges of the panels, as seen in Lisitng 10.15.

Listing 10.15   **The Accordion Content Style** (`accordion.css`)

```
.content
{
    padding: 10px;
}
```

All these styles are easily editable and can be modified to completely change the look of the accordion. It is now up to you to make it your own, or brand it for any project you would like to incorporate it with.

The completed accordion component will look very similar to Figure 10.1, aside from any content differences or additional panels you may add to the XML. This chapter's sample includes an example of how you can display an email thread in the accordion, which we will incorporate into an internal web mail application for the sample that we create in Part V, when we learn how to combine a database with Ajax.

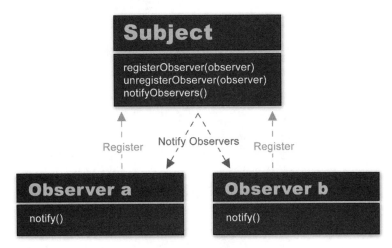

Figure 10.1   The completed accordion component is just one example of the many purposes they can serve in a web application.

11

Tree View

In this chapter, we will be creating an Ajax-enabled tree view component. This component will accept an XML file that will define the structure of the data and render it as a tree view in a specified HTML element or the document body. The tree view will have expand and collapse functionality and custom icons for folders. Each folder will have the capability to add HTML-enabled content, which in our case will be used to produce hyperlinks. These hyperlinks can be used for just about anything—for example, they can be used for internal or external website navigation or they can be used in a web application, as we will be doing in the final sample with our email application that will display specific folders with hyperlinks to emails.

This component will consist of two objects: `TreeManager`, which will control and bridge the gap between the Ajax engine and the graphical user interface (GUI), and `Tree`, which will render the GUI after parsing the response data it receives from `TreeManager`. A fully rendered tree view will look similar to Figure 11.1.

Figure 11.1   A fully rendered tree view.

Structuring the Data

In order to construct our tree view component, we must first have a way of defining the data. The data we will be defining will be requested by our Ajax engine, so we will create an XML structure to define it. The tree view component will render the XML exactly as we define it. This means that if we have a node named `Inbox` with a node value of `'New Mail'`, the tree view component will create a folder named `Inbox` and it will contain a text item equal to the node value that we defined. Therefore, all we need to do is define nodes and node values and leave the rest up to the component. The nodes will be represented as folders, and the node values will be represented as content in the form in which they are defined—whether they are HTML or simple text is up to us. The most important part is that the component will recursively create subfolders within the tree from any `childNode`s that are defined in order to render subcategories, which will ultimately create our tree view structure. The following code represents a sample XML structure for our tree view component. The sample in Listing 11.1 represents an email tree view structure, which will be a variation of what we use in our final sample.

Listing 11.1   The XML Structure That Defines Our Tree View (`tree.xml`)

```
<?xml version="1.0" encoding="iso-8859-1"?>
<Mail>
    <Inbox action="alert('This is the Inbox action');">
        <![CDATA[<a href="javascript:alert('Message from khadlock');">
        khadlock - Hi there</a><br/><a href="javascript:alert('Message from
        ➥khadlock');">
        khadlock - What's up</a><br/><a href="javascript:alert('Message from
        ➥ghopper');">
        ghopper - BUG FOUND</a>]]>
    </Inbox>
    <Outbox action="alert('This is the Outbox action');">
        <![CDATA[<a href="javascript:alert('Message from khadlock');">
        khadlock - No subject</a>]]></Outbox>
    <Sent action="alert('This is the Sent action');">
</Sent>
</Mail>
```

As you can see, this sample XML is very self-explanatory because there are only four nodes with node names of `Mail`, `Inbox`, `Outbox`, and `Sent`. Each of these items will be represented in the tree as a folder with the `Mail` folder as the parent folder, and the `Inbox`, `Outbox`, and `Sent` folders as subfolders in the tree. Each of the items has an attribute named `action`, which will specify the action that occurs when a user clicks the folder name. Within each node is an HTML node value that must be embedded in CDATA in order to properly parse. This HTML will be rendered as the contents of each folder. In this case, we are using hyperlinks as the contents of the folders, and these hyperlinks will represent the mail within each of these folders. Take a look at the `Inbox`'s node value, which includes multiple hyperlinks that are separated into different lines by break tags. We will see how simple it is to represent multiple pieces of mail in a folder in Part V, "Server-Side Interaction," when we populate these folders with database data using PHP and return it as XML to our component.

Now that we have a sample XML structure and before we create the actual tree component, we need to create a file to display the data. We will use an HTML file (see Listing 11.2) to load all the associated files, request the XML, and display the tree component. The first thing we must do is import a CSS file called `tree.css` (which we will create at the end of this chapter), all of the associated JavaScript files for the Ajax engine, and the two objects that will be used to create our tree view component. Now that we have the styles and JavaScript imported and once the page has completed loading, we can call an `initialize` method. This method will make a request through the `AjaxUpdater` object to get the XML file we just finished creating and send it to a method called `display` in the `TreeManager` object.

Listing 11.2   **Displaying the Data (`index.html`)**

```html
<html>
<head>
<title>Tree View</title>
<link href="css/tree.css" rel="stylesheet" type="text/css" />
<script type="text/javascript" src="javascript/Utilities.js"></script>
<script type="text/javascript" src="javascript/model/AjaxUpdater.js"></script>
<script type="text/javascript" src="javascript/model/HTTP.js"></script>
<script type="text/javascript" src="javascript/model/Ajax.js"></script>
<script type="text/javascript" src="javascript/view/Tree.js"></script>
<script type="text/javascript"
    src="javascript/controller/TreeManager.js"></script>

<script type="text/javascript">
function initialize()
{
    AjaxUpdater.Update("GET", "services/tree.xml", TreeManager.display);
}
</script>
</head>

<body onload="javascript:initialize();">
<div id="loading"></div>

</body>
</html>
```

After we have created a file to display the tree view component, we should probably create the objects that render it. We will start with the `TreeManager` object.

Handling the Response

The `TreeManager` object is the access point to the component. This object bridges the gap between the Ajax response and the `Tree` object in the view or the GUI.

`TreeManager` may be a small object, but it helps to separate the back-end response data from the GUI by adding an extra layer to act as a data controller, which is something we will cover in more detail in Chapter 15, "Model View Controller."

The `display` method (see Listing 11.3) first checks to see if the `ready` state of the Ajax object is successful. After it receives the `'OK'` string, it is ready to parse the response from the request. The difference between this controller and the controllers in the other components is that we do not actually parse any data from the response in this object; we simply pass it to the `Tree` object when we instantiate it. After we have a `tree` object that has received the response data, we simply use the `Utilities` object from Chapter 9, "Extending the Engine," to append the tree display directly to the body of the page. Alternatively, if we want to add it to a specific HTML element, we can append it to a specific element by name.

Listing 11.3   **Creating and Displaying the `TreeManager` (`TreeManager.js`)**

```
TreeManager = {};

TreeManager.display = function()
{
    if(Ajax.checkReadyState('loading') == "OK")
    {
        var tree = new Tree(Ajax.getResponse());
        Utilities.appendChild(document.body, tree.display());

        //tree.toggle();
    }
}
```

You will notice that this method also contains a `tree` object method called `toggle`. This method toggles tree items open and closed. Because the tree view will render itself in an expanded state by default, the `display` method has the capability to call the `toggle` method to change the tree view to a collapsed state by default instead. The next method is to set the custom icon (in our case, the folder) from an image that represents the expanded state to an image that represents the collapsed state. This method is called `toggleImage` and can be seen in Listing 11.4.

Listing 11.4   **Toggling Custom Folder Icons (`TreeManager.js`)**

```
TreeManager.toggleImage = function(id)
{
    if(Utilities.getElement(id) != null)
    {
        if(Utilities.getElement(id).src.indexOf('img/folder_o.gif') == -1)
        {
            Utilities.getElement(id).src = 'img/folder_o.gif';
        }
```

Listing 11.4   **Continued**

```
     else
     {
         Utilities.getElement(id).src = 'img/folder.gif';
     }
   }
}
```

This method can be changed to include any images that you choose as the icons for the categories. As you can see, it checks by id to see whether the specified category icon has an index of the expanded or collapsed version of the image. Based on which image it currently has, it chooses the other, which creates a toggle effect. Next, we will be creating the `tree` object, which will render the tree view for display in the GUI.

Rendering the GUI

The `Tree` object is the powerhouse in this component because it parses the response data that is received from the `TreeManager` object and creates a tree structure that is later appended to an HTML element or the HTML document body by `TreeManager`. In other words, this object pretty much does it all. The object is a prototype, which means it can be instantiated, and contains a constructor function. Listing 11.5 shows the code snippet for this constructor.

Listing 11.5   **Constructing a `tree` Object (`Tree.js`)**

```
function Tree(data)
{
    this.data = data;
    this.childArray = new Array();
    this.tree = '';
}
```

The `tree` object's constructor takes a data parameter, which is the response data from `TreeManager`, and sets the data to a local property called `data`. It also creates a new array called `childArray` and a property called `tree`. The `childArray` array is used to store all the child ids when the structure is created, and the `tree` property is used to concatenate a string version of the tree in HTML format, which is eventually added to the `innerHTML` property of the parent `div` for rendering. This parent `div` element is called `tree` and is created in the next method, which we will call `display`. This method renders all the data into an HTML element. The method is called from `TreeManager` after the `tree` object is created and populated to display the final tree view structure in the page. Listing 11.6 shows the `display` method code.

Listing 11.6   **Displaying the Tree (`Tree.js`)**

```
Tree.prototype.display = function()
{
    var tree = Utilities.createElement("div", {
          id: 'tree',
          innerHTML: this.traverse(this.data, 0)
          });

    return tree;
}
```

This method creates the HTML `div` element called `tree`, which we briefly discussed. This element simply acts as a container that holds the tree elements in its `innerHTML` property, including all of the nodes and node values. As you can see, we are calling the `traverse` method in the `innerHTML` property. This method recursively parses the XML structure and creates the tree view HTML, which is then added to this element.

The `traverse` method takes two parameters: a branch and a depth. The branch represents the node or category that is presently being parsed. For instance, with the current XML structure, we will start with the `Mail` branch or node as the first branch parameter, and then we will recursively dig deeper into the structure to parse the `Inbox`, `Outbox`, and `Sent` branches. The second parameter, which is the depth, represents the depth level of the tree. For instance, if we are parsing `Mail`, we are at a depth level of 0, but if we are parsing `Inbox`, we are at a depth level of 1, and so on. Coincidentally, the actual depth is not what is important here. Instead, it is that the depth be used as a unique id so that we can construct a reference id to each of the categories for later manipulation, such as expanding and collapsing a specific category. Listing 11.7 shows the method declaration and the parameters it receives.

Listing 11.7   **Traversing the XML (`Tree.js`)**

```
Tree.prototype.traverse = function(branch, depth) {}
```

Now that we understand the parameters, we can start parsing the data. Since every browser handles data differently, the first thing we need to do when we parse the data is check that the `nodeName` is a true `nodeName` and not a text or CDATA reference. We do this by simply checking the first character's code to make sure it is not equal to 35, which would mean it is the # symbol, used to represent text and CDATA references. The following is an example of the code that performs this check (see Listing 11.8).

Listing 11.8   **Checking for Folders (`Tree.js`)**

```
if(branch.nodeName.charCodeAt(0) != 35)
```

The next line of code is an example of why we need to keep a reference to the depth level of the tree. The id we construct may seem a bit convoluted, but it is necessary to keep a unique reference to each category (see Listing 11.9).

Listing 11.9   **Constructing a Unique Id (`Tree.js`)**

```
var id = branch.parentNode.nodeName+'_'+branch.nodeName+'_'+depth;
```

The reason that such a convoluted id is necessary is so there can be duplicate names within the same tree. Keeping reference to the parent node name, the current node name, and the depth level guarantees us no duplicate ids. The next bit of code (see Listing 11.10) puts our `childArray` to use. This is where we start pushing the ids to the array. These ids will then be easy to reference later, such as with the `toggle` method we may choose to call from the `TreeManager`.

Listing 11.10   **Storing Ids (`Tree.js`)**

```
this.childArray.push(id);
```

After we have created the ids and added them to the array, we can start creating the elements that will form our HTML string and represent the tree view in the GUI. This string will be concatenated into the tree property that we created in the constructor function. If a branch does not contain any `childNodes`, we will simply add an icon that represents an empty folder. If a branch does contain `childNodes` we will add a hyperlink that will contain our custom folder icon. This hyperlink will fire two methods: the `toggle` method from the `Utilities` object, and the `toggleImage` method from the `TreeManager` object. These methods will toggle the visibility of the contents within a specified folder and toggle the icon image between an expanded and a collapsed folder image. We will pass the `toggle` method the id that we created because it represents the element that contains the contents of each folder and causes this content to show and hide as we expand and collapse. We will pass the `toggleImage` method an id that represents the id of the `img` element we will create on the next line. This id will be used to target the specific image and change the `src` property. Listing 11.11 shows the code that handles this functionality.

Listing 11.11   **Adding Custom Icons and Defining Their Actions (`Tree.js`)**

```
if(branch.childNodes.length == 0)
{
    this.tree += "<img src='img/folder_empty.gif' border='0' class='folder'>";
}
else
{
    this.tree += "<a href='#' onclick=\"javascript:Utilities.toggle('"+ id +"');
        ➥TreeManager.toggleImage('expand_collapse_"+ id +"');
```

Listing 11.11   **Continued**

```
        ➥\" class='expand_collapse' onfocus='javascript:if(this.blur)
        ➥this.blur();'>";
    this.tree += "<img src='img/folder_o.gif'
        ➥id='expand_collapse_"+ id +"' border='0' class='folder'></a>";
}
```

This code may be a bit hard to read as a string, but it is simply the HTML that represents the functionality we just covered. As you can see, this code represents the hyperlink with an embedded image so that when a user clicks the image, the JavaScript functions are triggered and perform their specified duties.

The next couple lines of code create the folder name and associate the action attribute we specified in the XML to the action that occurs when a user clicks a folder name. Since we added these actions as attributes, we need to access them through JavaScript's `getAttribute` method (see Listing 11.12). This method is simple to use because we call it and pass the attribute name as a parameter of the method. Here is the code for this functionality.

Listing 11.12   **Parsing Folder Label Actions (`Tree.js`)**

```
var action = branch.getAttribute("action");
```

Now that we have parsed the action value and set an action variable to the value, we can use it in our hyperlink for the folder name. Following is the code that creates the hyperlink and adds this action to the `click` event (see Listing 11.13).

Listing 11.13   **Adding Folder Labels (`Tree.js`)**

```
this.tree += "<a href=\"#\" onclick=\"javascript:"+ action +"\"
class='container'>"+ branch.nodeName +"</a>";
```

As you can see, we have also added the `nodeName` of the branch as the text value in the hyperlink. This value will represent the name of the folder we specified in the XML at the beginning of this chapter. At this point, we have our custom folder icon with expand and collapse functionality, and the folder name that will render next to the folder icons for the first node in our XML. Now comes the harder part—recursively adding the values and the children of the tree. Before we start, you need to understand that we will be either adding node values to the current node (in other words, the contents of the folder), or we will be creating an entirely new category/ folder in the tree. The next piece of code will add an unordered list element with an embedded list item (see Listing 11.14). The embedded list item receives the id we created at the beginning of the method because this is the element that will contain the contents or node value for each folder or node. Within the embedded list, we will iterate through the branch's immediate children and recursively call the `traverse` method on each. The recursion will allow us to add the values or new folders to the tree. With each iteration, we need to increase the depth level by one to ensure that we are passing a unique depth id to the `traverse` method. After we finish adding the children, we can simply close the list item and the unordered list parent element.

Listing 11.14   **Iterating Through the Children (`Tree.js`)**

```
this.tree += "<ul><li id='"+id+"'>";
for(var i=0; i<branch.childNodes.length; i++)
{
    this.traverse(branch.childNodes[i], depth);
    depth++;
}
this.tree += "</li></ul>";
```

Now that we are recursively firing the `traverse` method, we need to identify what type of element to add to the tree. This element will either be a `div` element with the value for the folder, or a new folder element. We decipher this based on the first check we created in the method. This is the check that identifies whether the branch is a node or a text/CDATA value. If it is a node, we simply follow the same algorithm we just created; otherwise, we add the node value with the code in Listing 11.15.

Listing 11.15   **Adding Folder Contents/Values (`Tree.js`)**

```
var value = branch.nodeValue;
if(value != undefined)
{
    this.tree += "<div class='value'>"+ value +"</div>";
}
return;
```

This code parses the node value from the branch and creates a value variable. If this variable is not undefined, we add it to the `div` that holds the content values for each folder and append it to the tree string. After we have run out of node names, we simply return the `tree` property and add it to the `innerHTML` of the tree element that will be appended to either a specific `div` in the HTML page or, as in our case, the document body.

The last method in this object is the `toggle` method. In our example, the `toggle` method (see Listing 11.16) can be used by the `TreeManager` object to expand/collapse the entire tree view, but it also can be used by any other object in the application to accomplish the same goal.

Listing 11.16   **Toggling the Tree View State (`Tree.js`)**

```
Tree.prototype.toggle = function()
{
    for(var i=0; i<this.childArray.length; i++)
    {
```

Listing 11.16   **Continued**

```
        Utilities.toggle(this.childArray[i]);
        TreeManager.toggleImage("expand_collapse_"+this.childArray[i]);
    }
}
```

Adding Style to the Component

In order to stylize our component, we will create a CSS (Cascading Style Sheets) file
called `tree.css`. This file will contain element ids and classes that we created in the
`tree` object when we created the HTML string that was added to the current document. This file is simple and can be customized to look the way you would like, including link colors, spacing, and so on. Listing 11.17 shows this entire file.

Listing 11.17   **Styling the Component (`tree.css`)**

```css
body
{
    font-family: Verdana, Arial, Helvetica, sans-serif;
    font-size: 11px;
}

.container
{
    color: #333333;
    font-weight: bold;
    line-height: 21px;
    text-decoration: none;
}

ul
{
    margin: 2px 0px 5px 20px;
    list-style-type: none;
    padding: 0px;
}

li
{
    padding: 2px 0px 0px 0px;
}

.expand_collapse
{
    float: left;
```

Listing 11.17   **Continued**

```
    font-size: 9px;
    color: #333333;
    text-decoration: none;
}

.folder
{
    float: left;
    margin: 0px 0px 0px 0px;
}

.value a
{
    color: #999999;
    font-weight: normal;
    padding-left: 15px;
}
```

This file is fairly self-explanatory because each class and id is represented in the JavaScript file. If you are looking to create a new look for this tree, I would suggest modifying the colors and decoration for links, and replacing the folder image icons with any image you would like. This tree view component can be used to represent a lot of different data types and—with a little tweaking—can easily be used to represent other XML-based structures, such as RSS and podcasts.

12

Client–Side Validation

Client-side validation in web-based forms is an interaction designer's dream. It is a great way to inform users of their progress as they are using the form, rather than letting them get to the very end, only to discover they have a bunch of fields that must be updated with valid information. The problem here is that all forms are different, and what is valid in one may not be valid in another. If the forms are from different websites, we could just forget about finding any consistencies. This may not be incredibly surprising information and may seem like a battle not worth fighting, but if more developers were to use client-side validation, the Web would be a more form-friendly environment. Users would never be left wondering what information to enter into a field because the form would be smart enough to inform them on the spot before they even attempted to submit it.

This chapter will cover client-side validation with a combination of simple JavaScript and Ajax to inform users of valid and invalid information on the spot as they tab or click out of specified form elements.

Getting Started

The sample for this chapter is a login/registration page, which we will eventually plug in to our final sample application. This page will do one of two things: log in existing users or register new users. When new users arrive at the page, they will see a Register link at the top of the login form. When they click the Register link, the necessary form elements for registration will appear in the page, above the username and password form elements (see Figure 12.1).

While users begin filling out their user information, we will be checking their information against the existing information in the database to let them know if the information is already in use or present them with a visual identifier to inform them if they are in the clear. One way in which we are going to visually represent this information to the users is by changing the background color of the specific form element to red if it is already in use, or green if the element is valid. These visual identifiers obviously do not appear well in black and white, but the next identifiers will. They are simple string messages that state the status of the data next to the form element into which users are entering information, as shown in Figure 12.2.

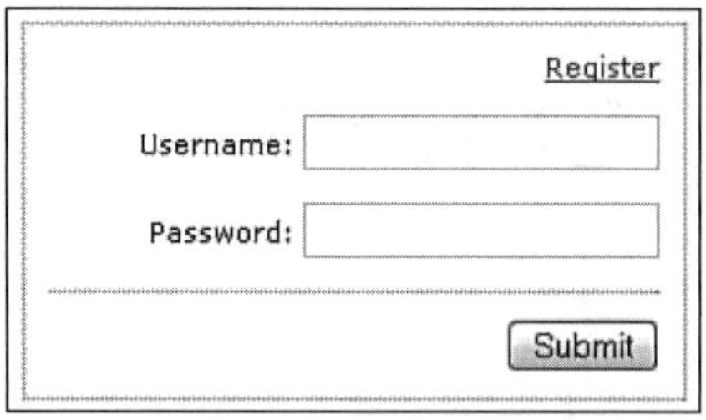

Figure 12.1   Our sample login form with optional, inline registration.

Figure 12.2   Validation provides visual feedback
to users as they enter information.

As you can see in Figure 12.2, we are not validating the first and last names. I chose to allow the same person to create a new account, as long as she uses a new email address and username (hence the reason we are validating these two fields). If we wanted to verify the first and last names, we would have to verify them together because there are a lot of people who share the same first name and sometimes the same last name. Another thing to be aware of is that we are running validation on the form elements only when the form is in registration mode. We only want to display feedback to users who are new to the application because we do not want to display verification on sensitive information that we are storing in the database.

This form may look very simple, but there is quite a bit of logic to make it a smart form. We first have the actual login/registration page, which contains a JavaScript validation object and fires a validation call each time specified form elements are exited. Behind the front-end code is a PHP object that runs validation on a user database when our JavaScript validation object makes an XHR to it. As if that were not enough, we have an instance of the PHP object included in the login/registration page for logging in existing users and registering new users. This chapter will cover each aspect of this process, but focus primarily on where we use Ajax to connect the JavaScript object to the back end. Let's get started by creating the JavaScript validation object.

Creating a Validation Object

Since we are validating user information, the JavaScript validation object that we are going to be creating will be called `UserValidator`. This object will have four methods: an `initialize` method for initializing all the object's local variables; a `setMode` method, which sets the form mode from login to register; a `validate` method, which is the Ajax part that will make XHRs to a PHP object; and an `onValidation` method, which will be used as the callback method for the XHR and ultimately display the feedback to the user. When the object is created, it automatically calls the `initialize` method to set the local object variables. When a request is made, the `validate` method is called, which sets the `onValidation` method as a callback so that it fires when the Ajax object responds. The `setMode` method is set when a user clicks the Register link because this is where the mode changes from login to register.

Getting started with this object is simple. First, we need to declare it and then call its `initialize` method as shown in Listing 12.1.

Listing 12.1 **Creating and Initializing the `UserValidator` Object (`UserValidator.js`)**

```
UserValidator = {};

UserValidator.initialize = function(formId, modeVal, fieldNum, submitId)
{
    UserValidator.currentSelector = '';
    UserValidator.currentForm = formId;
    UserValidator.mode = modeVal;
    UserValidator.fieldNumToValidate = fieldNum;
    UserValidator.submitId = submitId;
}
```

Declaring a Singleton object is nothing new, but we do have quite a few local object properties that are unique to this object and set within its `initialize` method. The first is a property called `currentSelector`, which will be used in our `validate` method to hold the current form field id that is being validated. The second is the `currentForm` property, which will be used to hold an id for the current form that is being validated. The third is the `mode` property, which will be used to check whether the page is in login or registration mode. The fourth is called `fieldNumToValidate` and will be used to hold a number that indicates how many form elements need to be validated before the Register button is enabled for a user to register. The last property is called `submitId`, which simply holds the id of the Submit button for the current form and will be used in the `setMode` method to change the value from login to register if a new user clicks the Register link. All of these properties will allow us create a form that interacts with the user. The `initialize` method is fired when the body in our login/registration page loads. Listing 12.2 shows how this method is added to our page.

Listing 12.2   **Initializing the `UserValidator` Object (`index.php`)**

```
<body onload="UserValidator.initialize('awadForm', 'Login', 2, 'submit');">
```

We are passing the values for the object properties as parameters of this method when the page loads.

The next method that we will create sets the mode for the form, switching it from login to registration in our case (see Listing 12.3). This method is called `setMode` and it takes one parameter, which is the new mode value. In our sample, this value will be `'Register'`.

Listing 12.3   **Setting the Mode from Login to Register (`UserValidator.js`)**

```
UserValidator.setMode = function(modeVal)
{
    UserValidator.mode = modeVal;
    Utilities.getElement( UserValidator.submitId ).value = modeVal;
    Utilities.getElement( UserValidator.submitId ).disabled = true;
    Utilities.getElement( UserValidator.currentForm ).action += "?mode="+ modeVal;
}
```

This method takes the new mode value and sets the local mode property, which we created in the `intialize` method, and the value of the Submit button to this new value. It then disables the Submit button until the form is validated based on the `fieldNumToValidate` property that we set in the `initialize` method and appends the mode value to the current form's action URL. Appending this value allows us to retrieve it when the post-back happens and use it to decipher whether we need to register a new user or log in an existing one.

Validating User Input

In order to validate the two fields that we specified in the `intialize` method, we have to create a `validate` method that takes a selector parameter and its value. The selector parameter is the id for the element that is being validated and the value parameter is the value of this element. Listing 12.4 shows this completed method, which we will cover in a moment.

Listing 12.4   **Validating Forms Against Database Data (`UserValidator.js`)**

```
UserValidator.validate = function(selector, value)
{
    if(selector != '' && value != '')
    {
        UserValidator.currentSelector = selector;

        var url = "serviceConnector.php?object=UserManager&method=
            ➥verifyUserInformation&params="+ selector +","+ value;
        AjaxUpdater.Update("GET", url, UserValidator.onValidation);
    }
    else if(selector != '' && value == '')
    {
        Utilities.getElement( selector ).style.backgroundColor = '#ffffff';
        Utilities.getElement( selector +"Message" ).innerHTML = '';
    }
}
```

Now that you have taken a look at the code, we can cover it line by line. The first thing we do is check to make sure that neither of the parameters is empty. If they are not empty, we set the `currentSelector` to the selector parameter and create a `url` variable to pass through an Ajax request. The `url` variable that we create consists of a `serviceConnector.php` file, an object parameter that is set to the `userManager` object that we will create soon, and a method parameter that is set to a `verifyUserInformation` method. The last part of the query is called `param` and is set to the selector and value parameters that were passed into the object. The parameters are concatenated into a comma-delimited list and the `url` variable is finally sent to the server through an Ajax request with the `onValidation` method set as the callback. Of course, there is always the possibility that the selector could be set, but the value parameter could be an empty string, so we have a condition that sets the selector element's visual feedback to the default state, just in case a user has already validated the element already.

In order to call this validation method from the client page, we need to add the code to the `onblur` for the form elements we want to validate. Listing 12.5 shows the body of the `index.php` sample page.

Listing 12.5   **Calling the Validation Method from the Form (`index.php`)**

```
<!DOCTYPE html PUBLIC "-//W3C//DTD XHTML 1.0 Transitional//EN"
"http://www.w3.org/TR/xhtml1/DTD/xhtml1-transitional.dtd">
<html xmlns="http://www.w3.org/1999/xhtml">
<head>
<meta http-equiv="Content-Type" content="text/html; charset=iso-8859-1" />
<title>AJAX for Web Application Developers</title>
<link href="css/user.css" rel="stylesheet" type="text/css" />
<script type="text/javascript" src="javascript/Utilities.js"></script>
<script type="text/javascript">
```

Listing 12.5   **Continued**

```
var jsFiles = new Array("javascript/utils/ErrorManager.js",
    ➡"javascript/utils/Alert.js", "javascript/utils/NumberUtil.js",
    ➡"javascript/utils/StringUtil.js", "javascript/model/AjaxUpdater.js",
    ➡"javascript/model/HTTP.js", "javascript/model/Ajax.js",
    ➡"javascript/utils/UserValidator.js");
Utilities.includeJS(jsFiles);
</script>
</head>
<body onload="UserValidator.initialize('awadForm', 'Login', 2, 'submit');">

<div id="login">
    <div style="color: #ff0000"><?=$error;?></div>
    <form id="awadForm" method="post" action="<?= $_SERVER['PHP_SELF']; ?>">
        <div id="register" style="display: none;">
            First Name: <input name="firstName" id="firstName" type="text" />
<br/><br/>

            Last Name: <input name="lastName" id="lastName" type="text" />
<br/><br/>

            E-mail: <input name="email" id="email" type="text"
                ➡onblur="javascript:UserValidator.validate(this.id, this.value);"
                ➡/><div
                ➡id="emailMessage"></div><br/><br/>
        </div>
        <a href="#"
            ➡onclick="javascript:document.getElementById('register').style.
            ➡display
            ➡= '';document.getElementById('registerButton').style.display =
            ➡'none';UserValidator.setMode('Register');"
            ➡id="registerButton">Register<br/><br/></a>

        Username: <input name="username" id="username" type="text"
            ➡onblur="javascript:if(UserValidator.mode == 'Register')
            ➡UserValidator.validate(this.id,
            ➡this.value);" /><div id="usernameMessage"></div><br/><br/>

        Password: <input name="password" id="password" type="password" />
<br/><br/>
        <div id="buttons">
            <input name='submit' type='submit' value='Login' id='submit'>
        </div>
    </form>
</div>

<div id="loading" style="display:none;"></div>

</body>
</html>
```

These validation calls are really simple and can be duplicated in any element that we want to add them to because they are getting their parameters from the current element to which they are attached. The only requirement is that there is an `id` attribute for the element that is calling the method. There is PHP code in the action that makes the form post back on this same page, which will require us to handle the login and registration within this page. It also has a PHP `$error` message that is displayed in this page if an error exists. This message will be covered in the next section when we add more PHP code to the top of this file to handle the login and registration.

Providing Visual Feedback

Visual feedback is important in web applications and often overlooked by developers. Adding visual feedback keeps users in touch with their interactions and does not leave them wondering what has happened to their data when they have clicked a button, exited a form field, and so on. Providing feedback with our `UserValidator` object is not difficult to accomplish because all we need to do is match element ids and change styles based on responses from our XHRs. Listing 12.6 shows this code and how it handles displaying visual clues to the user.

Listing 12.6   **Providing Visual Feedback to Users** (`UserValidator.js`)

```php
<?php
UserValidator.onValidation = function()
{
    if(Ajax.checkReadyState('loading') == "OK")
    {
        var color = '#ffffff';
        if(Ajax.getResponse().firstChild.data == 'success')
        {
            color = '#ff9999';
            Utilities.getElement( UserValidator.currentSelector +"Message" )
                ➡.innerHTML = 'Already in use.';
        }
        else
        {
            color = '#ccff99';
            Utilities.getElement( UserValidator.currentSelector
                ➡+"Message" ).innerHTML = 'OK';
            UserValidator.fieldNumToValidate--;
        }
        Utilities.getElement( UserValidator.currentSelector )
.style.backgroundColor = color;

        if(UserValidator.fieldNumToValidate == 0)
        {
            Utilities.getElement( UserValidator.submitId ).disabled = false;
```

Listing 12.6   **Continued**

```
        }
    }
}
?>
```

There are quite a few conditions in this method, but don't be intimidated—the code is very simple. The first thing we check is the ready state of the Ajax object, which we have already covered in the other components that we have created. After it verifies, we check the response to see if a success or failed message was returned from our server-side object, which we will be creating shortly. If the response is successful, it means we need to set the form element background to red and add a message stating that the data is already in use because this data already exists in the database. Otherwise, we set it to green and add an `'OK'` message. We also update the `fieldNumToValidate` property based on the condition of the response. The last thing we check is whether the `fieldNumToValidate` is equal to zero and, if it is, we enable the button.

Now that we have created the client side of the request, we need to check the database and respond with the XML based on matching data.

The Server Side

I know that we have not reached Part V, "Server-Side Interaction," yet, but this object truly requires us to dive into the server-side of the request. With that said, in this section, I do not plan on covering all the ins and outs of PHP or MySQL; rather, I will explain how to make the connection between the server and the client while explaining how to achieve it through the sample. We will create a server-side PHP object, in which we will make XHRs, through another intermediary PHP file that will bridge the gap between JavaScript and PHP. The PHP object will then check a database table for specific data, which we need to validate with our JavaScript object when we receive a response from the server. Let's start by creating the database table. Listing 12.7 shows the SQL code to create the table in your MySQL database.

Listing 12.7   **SQL Code to Create a User's Table** (`awad_users.sql`)

```
CREATE TABLE 'awad_users' (
  'password' varchar(50) NOT NULL default '',
  'username' varchar(25) NOT NULL default '',
  'email' varchar(100) NOT NULL default '',
  'lastName' varchar(50) NOT NULL default '',
  'firstName' varchar(25) NOT NULL default '',
  'id' int(11) NOT NULL auto_increment,
  PRIMARY KEY  ('id')
) ENGINE=MyISAM DEFAULT CHARSET=utf8;
```

We have already created the Ajax requests in the `UserValidation` object, so creating the server side will be a breeze. I honestly mean it when I say this: It may seem like a lot of steps to remember, but once you do it, you will be amazed at how simple it really is and how robust an application it can build. As I stated previously, we will need an intermediary PHP file, a PHP object, and a database. The intermediary file is the `serviceConnector.php` file that we are calling in our `UserValidation` object's Ajax requests. This file is very simple and is only needed to bridge the gap between the JavaScript and PHP objects. The first thing we will add to this page is a header to set the `content type` of the returned data to XML for the requesting Ajax object. The file will then include the PHP object called `UserManager.class.php`, which we will create shortly. This object will then be instantiated with the object variable that we are passing through our request. After the object is instantiated, the method we passed will be fired with the parameters in which we are passing. This file is so abstract that it can virtually be used for any public method, with any parameters passed as a comma-delimited list, in any object that we choose to include in this page. This lends the file quite a bit of power, which is why we will need to add some sort of security to it in Part V, "Server-Side Interaction." Listing 12.8 shows how we accomplish this functionality with this intermediary file.

Listing 12.8   **Bridging the Gap Between the Client and the Server (ServiceConnector.php)**

```php
<?php

header("Content-Type: application/xml; charset=UTF-8");

require_once("classes/UserManager.class.php");

$o = new $_GET['object']();
echo $o->$_GET['method']( $_GET['params'] );

?>
```

As I said, this file is extremely simple, yet it packs a lot of power and can basically be used in any situation where you need to make this sort of connection by simply including another object. The object that we are using in this case is for user management, which will be incorporated into our final sample. The methods it contains will look very familiar since we already created the requests in our `UserValidation` object. The methods this object consists of are listed in Table 12.1.

Table 12.1   The Methods of the `UserManager` Class (`UserManager.class.php`)

Methods	Function
`constructor`	Creates the database connection object
`verifyUserInformation`	Checks the database to see whether the data passed in as a parameter exists in the database
`register`	Registers a new user
`insertWelcomeMessage`	Used by the `register` method to insert a welcome email in a new user's inbox
`login`	Logs in an existing user

The Constructor

Before we create the `constructor` function, we first need to create a private local class variable called **dbConnector**, which we will use to get the Singleton instance of the database connector object from the **DatabaseConnector.class.php** in the constructor. After we create this variable and set it to the Singleton object, we fire its **init** method to make the initial connection and select our database. This object can be used in each of our other methods to connect to the database and make queries. Listing 12.9 shows this code in action.

Listing 12.9   Creating the Object Constructor (`UserManager.class.php`)

```php
<?php
require_once("classes/database/DatabaseConnector.class.php");
require_once("classes/utils/Constants.class.php");

class UserManager
{
    private $dbConnector;

    public function UserManager()
    {
        $this->dbConnector = DatabaseConnector::getInstance();
        $this->dbConnector->init();
    }
}
?>
```

> **Note**
>
> A very important thing to remember in order to connect to your database is to change the static variables in `Constants.class.php`.

These variables look like the code in Listing 12.10.

Listing 12.10   **Changing the Database Connection Information**
                 (Constants.class.php)

```php
<?php

class Constants
{

    // Datbase connection
    static $DB_USER = "USERNAME";
    static $DB_PASSWORD = "PASSWORD";
    static $DB_HOST = "localhost";
    static $DB_NAME = "DB_NAME";

    // Database Tables
    static $AWAD_EMAIL = "awad_email";
    static $AWAD_USERS = "awad_users";

    // Password
    static $PASSWORD = "TEMPPASSWORD";

    // Return Values
    static $SUCCESS = "<xml>success</xml>";
    static $FAILED = "<xml>failed</xml>";

    public function Constants() {}

}

?>
```

These variables should contain the connection information for your database. These are the only items that you will have to modify in `Constants.class.php` in order to get the sample to work on your server. For security reasons it is also a good idea to put the `Constants` file in a secure directory that is not accessible from the Web. `DatabaseConnector.class.php` will never need to be modified because it is configured to connect to any database with this information.

Verifying User Information

All of our XHRs for client-side validation were made to this method. If we take a look back at the Ajax requests that we created in our `UserValidation` object, they specify the `UserManager` object, the method name, and the parameters necessary to verify data against the database. After the connection has been made between the client and object, the parameters are used to select the specified data from the database to see whether there is a match. If there is a match, the method returns `true`; otherwise, it returns `false`. You will notice we are returning these messages in the form of XML through the `Constants.class.php` file. This is to make the response a valid DOM object, which will then be accessible via Ajax. See Listing 12.11 for an example.

Listing 12.11   **Verifying User Information in the Database (`UserManager.class.php`)**

```php
<?php
public function verifyUserInformation($params)
{
    $param = split(",", $params);
    $selector = $param[0];
    $selectorValue = $param[1];

    $this->dbConnector->connect();
    $table = Constants::$AWAD_USERS;
    $query = "SELECT * FROM $table WHERE $selector='$selectorValue'";
    $result = mysql_query($query);
    $this->dbConnector->complete($query);

    if(mysql_num_rows($result) == 0)
    {
        return Constants::$FAILED;
    }
    else
    {
        return Constants::$SUCCESS;
    }
}
?>
```

Registering and Logging In a User

Although these methods do not have anything to do with Ajax, they do allow us to obtain users on which to run our validation requests. Therefore, I am including them in order to get us started. The first method I am displaying is the `register` method in Listing 12.12.

Listing 12.12   **Registering New Users (`UserManager.class.php`)**

```php
<?php
public function register($firstName, $lastName, $email, $username, $password)
{
    $password = md5($password);
    $this->dbConnector->connect();
    $table = Constants::$AWAD_USERS;
```

Listing 12.12   **Continued**

```php
$query = "SELECT * FROM $table WHERE username='$username' AND
    ➥password='$password' AND email='$email'";
$result = mysql_query($query);

if(mysql_num_rows($result) == 0)
{
    $query = "INSERT INTO $table (firstName, lastName, email, username,
        ➥password)
VALUES ('$firstName', '$lastName', '$email', '$username', '$password')";
    $this->dbConnector->complete($query);
    $this->insertWelcomeMessage($username);
    return Constants::$SUCCESS;
}
else
{
    return Constants::$FAILED;
}
}
?>
```

This method simply takes the data that was entered into the form in our `index.php` file and adds it to our database.

Note

The `register` method also fires a method called `insertWelcomeMessage`, which is not covered in this chapter, but is included in the code sample. This method creates a welcome email by default for new users.

The next method is a login method for existing users (see Listing 12.13).

Listing 12.13   **Logging In Existing Users** (`UserManager.class.php`)

```php
<?php
public function login($username, $password)
{
    $password = md5($password);
    $this->dbConnector->connect();
    $table = Constants::$AWAD_USERS;
    $query = "SELECT * FROM $table WHERE username='$username' AND password=
        ➥'$password'";
    $result = mysql_query($query);
    $this->dbConnector->complete($query);

    if(mysql_num_rows($result) == 0)
    {
```

Listing 12.13   **Continued**

```
            return Constants::$FAILED;
        }
        else
        {
            return Constants::$SUCCESS;
        }
    }
?>
```

These two methods are fired from the `index.php` file when the form posts back on itself. Listing 12.14 shows the code that needs to be added to the top of our index page to handle registration and login.

Listing 12.14   **Handling User Logins and Registration (`index.php`)**

```php
<?php

require_once("classes/utils/Constants.class.php");
require_once("classes/UserManager.class.php");
$uManager = new UserManager();

$error = '';
if($_GET['mode'] == 'Register')
{
    if($_POST['firstName'] != '' && $_POST['lastName'] != '' && $_POST['email']
       ➥!= '' && $_POST['username'] != '' && $_POST['password'] != '')
    {
        $response = $uManager->register($_POST['firstName'], $_POST['lastName'],
            ➥$_POST['email'], $_POST['username'], $_POST['password']);

        if($response == Constants::$SUCCESS)
        {
            header("Location: mail.php?username=". $_POST['username']);
        }
        else
        {
            $error = 'The username or password that you have choosen is in use.';
        }
    }
    else
    {
        $error = 'Please complete all of the form fields.';
    }
}
else
{
```

Listing 12.14   **Continued**

```php
    if(isset($_POST['username']) && isset($_POST['password']))
    {
        $response = $uManager->login($_POST['username'], $_POST['password']);

        if($response == Constants::$SUCCESS)
        {
            header("Location: mail.php?username=". $_POST['username']);
        }
        else
        {
            $error = 'The username and password that you have entered do
not match any records.';
        }
    }
}

?>
```

When the form is posted, it posts back on itself and runs the PHP at the top of the page. It first sets the error variable for later use and then checks the mode of the form. If the mode is equal to `register`, it runs the register code; otherwise, it runs the login code. In the registration code, it verifies that all the fields were completed and then registers the user through the `UserManager` object. If the fields are not completed, we set an error message to display to the user. In login mode, we verify that the Username and Password fields are completed and, if they are, we log in the user through the `UserManager` object. After we receive a successful response, we redirect the user into the application. We set an error message again if there are any failures during this process.

Now that we have created this code, we can really use it for any web application. This reusability is the great thing about writing server-side classes and client-side objects.

13

Data Grid

Data consolidation is a typical problem that developers face when designing a web application GUI because handling large amounts of data is common practice in dynamic applications. Using a data grid to display large amounts of data is beneficial for consolidation and usability. Data consolidation and better usability occur naturally because the function of a data grid is to format the data into rows and columns, which ultimately creates a structured grid that is much easier to read. A data grid formats the data into rows of different content. Within each of the rows are columns that separate corresponding content.

This way of structuring data is common practice among web applications. The component that we build in this chapter will make the process of structuring a data grid as easy as structuring the XML data that you will be passing it. Therefore, you will never have to touch the JavaScript objects after they are created—unless, of course, you would like to add additional functionality. This is because all the styling will be done in a CSS file in order to help you design the GUI for the grid and match any application that you are developing.

Getting Started

Before we create any of the JavaScript objects, which will become our data grid component, we will need to create an XML file to hold our data and an HTML file to display the component. This section is a brief description of how to create the files we need in order to get started. The XML for this chapter is actually the same structure we created in Chapter 3, "The Response." This chapter will take the XML and render it into a custom data grid component that we will create step by step in the next section. The only difference is that we will modify the actions to become alerts in order to show an example of how the actions work. Here is an example of the new action in the `action` attribute:

```
<items action="alert('Grace Hopper');" icon="img/mail.gif"> </items>
```

After we have an XML structure defined, we must create an HTML page to display the data. We will create an index page that contains the corresponding JavaScript files that we will need in order to make an XHR and display the data in the data grid. The index will wait for the body of the document to load, and then fire an update call on the `AjaxUpdater` to load the corresponding XML data. We will also specify the `DataGrid`'s display method as the callback because this is the method that will handle rendering after we create the object. Take a look at Listing 13.1 to get an idea of how the HTML needs to be structured.

Listing 13.1   **The Container for Displaying the Component** (`index.html`)

```
<html xmlns="http://www.w3.org/1999/xhtml">
<head>
<title>DataGrid</title>
<link href="css/datagrid.css" rel="stylesheet" type="text/css" />
<script type="text/javascript" src="javascript/Utilities.js"></script>
<script type="text/javascript" src="javascript/utils/NumberUtil.js"></script>
<script type="text/javascript" src="javascript/utils/StringUtil.js"></script>
<script type="text/javascript" src="javascript/model/AjaxUpdater.js"></script>
<script type="text/javascript" src="javascript/model/HTTP.js"></script>
<script type="text/javascript" src="javascript/model/Ajax.js"></script>
<script type="text/javascript" src="javascript/view/DataRow.js"></script>
<script type="text/javascript" src="javascript/view/DataColumn.js"></script>
<script type="text/javascript" src="javascript/controller/DataGrid.js"></script>
<script type="text/javascript">
function initialize()
{
    AjaxUpdater.Update("GET", "services/email.xml", DataGrid.display);
}
</script>
</head>

<body onload="javascript:initialize();">
<div id="loading"></div>

</body>
</html>
```

There is nothing complicated about this HTML file—it's really just a matter of importing all the correct JavaScript files and making the XHR when the page has completed loading. One last item to add is the loading `div`, which will display a message regarding the status of the XHR. Now that we have the data and the display page created, let's dive into the code of the data grid component.

Creating a DataGrid Object

Data grid components offer a great way to display large amounts of data. This section will show you how to create a `DataGrid` object that will load XML, parse it, and delegate it to two other objects called the `DataRow` and the `DataColumn`, which we will create in the next section.

We first need to define and instantiate the `DataGrid` object before we can begin to use it. Listing 13.2 shows the code for accomplishing this. After the data grid has been defined, we will define its first method called `init`. This method creates the object properties, which in our case is simply a new array called `rows`.

Listing 13.2   **Defining and Instantiating the `DataGrid` Object (`DataGrid.js`)**

```
DataGrid = {};

DataGrid.init = function()
{
    rows = new Array();
}
```

The data grid that we will create accepts an XML file with the structure that we created earlier. The XML acceptance occurs when the display method is invoked as the callback of an XHR. When the display method is invoked, it checks the `readyState` of the XHR and displays a loading message in the `loading div` that we added to our HTML. The loading message displays until the status reaches a completed state and returns the `"OK"` status code, which we added to the `HTTP` object in Chapter 9, "Extending the Engine."

```
if(Ajax.checkReadyState('loading') == "OK"){}
```

The first element that is created is an actual data grid `div` element. This element will be used as the container for all of the rows and columns that will eventually format the parsed XML data. The data parsing begins with retrieval of the categories, which provides us with an array that we will iterate to target each category's value. While iterating through the categories, we create `titlebar` elements, which will hold the category values and display them as the titles of each column in the grid. During the iterations, we will target each category value and add it to the `innerHTML` attribute of a `category div` element. After we have the `titlebar` and category element populated, we can append the `titlebar` element with the category. Listing 13.3 shows the code to create the categories.

Listing 13.3   **Creating Category Titles** (DataGrid.js)

```
var datagrid = Utilities.createElement("div", {id:'datagrid'});
var categories = Ajax.getResponse().getElementsByTagName('category');
for(var i=0; i<categories.length; i++)
{
    var titlebar = Utilities.createElement("div", {id:'titlebar',
        ➥className:'titlebar'});
    var categoryText = Ajax.getResponse().getElementsByTagName
        ➥('category')[i].firstChild.data;
    var category = Utilities.createElement("div", {id: 'title', className:
'title',
        ➥innerHTML:categoryText });

    Utilities.appendChild(datagrid, Utilities.appendChild(titlebar, category));
}
```

This code would essentially leave us with the following HTML structure:

```
<div id="titlebar">
    <div id="category">value1</div>
    <div id="category">value2</div>
    <div id="category">value3</div>
</div>
```

Now that we have the category titles created, we need to display the rest of the data in a grid structure. We begin by targeting the row elements in the XML. This provides us with an array of rows in which we can iterate for the rest of the data. We need to target the items within the row tags and create an `items` array from the results. With this array, we can get the value of the attributes that each group of items contains. The first attribute is the `action` attribute, and the second is the `icon` attribute. Targeting these attributes provides us with their values. The next line of code requires a utility object that we will create shortly, which is called `NumberUtil`. We are calling its `getParity` method to decipher whether the value that we are passing it is an even or odd number. This value is eventually used in the `DataRow` object to decide which color the row will be. All of these values are passed as parameters to the `DataRow` object that we create and pushed to our `rows` array for later retrieval. The `DataRow` takes its parameters in the following order: `id`, `items` array, `action`, `parity`, and `icon` (see Listing 13.4).

Listing 13.4   **Parsing Row Data** (DataGrid.js)

```
var row = Ajax.getResponse().getElementsByTagName('row');
for(var i=0; i<row.length; i++)
{
    var items = Ajax.getResponse().getElementsByTagName('items')[i].childNodes;
    var action =
        ➥Ajax.getResponse().getElementsByTagName('items')[i].getAttribute
        ➥('action');
```

Listing 13.4   **Continued**

```
    var icon =
        ➥Ajax.getResponse().getElementsByTagName('items')[i].getAttribute
        ➥('icon');

    var parity = NumberUtil.getParity(i);
    rows.push( new DataRow(i, items, action, parity, icon) );

    Utilities.appendChild(datagrid, rows[i].display());
}
```

After we have parsed all the item data and created all the data rows, we append each row to the `datagrid` `div` element that we created at the beginning of the method. As you can see in Listing 13.5, we are calling the display method from the `DataRow` object, which will return all the HTML that we will be creating in the `DataRow` object.

Listing 13.5   **Displaying the DataGrid Component (DataGrid.js)**

```
DataGrid.display = function()
{
    if(Ajax.checkReadyState('loading') == "OK")
    {
        var datagrid = Utilities.createElement("div", {id:'datagrid'});
        var categories = Ajax.getResponse().getElementsByTagName('category');
        for(var i=0; i<categories.length; i++)
        {
            var titlebar = Utilities.createElement("div", {id:'titlebar',
                ➥className:'titlebar'});
            var categoryText =
                ➥Ajax.getResponse().getElementsByTagName('category')[i].
                ➥firstChild.data;
            var category = Utilities.createElement("div", {id: 'title', className:
                ➥'title', innerHTML:categoryText });

            Utilities.appendChild(datagrid, Utilities.appendChild(titlebar,
category));
        }

        var row = Ajax.getResponse().getElementsByTagName('row');
        for(var i=0; i<row.length; i++)
        {
            var items =
                ➥Ajax.getResponse().getElementsByTagName('items')[i].childNodes;
            var action =
                ➥Ajax.getResponse().getElementsByTagName('items')[i].getAttribute
                ➥('action');
            var icon =
                ➥Ajax.getResponse().getElementsByTagName('items')[i].getAttribute
                ➥('icon');
```

Listing 13.5   **Continued**

```
            var parity = NumberUtil.getParity(i);
            rows.push( new DataRow(i, items, action, parity, icon) );

            Utilities.appendChild(datagrid, rows[i].display());
        }

        //Utilities.appendChild(document.body, datagrid);
        Utilities.appendChild(Utilities.getElement('list'), datagrid);
        AjaxUpdater.saving = false;
    }
}
```

The last line of code to include in the `DataGrid` object is triggering the `init` method to invoke the object's properties. Listing 13.6 shows us how to accomplish this.

Listing 13.6   **Initializing the `DataGrid` Object (`DataGrid.js`)**

```
DataGrid.init();
```

The `NumberUtil` object that we were using to get the parity is a simple utility object that can handle number-related functions. Although the object is currently handling only parities, it can be scaled to contain additional methods of your choice, such as complicated calculations that you may need to use multiple times and so on. Listing 13.7 shows the object in its entirety.

Listing 13.7   **The `NumberUtil` Object (`NumberUtil.js`)**

```
NumberUtil = {};

NumberUtil.getParity = function(num)
{
    if(num % 2 == 0)
    {
        return "even";
    }
    else
    {
        return "odd";
    }
}
```

Now that we have completed the `DataGrid` object, we need to create the rows and columns to structure the data. Let's get started by creating a `DataRow` object.

Displaying the Data

Displaying data in the grid requires the ability to create rows and columns. These rows and columns need to handle rendering data into a structured display. This display will represent the data grid and typically handle interactive functionality, which in our case will invoke the actions that we are setting in the XML.

Creating a DataRow Object

The `DataRow` object separates data of matching groups into rows, which will eventually be subdivided into columns. Since the object is a prototype, in order to create and instantiate the object, we need to build a constructor function for the object. As you can see in the constructor function in Listing 13.8, we are passing the five parameters that were used in the `DataRow` objects that we instantiated in the `DataGrid` object. These parameters are `id`, `items` array, `action`, `parity`, and `icon`.

Listing 13.8   **Constructing the `DataRow` (`DataRow.js`)**

```
function DataRow(id, items, action, parity, icon)
{
    this.id = id;
    this.icon = icon;
    this.items = this.getAllItems(items);
    this.action = action;
    this.parity = parity;
}
```

The parameters that we accept in the `DataRow` constructor are set to local properties within the object. All of these parameters are directly translated into local properties except for the `items` array. This parameter calls another method in the object called `getAllItems`, which parses the node values from the items and returns an array of `DataColumn` objects, which is then set to the local `items` array. We will create the `getAllItems` method in just a bit.

The display method is what we called in the `DataGrid` object to return the HTML for each of the rows. We then took this data and appended it to the `datagrid div` element. Take a look at Listing 13.9 to see how we create the HTML elements for the rows in the display method.

Listing 13.9   **Displaying a `DataRow` (`DataRow.js`)**

```
DataRow.prototype.display = function()
{
    var row = Utilities.createElement("div", {
        id: 'row_'+ this.id,
        className: 'row_'+this.parity,
        onclick: this.getAction(this.action),
```

Listing 13.9   **Continued**

```
        onmouseover: this.rollOver('row_'+ this.id),
        onmouseout: this.rollOut('row_'+ this.id)
        });

    for(var i=0; i<this.items.length; i++)
    {
        Utilities.appendChild(row, this.items[i]);
    }
    return row;
}
```

The display method is the control center for the object. It not only contains all the code
to render the rows, but it also holds all the event handlers. This method is used as the
access point from other objects and combines all of the other methods in the object to
return a complete row element with interactive event handlers to the front end or the
GUI. After the element is constructed, we need to iterate the `items` array, which
includes `DataColumn` elements, to the current row. The row element this method creates
has a unique id, a class name, and `onclick`, `onmouseover`, and `onmouseout` events. The
unique id is used to uniquely identify the row, which can be used to provide us with a
way to target the object by name. The class name is where the parity comes into play.
The parity provides us with a way to concatenate two different class names: `row_even`
and `row_odd`. In our sample, these classes differ by providing background colors that
alternate from even to odd rows, leaving us with a way to distinguish one row from the
other. Of course, these classes could be modified to display the rows in other unique
ways, but I'll leave that part up to you. The events that are created give our row interac-
tivity and enhance the user experience of the component. The first event is the `onclick`
event that we set to the `getAction` method and pass the `action` property as a parameter. This method takes the `action` and returns a function to the event. Therefore, when
the row is clicked, a function is invoked. This function then evaluates the `action` and
fires it after it validates. Take a look at Listing 13.10 to see this method in action.

Listing 13.10   **Creating an Action from the Parsed XML (`DataRow.js`)**

```
DataRow.prototype.getAction = function(action)
{
    return function()
    {
        eval(action)
    }
}
```

The next event handler that we are adding in the row element is the `onmouseover`. This
event is set to the local rollover method within the object. In the sample, we are using

the rollover method to handle the styles for the rows. In this case, we are simply changing the color and setting the cursor to the hand pointer to distinguish the row as a clickable item (see Listing 13.11).

Listing 13.11   **Rolling Over a Row (`DataRow.js`)**

```
DataRow.prototype.rollOver = function(id)
{
    return function()
    {
        Utilities.getElement(id).style.backgroundColor = '#999';
        Utilities.getElement(id).style.cursor = 'pointer';
    }
}
```

The last event handler is the `onmouseout` event, which calls a method called `rollout`. This method is very similar to the rollover method because it also changes the color of the background, but in a different way. When a user rolls out of the row, we want the row color to return to its previous state. Therefore, we need to reset the color in this method, but it gets a little trickier. We have the alternating colors from one row to the next, so in order to handle this, we need to check the parity of the object calling it and base the background color on the parity.

There is another item of interest in this method, which we have covered in previous chapters: the scope of the `this` keyword. When the JavaScript object is created, the scope works fine, but during runtime the events associated with an element will not know the scope of the `this` keyword or even what `this` refers to. Therefore, we need to set a variable called `_this` to `this`, which is equal to the object scope, when we create the method in the object. This allows the variable to scope properly when we fire an event during runtime and ultimately allows us to read specific properties based on the current object. Listing 13.12 shows the rollout method in its entirety.

Listing 13.12   **Rolling Out of a Row (`DataRow.js`)**

```
DataRow.prototype.rollOut = function(id)
{
    var _this = this;
    return function()
    {
        if(_this.parity == "even")
        {
            Utilities.getElement(id).style.backgroundColor = '#eaeaea';
        }
        else
        {
            Utilities.getElement(id).style.backgroundColor = '#fff';
        }
```

Listing 13.12   **Continued**

```
        Utilities.getElement(id).style.cursor = 'none';
    }
}
```

The last method in the `DataRow` object is one that I have previously mentioned. This `getAllItems` method takes an array of nodes and creates `DataColumn` objects, which it appends to an array and returns to the `DataRows items` array (see Listing 13.13).

Listing 13.13   `DataRow.js`

```
DataRow.prototype.getAllItems = function(items)
{
    var columns = new Array();
    for(var i=0; i<items.length; i++)
    {
        for(var j=0; j<items[i].childNodes.length; j++)
        {
            var copy = StringUtil.trim(items[i].childNodes[j].nodeValue, 50);
            columns.push(new  DataColumn(j, copy).display());
        }
    }
    return columns;
}
```

The first thing we do is create a new column array, and then we begin to iterate through the `items` array that was passed as a parameter. While iterating through this loop, we will need to nest another loop, which iterates the `childNodes` in the items. Now that we are iterating at the value depth for the items, we can target the `nodeValue` for each item. We then take this value and pass it to a `trim` method in an object called `StringUtil`, which takes a string and a number as parameters. This method returns a trimmed version of the string at the number of characters specified as the second parameter. After we retrieve this trimmed version of the copy, we use it as a parameter in the `DataColumn`. We then push an HTML version of the `DataColumn` to the `columns` array by invoking the `display` method for the object. After we have completed iterating and constructing the `columns` array, we return it.

Now that we know how to create a `DataGrid` object and construct `DataRows` to be displayed within it, we will complete our grid by creating the `DataColumn` object.

Creating a DataColumn Object

The `DataColumn` object handles separating groups of corresponding data into columns. The `DataColumn` object takes two parameters, `id` and `copy`, which both get scoped to local properties in the constructor function. This object is very small because it simply constructs itself and displays its data. The display method handles the creation of column divs. Each column `div` contains a unique id, a class name of `column` and `innerHTML`, which is equal to the `copy` parameter that was passed to it by the `DataRow` object. After the column is constructed, it is returned to the object that calls it. See Listing 13.14 for an example.

Listing 13.14   `DataColumn.js`

```
function DataColumn(id, copy)
{
    this.id = id;
    this.copy = copy;
}


DataColumn.prototype.display = function()
{
    var column = Utilities.createElement("div", {
      id: 'column'+ this.id,
      className: 'column',
      innerHTML: this.copy
      });

    return column;
}
```

Adding Design to the Component

The CSS for the `DataGrid` handles the design for the each component's GUI elements. The first item we will set a class for is the `datagrid` element (see Listing 13.15). This class will simply define the width of the grid component, but we could easily add a background color or a border, for example, to make it more appealing.

Listing 13.15   **Styling the `datagrid` Element (`datagrid.css`)**

```
#datagrid
{
    width: 600px;
}
```

The next two classes are related to the parity method that we used in the `DataRow` object. Depending on whether the row is even or odd, we assign one of these classes. Each class is composed of a float, which aligns the rows to the left. It also contains a width and a background color (see Listing 13.16).

Listing 13.16   **Styling Alternating Rows** (`datagrid.css`)

```
.row_even
{
    float: left;
    width: 600px;
    background-color: #eaeaea;
}

.row_odd
{
    float: left;
    width: 600px;
    background-color: #fff;
}
```

The last three classes represent the titles and the columns of the grid. The `titlebar` and the `title` classes handle the design for the category titles in the grid, setting the background properties for the bar and the font rendering from the title itself. The last class is the `column` class, which floats the columns to the left and aligns each one in its respective row. This class also sets the width and the padding around the content within each of the columns. See Listing 13.17 for an example.

Listing 13.17   **Styling Titles and Columns** (`datagrid.css`)

```
.titlebar
{
    float: left;
    width: 140px;
    padding: 5px 50px 5px 10px;
    background-color: #666;
}

.title
{
    font-weight: bold;
    color: #fff;
}

.column
{
    float: left;
    width: 140px;
    padding: 5px 50px 5px 10px;
}
```

The beautiful part of using CSS and `div` elements for the component is that these classes can be modified to render the data grid in a million different ways. This means that you can reuse this component in any situation and make it fit within any design necessary. The objects can also be easily modified to include additional functionality, such as resizable rows and columns or an action column for adding, editing, and deleting information from the grid. These are only a few ideas—I am sure you already have many of your own.

IV

Ajax Patterns

14

Singleton Pattern

In Part II, "Creating and Using the JavaScript Engine," we covered two advanced ways of creating JavaScript objects, the creation of the Ajax engine, and how to debug and put the engine to use in your web applications. We also covered extending the engine, which we will continue to do in this part of the book. I will show you how to take your Ajax applications to the next level by using design patterns in your code to help you optimize and build scalable applications that can be easily updated with future features.

Design patterns help solve common programming problems. For instance, the Singleton pattern solves the problem of having to instantiate multiple instances of an object throughout an application by simply giving our application one reference that never changes. This is how the Singleton pattern specifically solves a common programming problem. Throughout this part of the book we will learn many design patterns and how to apply them to our Ajax applications. This particular pattern is a simple one to grasp, but extremely useful. The patterns will get more advanced as we move along through the rest of Part IV "Server-Side Interaction."

Objects that utilize the Singleton pattern provide a consistent reference for other objects in the web application. A *Singleton object* is one that cannot be instantiated more than once. This means that multiple instances of the object cannot be created. You might be asking why you would want an object that cannot be instantiated by other objects in a web application. This chapter will explain why, help you understand how this pattern is useful, and show you how to use this pattern in your Ajax applications by creating an object that handles all of your Ajax updates.

An Overview of the Singleton Pattern

Imagine having a large-scale Ajax application with dozens of objects. In this application, you would like to add an object that handles all your Ajax updates. We will call this object the `AjaxUpdater`. All the objects in your web application will communicate through this object if they need to make an XHR at any time. Not only will this object handle all the requests, it will also handle delegating the responses to specified callback methods. In other words, when the response has been received, the `AjaxUpdater` will notify the requesting object if a callback method was specified during the request. This situation would require the use of the Singleton pattern because we would need a consistent object reference for the dozens of objects in our application that might be making XHRs. This pattern will also help separate this important functionality into a specific object for more flexibility, and help keep the web application decoupled for easy updates and future additions to the code. It might seem odd at first to separate your code into so many different objects, but as your application grows it will keep your code extremely easy to update and save you a lot of time in the long run.

Creating an Object Using the Singleton Pattern

Creating a JavaScript object with the Singleton pattern is so simple and intuitive that you might not have even realized that you made one in Chapter 6, "Creating the Engine," when you created the `Ajax` object. To instantiate a Singleton object, simply write the following line of code:

```
AjaxUpdater = {};
```

Instantiating the object is truly this simple and, as you can see, it only allows us to create the one reference to the object within the object itself. This object will then be used throughout the rest of the web application for constant reference. Now that we have our object instantiated, all we have to do is call it by name from anywhere in the application to access its properties and methods.

Creating properties and methods in a Singleton object is just as simple as instantiating the object. Write the name of the object, followed by the name of the method, and then point it to a new function, with any associated parameters if necessary. Take a look at the example of the `initialize` method in Listing 14.1.

Listing 14.1   **Creating a Method in a Singleton Object** (`AjaxUpdater.js`)

```
AjaxUpdater.initialize = function()
{
    AjaxUpdater.isUpdating = false;
}
AjaxUpdater.initialize();
```

The `initialize` method needs to be invoked after it is created in order to initialize the object before we can use the rest of its methods. It also prevents JavaScript from throwing an error because the method will not have existed at this point. This method initializes the `AjaxUpdater` and, although it does not accept any parameters, it is used to set all the local properties for the object. If this object is not initialized, the properties of the object will not be properly instantiated when we try to access their values, resulting in unexpected behaviors. Creating a property in a Singleton object is as simple as typing the name of the object, followed by the property you want to create.

```
AjaxUpdater.isUpdating = false;
```

In the preceding example, we are creating a Boolean property named `isUpdating`. This property is set to `false` by default because the object is not currently active, which means that it is not currently updating any requests or waiting for any responses. The `isUpdating` Boolean will be used to determine whether the object is currently updating a request or waiting for a response from the Ajax engine. This property will be extremely useful when we have an application with numerous requests because we might need to decide whether to make a new request based on its value, or we might want to check it if a user is trying to exit the page while a request is in transit to warn him of any potential data loss. There are many other uses for this Boolean value, as we will discover when our application grows larger and has numerous active requests.

After we have our object instantiated and all its properties are initialized, we can create the rest of the methods it will contain. The methods we will be creating will help this object handle all of our Ajax requests and delegate the server-side responses to the correct callback methods. The method we will use the most throughout our web application is the `Update` method. This method will handle making all the requests and delegating all the responses to the appropriate callback methods. The object takes three parameters to provide maximum flexibility to our object's XHRs. The first parameter is called `method` because it represents the method in which we want to handle the requests. As we learned in Chapter 2, "The Request," there are three possible values for this parameter: `GET`, `POST`, and `PUT`. The second parameter is a called `service`. This parameter represents the key/value pair, XML, or any other type of data that we would like to pass to the server side to be saved to a database or used to retrieve specific data. The third is an optional parameter named `callback`. This parameter represents the callback method that other objects will register to use when making a request. This method can be located in any other object, as long as it is scoped properly during the request. If this parameter is not passed, we default to a callback parameter that we will create as part of the `AjaxUpdater` object next. Listing 14.2 shows how the `Update` method is constructed.

Listing 14.2   **The `Update` Method in the `AjaxUpdater` (`AjaxUpdater.js`)**

```
AjaxUpdater.Update = function(method , service, callback)
{
    if(callback == undefined |¦ callback == "")
    {
        callback = AjaxUpdater.onResponse;
    }
    Ajax.makeRequest(method, service, callback);
    AjaxUpdater.isUpdating = true;
}
```

The first section of code in the `Update` method is an `if` statement, which checks for the callback parameter. We check to see if this value is undefined or an empty string. If it is, we set it to a default method named `onResponse`, which is a method that will exist in the `AjaxUpdater` object. When we are sure that we have a callback method set, we move on to make our XHR through the `Ajax` object. We already know how the engine handles XHRs at this point—the only difference here is that we are encapsulating it into our new `AjaxUpdater` object and abstracting the `Ajax` object from the rest of our application. As I mentioned at the beginning of this section, the `Ajax` object also uses the Singleton pattern because we do not want multiple `Ajax` objects floating around a large web application because it would get very unwieldy. The XHR is made by directly calling the `Ajax` object's `makeRequest` method and passing it three parameters. The first parameter is the method in which we want to send the data, which we have passed to the `Update` method. The second parameter is the service parameter that we passed to the `Update` method, which contains an XML or server-side file and additional query strings. The last parameter is the callback method that was either passed to the `Update` method or set to the default response method in the `if` statement. This method will make an XHR according to the data we provide it and respond to the callback method we pass to it, regardless of where it is located in the application. As you can see, we are also setting the `isUpdating` Boolean from the `initialize` method to `true` based on the fact that a request is in progress when this method is invoked.

The `onResponse` method that we use as a default callback method is very simple and can be used for any default response that you would like; see Listing 14.3. In the example, I am simply using it as a way to reset the `isUpdating` Boolean back to `false`, but you could use it to display a default, custom loading message, and so on.

Listing 14.3   **The onResponse Method in the `AjaxUpdater` (`AjaxUpdater.js`)**

```
AjaxUpdater.onResponse = function()
{
    if(Ajax.checkReadyState('loading') == "OK")
    {
        AjaxUpdater.isUpdating = false;
    }
}
```

If we do not use this default callback method, we will need another way to set the `isUpdating` Boolean to false. I have decided to set this variable directly in the `Ajax` object's `checkReadyState` method. When the `readyState` of the response reaches level 4, we know that the response has completed and is no longer updating. Listing 14.4 shows an example of where to add this code to the existing method.

Listing 14.4   **Updating the `AjaxUpdater` Status**

```
Ajax.checkReadyState = function(_id)
{
    switch(this.request.readyState)
    {
```

Listing 14.4   **Continued**

```
    case 1:
        document.getElementById(_id).innerHTML = 'Loading ...';
        break;
    case 2:
        document.getElementById(_id).innerHTML = 'Loading ...';
        break;
    case 3:
        document.getElementById(_id).innerHTML = 'Loading ...';
        break;
    case 4:
        AjaxUpdater.isUpdating = false;
        document.getElementById(_id).innerHTML = '';
        return this.http.status(this.request.status);
    }
}
```

As you can see, this has been a simple addition to the object, but it will cover all of our responses in future requests.

Using the Singleton Object

In the previous section, we learned how to create an object using the Singleton pattern. Now we will discover how to access it from other objects in a web application. The `AjaxUpdater` object can be used in any other object throughout your web application, all we need to do is import the file.

```
<script type="text/javascript" src="../javascript/utils/AjaxUpdater.js"></script>
```

Because the object instantiates itself, it is usable from the moment the file is loaded and can be called directly by name from any object that is loaded into the same page. Using a Singleton object method and property, such as the `AjaxUpdater`, is extremely easy. The following line of code makes an XHR and sets a callback method, which waits for the response from the server through the Ajax engine:

```
AjaxUpdater.Update("GET" , "services/accordion.xml", Accordion.display);
```

This method is called by name because it resides in the same page as the object that is making the request. The only code we would need to write at this point is the callback method that handles the response. You can refer to Listing 14.3 to get an idea of how this method would be written, although if you were to write a custom callback method, you would be doing so because you want to parse a custom response. Therefore, you would write additional code in the method to handle any custom actions you would like to accomplish. As an example, I have included a snippet of code in Listing 14.5 that we will cover in Chapter 16, "The Observer Pattern," to show you how a custom response handler might look and how you can get started parsing the response.

Listing 14.5   **Accessing a Method in a Singleton Object**

```
Accordion.display = function()
{
    if(Ajax.checkReadyState('loading') == "OK")
    {
        var p = Ajax.getResponse().getElementsByTagName('panel');
        for(var i=0; i<p.length; i++)
        {
            var title =
              ➡Ajax.getResponse().getElementsByTagName('title')[i].
              ➡firstChild.data;
        }
    }
}
```

This snippet of code does not actually result in anything useful, but it gives us an idea of how we would construct a custom response handler. First, we would start with the code in Listing 14.5 to make the XHR and pass this method as the callback. When we receive the response, we need to parse the XML that is returned by accessing the response data through the Ajax engine's `getResponse` method that we created in Part II. Once we have this response data, we can target elements by name with the JavaScript `getElementsByTagName` method. In this case, we get an array of panels that we iterate. While iterating through the panels, we can retrieve specific child data from the response, such as the title of each panel.

As you can see, the `AjaxUpdater` might be a small object, but it packs a lot of power and is the perfect candidate for the Singleton pattern. In this chapter, the Singleton pattern made the `AjaxUpdater` accessible from anywhere in the application and gave us a consistent reference to the object so that we did not have to worry about having the current information. Separating important pieces of functionality into separate objects provides us with layers of abstraction that keeps our code clean and easily scalable. Now that we have covered this simple design pattern, let's move on to discover a few more complex patterns that will help us optimize the code in our Ajax applications.

15

Model View Controller

The Model View Controller (MVC) pattern is the separation of an application's graphical user interface (GUI) from its core logic. There is no absolute design for the MVC, but as with any design pattern, it should adapt to the situation you are faced with when developing. Patterns are available to help solve or manage common problems when developing, but will only hinder that development if we restrict ourselves to absolute or strict guidelines. These lines must be blurred from one application to the next based on the situation at hand. This is why most experienced developers use multiple patterns in an application to accomplish or satisfy unique situations that occur because, as we all know by now, no two applications are the same. With that said, each application has common problems, and this is where patterns can come into play.

The MVC has existed since 1978, the year I was born. Obviously, due to technological advances, the implementations of this pattern in present applications will not fit the exact mold of the original pattern. In this book, we will take this and the rest of the patterns we have covered so far and implement them in a way that is appropriate to our project. A word of advice: Do not get hung up on conforming to any strict mold; rather, be free to make the best decisions based on the problem at hand. The goal with this pattern is to prevent having to make changes to the core logic in order to modify anything in the GUI. This chapter will explain how to accomplish this goal.

An Overview of the Pattern

Anyone who knows me will tell you I am a big fan of organization and order, especially when it comes to sensible code management, which is why I really like this pattern. I look at the MVC as more of a way to structure and organize certain objects of a code base in an application; whether it is a web or desktop application, the same idea applies. Keeping the core server logic separated from the view or the data that the user is interacting with by adding a central layer, called the *controller*, not only keeps our code organized, it also creates a logical data flow that is easier to manage. Believe it or not, in theory this pattern exists in every web application—it is simply not always organized into separate layers or there are variations of organization. Take a look at Figure 15.1, which shows the MVC pattern as it applies to our Ajax application.

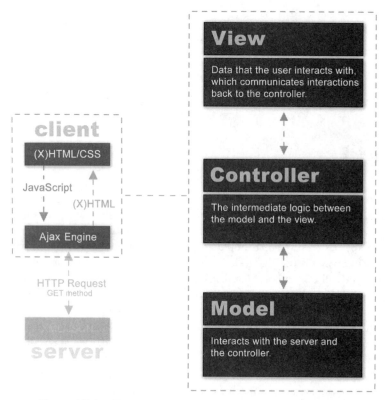

Figure 15.1   The MVC pattern applied to the sample project.

After taking a look at Figure 15.1, it is obvious this pattern exists in all applications. Even if there is only one code file in an application, the underlying data flow is always present. For example, all applications must make decisions based on user interaction and interact with the server by storing or retrieving data—whether it is attached to a database or simply making HTTP requests—and respond to the user with new data. The controller would be the decision making, the model would be the server interaction, and the view would be the response to the user. In theory, the XHR is exclusively an MVC pattern because it takes user input, interacts with the server via the HTTP request, and responds to the user via the `responseText` and `responseXML` properties. The difference is in the structure and design, which are definitely debatable and open to interpretation. Reusable objects are the ultimate goal of any application, and decoupling the objects is what makes this pattern powerful. Therefore, this pattern may exist in all code in theory, but it is not until we pair it with an object-oriented and structured design that its true power is unleashed.

Creating the Pattern

Usually when you read about the MVC pattern, it is not related to JavaScript. However, as I am sure you have noticed, we have already begun to implement this pattern with the components we have built. Each of the components consists of at least one controller and one view object, whereas the model consists of the objects that interact with the server, such as the `Ajax`, `AjaxUpdater`, and `HTTP` objects that we created in Part II, "Creating and Using the JavaScript Engine." Creating this pattern is as simple as starting with the folder structure in the code folder of our application. Since this pattern is related to the JavaScript code we are creating, we will create this structure within the `javascript` directory as in Figure 15.2.

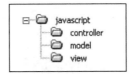

Figure 15.2   Directory structure for the MVC pattern.

This is obviously trivial and might seem like a waste of time to cover, but it is the basis for the structure we will utilize when creating objects we would like to fit into this pattern. Let's take the `Accordion` component from Chapter 10, "Accordion," as an example. This component is composed of two objects: `Accordion` and `Panel`. Figure 15.3 shows the previous MVC structure with the `Accordion` component and associated model objects.

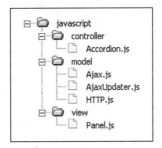

Figure 15.3   MVC directory structure with the Accordion component.

The `Accordion` object is the controller for this component because it interacts with another controller (`AjaxUpdater`) and ultimately the model (`Ajax`), and responds to the panel with the information from the server. The `Panel` object represents the view and presents to the user the different panels the accordion is composed of. When a user interacts with a panel, the panel interacts with the `AjaxUpdater`. This controller then sends a request to the model, which is our `Ajax` object. Therefore, we end up with multiple MVC triads working together to accomplish a task. Take a look at Figure 15.4 for a graphic view of how the data flows between the objects in this pattern.

Figure 15.4   Graphical view of how the Accordion uses the MVC pattern.

This is a good example of how the pattern can fluctuate. You can use multiple objects from different aspects of the MVC structure to work together as one whole unit, yet keep those objects completely decoupled.

Using the Pattern

As we have covered, there are many ways to use this pattern. This pattern can be combined with other patterns that are completely different, or the same pattern in combination with other MVC triads. As an example, we could have one MVC in our PHP code and another MVC in our JavaScript code. There are also many different ways to interpret the MVC pattern—no one way is the absolute and only way because the best solution for a situation is always the one that works best. As I said, this pattern can be used to simply organize your JavaScript and your PHP code into separate MVC patterns of their own, or it can be used to organize all your code into one combined MVC pattern. In the last section, we covered how we already combined our JavaScript objects for the `Accordion` component into an MVC pattern, whether or not we knew we were doing it when we built the accordion. Figure 15.5 shows a graphical representation of the PHP and the JavaScript organized into one combined MVC pattern.

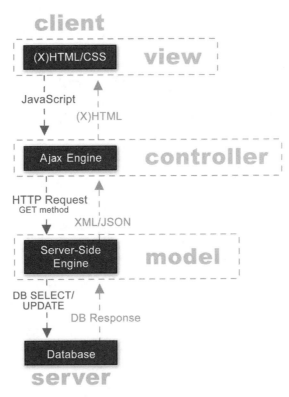

Figure 15.5   Graphical representation of the PHP and JavaScript organized into one combined MVC pattern.

In conclusion, this pattern is a great way to abstract our code into layers so that all objects have a common pattern for interacting with other objects. By following this pattern, we avoid having mixed connections, which could ultimately lead to tracking down what objects are connected to others. Finding an issue is usually harder than fixing the issue itself, which is why when following common patterns, the maintenance tasks become easier to manage because there is a logical flow to the application. This allows us to focus more quickly on specific areas that may be causing issues, which is the power of this pattern because it becomes more than handling a programming task—it becomes a way to structure and manage large amounts of data in a more efficient manner.

16

The Observer Pattern

As you have been learning throughout this part of the book, design patterns are extremely useful when developing large-scale applications. Design patterns provide code flexibility and help establish a way of handling common situations that occur in the logic of an application. The Observer pattern is an extremely important addition to the sample application because it creates a way of handling an unlimited number of objects as a collection with only a few object methods. Let's learn more about how this pattern accomplishes so much with so little.

Pattern Overview

The Observer pattern is a design pattern that is used to observe the state of an object in an application. The observed object allows other objects to register and unregister as observers. The observers are notified when specific events that they are observing are fired. The observed object has three distinct methods, which are outlined next.

Register Observers Overview

The Observer pattern essentially allows an unlimited number of objects to observe or listen to events in the observed object (or subject) by registering themselves. After observers are registered to an event, the subject will notify them when the event is fired. The subject handles this by storing an observer collection and iterating through it when the event occurs in order to notify each observer.

Notify Observers Overview

When an event is fired in the subject, the observers are notified via the methods they provide to the observer when they are registered. Each observer specifies its own `notify` method and defines what happens when the notification occurs. For instance, you may have an object that registers to an error-handling object and specifies a `notify` method that handles displaying the error to the user. On the other hand, you may also have a completely different object that specifies a `notify` method, that sends an email to the developer each time an error occurs in the web application. The power of this pattern is in the fact that both of these objects can be registered and notified by the same subject.

Unregister Observers Overview

If an object no longer wants to be notified by the subject it is registered with, it can unregister itself. There are a number of instances in which this method is useful, one of which is when you do not want an object to be notified more than one time. After an object has been notified, it can unregister itself and the subject will remove it from the observer collection. For example, imagine that you want to wait to fire a method until another method has occurred. If it follows the Observer pattern, you can register to this method and wait for notification before moving forward. Take a look at Figure 16.1 for an example.

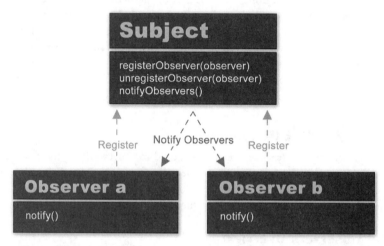

Figure 16.1   The Observer pattern allows multiple objects to observe
one event and be notified when that event is invoked.

As you can see, the Observer pattern can affect numerous objects with only one event. In this chapter, we will create an error-handling object that we will call the `ErrorManager`. This object will follow the Observer pattern and notify any registered objects if an error occurs.

Creating an Error-Handling Object

An error-handling object is essential when building and releasing large web applications that use heavy amounts of JavaScript. While building, error handling is very useful for identifying bugs in your code so that you can easily track them down and progressively finish building the application. When releasing an application, error handling is even more important because users need to know how to handle issues that may arise and cannot do so without feedback from the application, which can tell them what went wrong. It is also important after releasing because you or your fellow developers will be able to identify what went wrong when a user is contacting you with an issue. To handle errors, let's create an object called `ErrorManager` as in Listing 16.1.

Listing 16.1   **Instantiating `ErrorManager` (`ErrorManager.js`)**

```
ErrorManager = {};
```

The core of this object is JavaScript's intrinsic `onerror` event. This method listens for errors and fires an event that can point to any custom `callback` method that you specify. The `onerror` event also has the capability to pass three parameters to the `callback` method, to provide detailed information regarding any errors that occur. The three parameters that the event passes are the actual error message, which identifies what error occurred; the URL of the document where the error occurred; and the line number in the document where the error occurred. These parameters can have a number of uses. They can be used to provide feedback to users regarding any errors that occur, or they can be used to provide feedback to the developer so that he is aware of any issues that occur during user interaction after an application has been released or is being tested. We will set this event to a local callback in the `ErrorManager` object, but first we need to create the observer methods.

Register Observers

The `onerror` event will be used to notify the subject, which is the `ErrorManager` object of any errors that occur. `ErrorManager` will then notify any objects that have been registered and stored in its collection. There are three methods we will create, which we discussed in the previous section. The methods that will handle all the observation functionality are called `registerObserver`, `notifyObservers`, and `unregisterObserver`. These methods must be the first written in the object after the object has been declared. Listing 16.2 shows the `registerObserver` method.

Listing 16.2   **Registering Observers (`ErrorManager.js`)**

```
ErrorManager.registerObserver = function(_observer)
{
    ErrorManager.observerCollection.push(o);
}
```

The `registerObserver` method does exactly that: It registers an observer by adding it to an `observerCollection`, which is a property of the object and is essentially an array that is specifically used to store observers. Observers that are added to this collection need to specify the object name plus the method they want to use as the notification callback in a *codestring*. A codestring is a string representation of any code. In this case, it would be a method call in the form of a string:

```
"Object.notify"
```

The collection will be declared in an `initialize` method that we will create as soon as we have finished adding the observer methods to the object so that we keep the scope of the object members intact.

Notify Observers

The next method, called `notifyObservers` (see Listing 16.3), iterates through the `observerCollection` and fires the `callback` methods that the observers specified.

Listing 16.3   **Notifying the Observers (`ErrorManager.js`)**

```
ErrorManager.notifyObservers = function(message, url, line)
{
    for(var i in ErrorManager.observerCollection)
    {
        eval(ErrorManager.observerCollection[i] +"('"+message +"',
          ➥'"+ url +"','"+ line+"');");
    }
}
```

While iterating through the `observerCollection`, the `notifyObservers` method calls the observers by using JavaScript's intrinsic `eval` method to create a method from the codestring that was passed to the `registerObserver` method. The `eval` method determines whether the codestring is valid and executes the code if it is valid. I have also added the additional power of passing the error parameters from the `onerror` method to the `notify` methods. This allows the observers to be aware of the error that occurred and act on it as they see fit. For example, an object may register to the `ErrorManager` and receive notification when an error occurs. Based on the parameters we are passing to the `callback` method, the line of code where the error occurred may be used to highlight the corresponding issue in the GUI. This allows our objects to provide feedback to the user as to what went wrong. The best part about this pattern is that there can be an unlimited number of objects registered to the subject and they can all handle errors in different ways, depending on what portion of the application they manage. This allows for complete flexibility in your application and keeps the objects extremely decoupled, while allowing them to communicate with each other.

Unregister Observers

The next method is the `unregisterObserver` method, which is used to remove observers from the collection so that they are no longer notified when an event occurs. Listing 16.4 shows the method as it is used in `ErrorManager`.

Listing 16.4   **Unregistering Observers (`ErrorManager.js`)**

```
ErrorManager.unregisterObserver = function(_observer)
{
    for(var observer in ErrorManager.observerCollection)
    {
        if(_observer == ErrorManager.observerCollection[observer])
        {
            ErrorManager.observerCollection.splice(observer, 1);
        }
    }
}
```

This method receives a codestring as did the `registerObserver` method. It then uses this string while iterating through the collection by checking to see whether there is a matching codestring in the collection. When and if there is a match, the codestring is removed from the collection. In order to remove the string from the collection, we need to use the JavaScript `splice` method to remove the specified index in the collection. After the observer has been removed from the collection, it will no longer be notified of any events that it was once registered to, although the object may register again at any time.

Once we have these three methods created, we need to initialize the object and all its properties. Listing 16.5 shows our `ErrorManager`'s `initialize` method.

Listing 16.5   **Initializing the `ErrorManager` (`ErrorManager.js`)**

```
ErrorManager.initialize = function()
{
    ErrorManager.observerCollection = new Array();
    ErrorManager.registerObserver("ErrorManager.emailError");
    onerror = ErrorManager.notifyObservers;
}
ErrorManager.initialize();
```

As you can see, the `initialize` method is very important to this object. It must be called as soon as it has been created to allow proper scoping of its properties. As I mentioned earlier, it handles the creation of the `observerCollection` that we used throughout all of the observer methods. The `observerCollection` is nothing more than a simple array that is used to collect the observers as they are registered. The next two lines of code in this method register two methods from the `ErrorManager`: a method named `emailError` and another named `alert`. These two methods will be notified when any JavaScript error occurs in the application. Now that we have the observer methods created and the objects' properties are available, we can set the local `callback` method to JavaScript's intrinsic `onerror` event. This event becomes the core of this object; without it, the object would not function. Anytime a JavaScript error occurs, this event fires the callback, which in this case is the `notifyObservers` method. It may look as if we are defining a variable, but since this is an intrinsic JavaScript event it knows how to handle the assignment. This method then handles notifying all the observers of the error that occurred, along with all the details, including the message, URL, and exact line of code.

The first notify method that we will create is the `emailError` method (see Listing 16.6) that we registered in the `initialize` method. This method contains the functionality to send an email to specified developers listing all the details of the error.

Listing 16.6   **Emailing Errors (`ErrorManager.js`)**

```
ErrorManager.emailError = function(message, url, line)
{
    var error = "<b>Error:</b> <font color=red>"+ message +"</font><br/>";
    error += "<b>URL:</b> "+ url +"<br/>";
    error += "<b>Line:</b> "+ line +"<br/>";

    var page = "classes/ErrorManager.class.php";
    var subject = "My Ajax Application Error";
    AjaxUpdater.Update('POST', page +"?subject="+ subject +"&message="+ error,
      ➥this.catchResponse);
}


ErrorManager.catchResponse = function()
{
    if(Ajax.checkReadyState('loading') == "OK")
    {
        // Handle the response from the server-side
    }
}
```

Take a look at the parameters the `emailError` method accepts. They are the three parameters that we previously discussed. We will use these parameters to create an HTML-formatted email that we will ultimately send to ourselves or the developer of our application. After we have the error formatted as HTML, we will identify the variables that will be used as the parameters in the email. The first parameter is the page that we are requesting through Ajax, which is an `ErrorManager` class that we will create with PHP shortly, and the second is the subject of the email. After we have our variables identified for the request, we will send it to the `AjaxUpdater`'s `update` method, which we created in Chapter 14, "Singleton Pattern." This request will be made through the

POST method to the page that we specify, which in this case is an ErrorManager class that we will create with PHP. The request is sent along with a query string that consists of the variables we defined, such as the subject and HTML error. We will also specify a callback method, named catchResponse, which we can use to handle the response from the server. After all this information has been passed to the AjaxUpdater, it will make the request through the Ajax object to the PHP page specified.

Although we have not covered server-side interaction with Ajax, in this section we will be jumping ahead a bit in order to add the functionality to send the email. Later, in Part V, "Server-Side Interaction," we will take an in-depth look at server-side interaction. The PHP ErrorManager class is a fairly small class, so it will be a good object in which to make our first server-side interaction. Listing 16.7 shows the class in all its glory.

Note
The PHP classes used throughout this book require PHP version 5.0.

Listing 16.7   ErrorManager **PHP Class** (ErrorManager.class.php)

```php
<?php

$errorManager = new ErrorManager();
$errorManager->send($_GET["subject"], $_GET["message"]);

class ErrorManager
{

    public function ErrorManager() {}

    public function send($_subject, $_message)
    {
        $headers = "From: noreply@sample.com\r\n" .
                    "Reply-To: noreply@sample.com\r\n" .
                   "MIME-Version: 1.0\r\n" .
                   "Content-Type: text/html; charset=utf-8\r\n" .
                   "Content-Transfer-Encoding: 8bit\r\n\r\n";
        mail("you@yourdomain.com", $_subject, $_message, $headers);
    }

}

?>
```

As I mentioned, this class is fairly small because it only consists of one method. It is important to notice that we are instantiating the object in the same file. This allows us to make requests directly to the class without having to create an intermediate file that does it for us. Either way is perfectly fine, but I find this way to be a bit cleaner and easier to manage. After the object is instantiated, we call the `send` method and pass it two parameters, which are the `subject` and `message` parameters. You may recognize these parameters from the `ErrorManager` object that we created in JavaScript. These are the `onerror` parameters that are sent to the `callback` method and ultimately passed through the request to this class. Therefore, this method is invoked as soon as the page is requested. The request is then handled by the `send` method, which sends an email based on the parameters that are sent to it. However, before it sends the email, it also specifies the headers, such as the from email address, the reply-to email address, and the MIME version, content type, and content-transfer encoding, which are all used to handle the HTML format that we are passing through the request. After the headers have been identified, we will use PHP's intrinsic mail function, which allows you to send an email.

The only requirement is that the server you are using to run the web application must have access to a mail application. In order to get more information about the mail function, you may visit the PHP manual at www.php.net and search for *mail* in the function list. This page will provide you with additional information regarding the function and samples to show you how to make our `ErrorManager` class more robust. For example, you may want to add error handling in the `ErrorManager` class in case the email is not sent for any reason. If an error occurs, you can then respond to the client-side Ajax engine and ultimately the `catchResponse` method in the JavaScript `ErrorManager` with the response. The JavaScript `ErrorManager` can then handle the response by trying to send another email if there was a failure or simply notifying the user of the error that occurred as an alternative to sending the email.

Now that we have a fully functional `ErrorManager` object, we can use it throughout our application. Let's see how.

Using the Error-Handling Object

Error handling is essential to a successful web application, but it is often overlooked and deemed a boring chore to developers. Using the Observer pattern for Ajax error handling allows us to create an extremely intuitive user experience and is actually quite interesting to program. As you learned in Chapter 9, "Extending the Engine," with HTTP status codes, we can also provide immediate feedback and options to the user when errors occur without disrupting the flow of experience or leaving a user with questions regarding what to do next. Imagine having an object that can control all the alerts in your application. I have created one that is named `Alert`. This object registers an error method with the `ErrorManager` object immediately after it is instantiated. This method accepts the three parameters the `notifyObservers` method passes to observers in its collection. It then concatenates an error string that is displayed in an alert box to the user (see Listing 16.8).

Listing 16.8   **Alert** Object (`Alert.js`)

```
Alert = {};

ErrorManager.registerObserver("Alert.error");

Alert.error = function(message, url, line)
{
    var error = "Error: "+ message +"\n";
    error += "URL: "+ url +"\n";
    error += "Line: "+ line;
    alert(error);
    //ErrorManager.unregisterObserver("Alert.error");
}
```

After the error method is called, you can unregister it as an observer by uncommenting the last line in the method. This is only one simple example of how to use the Observer pattern in a web application. There are millions of ways this pattern can bring power to your applications.

17

Data Reflection Pattern

The Data Reflection pattern is a pattern that keeps web application content in sync with the database and with the file it is requesting. This pattern can be used in a number of ways. In our sample, it will be used as a way to keep a user's email data current by allowing the application to receive new emails from other users. This means that if a user sends email to another user, the receiving user will get this new email whenever the data happens to be reflected in the back end of the application. This reflection will be based on a delay or time interval that we set in the code. Or, the functionality could also be extended into a user preference, which would allow a user to choose how long a delay he has for email checking, such as current desktop applications have. The limits are based on your application and what pieces of it could benefit from using this pattern because it provides niche functionality that is not always going to be necessary.

In this chapter, we will learn different ways this pattern can be useful in a web application, as well as specific sections of an application that might benefit from it.

An Overview

The Data Reflection pattern keeps the web application content in sync with the database. This happens because the pattern runs in the back-end code and updates data that has changed while a user is logged in and using the application. As a typical XHR model does, the Data Reflection pattern starts with the user interface, where a user interacts with an element and the application makes a request. The major difference is that this pattern programmatically consists of JavaScript's `setTimeout` method. This method continuously makes XHRs through the Ajax engine to either call a server-side language and check for database updates or to check an XML file for updates. If there are updates, the new data is returned to the Ajax `callback` method and the application content is updated (or reflected); otherwise, there is nothing to reflect and therefore we do not complete the request. Figure 17.1 shows the data flow of the as it continually makes XHRs to the server-side language.

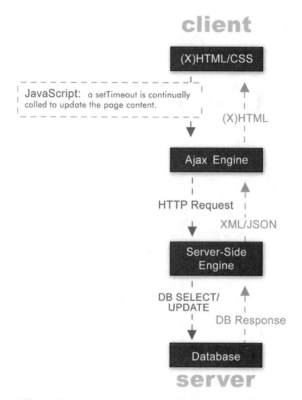

Figure 17.1   The constant data flow of the Data Reflection pattern.

This figure shows the data flow as the pattern makes requests to a server-side script and ultimately the database, but keep in mind that the pattern could loop back by requesting an XML file as well. Figure 17.1 shows the client on the front end of the application, with the `setTimeout` method continually making a request through the Ajax engine. When the Ajax engine receives the request, it either sends a `POST` or `GET` as an HTTP request to a server-side language or engine. The server-side engine checks the database for updates and does one of two things depending on the results. The results could yield no changes, which would cause the server-side script to respond to the Ajax engine with no updates, or the script could respond with updates that exist in the database. If there are updates in the database, the engine can respond with XML or JSON, which the Ajax engine will delegate to a `callback` method. The `callback` method will parse this data and reflect the changes in the user interface or the GUI as (X)HTML and/or CSS. This might seem like a lot of steps, but after we have the Ajax engine and the server-side engine running, we will not have to modify them any further. This means that after the application is set up, we should not have to touch the code and the users will keep the application running with fresh data. Now that we have an understanding of the Data Reflection pattern, let's step it up a notch and add more layers to the pattern. In this next section, we will extend this pattern to satisfy multiple users and allow them to interact with our application simultaneously with real-time updated content.

The Multi-User Pattern

The Data Reflection pattern can be extended to accommodate much more functionality. A perfect example of this is the Multi-User pattern. It is based on the Data Reflection pattern, yet it delegates the functionality between multiple users to provide them all with updated information from other user requests. Take a look at Figure 17.2 to get an idea of how the data flows from one user to the next in this pattern.

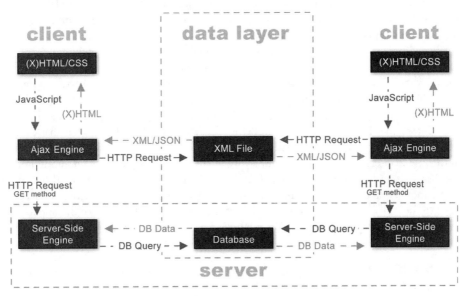

Figure 17.2   The Multi-User pattern as an extension of the Data Reflection pattern.

An example of this pattern is a chat application. Imagine multiple users from remote locations typing data into a chat window and clicking Send. Each time a user clicks the Send button, an XHR is made to update the database or file that is currently holding the chat content. While the users are chatting back and forth, this pattern is consistently polling from the server in the background to see whether there are any content updates on the server that a user does not yet have. If a user is up to date, nothing happens, but if she is not, she receives the latest content from the server. This is just one of a million examples of how we can use this pattern, but the same concept applies as far as the functionality works and the data flows in the back end of the application. Think about any situation that can possibly have multiple users and this pattern can be applied over and over again without changing the base code that we will write in the next section. Let's take a look at this code and how it will apply itself to the functionality in our application.

Creating the Pattern

Now that we understand the power of this pattern, we will learn how to put it to use in our application. Up to this point, we have created all the components that are needed to create an email application, but we are missing the object that ties them together in some way. In this section, we will create an object named `Email`, which will perform all the duties that are necessary to gather data for each of the components. But rather than focus on the details of each method and the population of different components, we will focus on how to add the Data Reflection pattern to the object. Therefore, we will create all the methods, but we will not add code to them until Chapter 21, "Interacting with a Database: The Server Side," when we connect the object to a database with PHP. So, let's get started by defining the methods we will need to populate the different components and make our application function.

We will start by identifying the actions you would typically associate with an email application. The first actions that come to mind are sending, receiving, and composing an email. Next, we will focus on how we would like to show email threads. I have chosen to use the accordion component that we built in Chapter 10, "Accordion," to display all the emails in a particular thread as a group. The first email in the group, which is the one that initiated the thread, is the email that will display in the inbox. The replies that came afterward will only display in the accordion as part of the thread, but we will focus more on this in Chapter 21. Since we are displaying emails in a thread, we will add a method that displays them as a threaded group. Last, we will create an `initialize` method to set the local variables, and we will also create a `display` method to be used as an access point to the object, which will fire the correct methods when the body of the application has loaded. Therefore, we have six methods we need to create, as follows:

- `Email.initialize`
- `Email.display`
- `Email.showThread`
- `Email.getMail`
- `Email.sendMail`
- `Email.compose`

Each method is prefixed with the `Email` object since this will be the name of the object that contains them. Now that we have these methods, we can move on to the focus of this section, which is adding the Data Reflection pattern to the `Email` object. The first thing we will do is add a method that creates a Data Reflection pattern. We will appropriately name the method `dataReflection` and it will receive two parameters: a `callback` method and a time delay. The `callback` method represents the method we want to be called each time the data is reflected. In our case, we will call back the `display` method because it is our access point and will naturally create a consistent loop for the pattern, which will continually reflect the database data. The time delay represents the amount of time in milliseconds in which we would like the method to be called. For example, if we would like to set it to reflect every minute, we would use 60,000 milliseconds. Within the `dataReflection` method is JavaScript's `setTimeout` method, which will take these two parameters and fire when the time delay has been reached. Following is the `dataReflection` method, which we will add to the `Email` object.

```
Email.dataReflection = function(callbackMethod, delay)
{
    setTimeout(callbackMethod, delay);
}
```

Since the `display` method is the access point to our object, we will plant the first `dataReflection` pattern within this method and create a loop that continually does callbacks on the `display` method. The `display` method for our object will receive a username when we add the server-side code to it in Chapter 21 because we will need to have a value to check against in the database so that we can provide the appropriate email data back to the current user. This means that the `callback` method will need to have this value as well. Here is the code that we will add to the `display` method, with the `username` parameter as a value in the `callback` method.

```
Email.display = function(username)
{
    Email.dataReflection("Email.display('"+ username +"')", 60000);
}
```

As you can see, calling this method is trivial because it is really just a wrapper for the `setTimeout` method. Although it is simple, this pattern is actually quite powerful when put to use with a database.

18

Interaction Patterns

There are many interaction patterns emerging in the budding presence of Ajax. Web applications can now have front-end functionality that is much more complex, such as interacting with the database without a browser refresh. Not refreshing the browser is much more than a code trick that is just done for kicks—it allows developers to create extremely complex front-end functionality that interacts with the database and feels like any other application, regardless of whether it is on the desktop or the Web. In this chapter, we are going to cover two interaction patterns I have found much use for. The patterns we will be discussing are creating a pseudo-history and a drag-and-drop interface. Both of these objects will be completely flexible, allowing for extensibility, which I'm sure will provide you with some additional ideas. Let's get started creating a history, and then we will dive into the drag-and-drop interface.

Creating a History with Cookies

History is a known issue with Ajax because when a page is not refreshed, it is not added to the browser history. In this section, we will create a solution that will solve many issues with regard to application history and can also be used to provide additional functionality to an application, such as Undo. Although this object will not completely fix the Back button issues, which occurs due to a user never leaving the same page and therefore never creating a history, it will allow users to click the Back button and come back to the site where they left off if they allow cookies to be saved to their local machine.

The Historian Object

The `Historian` object will be a different type of object than the others we have created in the book. It uses the object constructor method, which we covered in Chapter 5, "Object-Oriented JavaScript." We are using this method because I want to lend flexibility in terms of being able to use multiple `Historian` instances in one application, during one session. This could come in handy if we wanted to save a separate history for specific features in an application. The `Historian` object will save data to a cookie to allow users to leave the page and come back to where they left off. The first thing we will do is create a constructor for the object and, since it saves a cookie, we will pass the URL that the cookie should be saved to. The following code snippet shows how we are going to accomplish this:

```
function Historian(url){} .
```

After we have the constructor completed and we are able to pass a unique URL, we will create a local array called `collection` and a method called `push`. The `push` method will enable us to add data to the array, and will ultimately save the array to a cookie at the URL specified as the constructor's parameter. It checks to see whether the collection contains the value we are pushing through a custom method that we will create called `containsValue`. If the value does not already exist, we will push the new value and save the `collection` array. The following code shows how we will push new values to the collection, call another method to save the data to a cookie, and check the collection to make sure that the value does not already exist.

```
this.collection = new Array();

this.push = function(_index)
{
    if(!this.containsValue(this.collection, _index))
    {
        this.collection.push(_index);
        this.save(this.collection, 1, "/", url, false);
    }
}

this.containsValue = function(_arr, _val)
{
    for(var i=0; i<_arr.length; i++)
    {
        if(_arr[i] == _val)
        {
            return true;
            break;
        }
    }
    return false;
}
```

The **save** method we are calling from the **push** method is what creates and stores the cookie. It receives five parameters, all of which are required to create the cookie:

- The value we are saving, which in this case is our **collection** array
- The number of days for which it is saved
- The path on the server where it is saved
- The domain we are passing through the constructor
- A Boolean for whether the cookie is saved securely

After the method is triggered, it simply creates a **date** object in order to set the expiration date relative to the amount of days that are passed to the method. After we configure the **date** method, we create the cookie with all the data we have received:

```
this.save = function(value, days, path, domain, secure)
{
    var expdate = new Date();
    expdate.setTime(expdate.getTime() + days *24*60*60*1000);

    document.cookie= "history=" + escape(value) +
        ((expdate) ? "; expires=" + expdate.toGMTString() : "") +
        ((path) ? "; path=" + path : "") +
        ((domain) ? "; domain=" + domain : "") +
        ((secure) ? "; secure" : "");
}
```

Now that we have a way to save the data as a cookie, we need to create a method for retrieving it. We will create a method called **getSaved**, which will retrieve the cookie, and if one exists, repopulate the collection with the saved data. Since cookies are saved as strings, we need to parse the saved data in a number of ways in order to retrieve the values we need. The first few things we will do are get the cookie, set a variable to the prefix that we saved the data as, and look for an index of the prefix in the cookie. If a prefix does not exist, the method will simply return a null value. Otherwise, we will have an index in which to look for the values, which we will set to a variable called **begin**. Last, we will return the **unescape**d value of the cookie after performing a substring from the begin number plus the prefix length to the end of the cookie string.

```
this.getSaved = function()
{
    var dc = document.cookie;
    var prefix = "history=";
    var begin = dc.indexOf(prefix);
    if (begin != 0)
    {
```

```
        return null;
    }
    return unescape(dc.substring(begin + prefix.length, dc.length));
}
```

Now that we have created this method, we can set the collection to the returned value of the method. We will do this by simply adding a **try**, **catch** to the object directly after the getSaved method. We will use the **try**, **catch** in in order to determine whether the code will perform before we follow through with it. We will try to set the collection to the getSaved data after we split it at all the commas into an array value. If we get an error, we will simply catch it and set the collection to a new array.

```
try
{
    this.collection = this.getSaved().split(",");
}
catch(err)
{
    this.collection = new Array();
}
```

In order to clean up and clear the cookie through the **Historian**, we will create a method named **clear**. This method takes two parameters: the path and the domain of the cookie. It first checks to see whether any data is saved in the cookie by calling the getSaved method. If the method returns a value other than **null**, we simply set a new cookie with all the previous data to a past date, which renders the cookie expired and therefore clears it from memory.

```
this.clear = function(path, domain)
{
    if(this.getSaved())
    {
        document.cookie = "history=" +
            ((path) ? "; path=" + path : "") +
            ((domain) ? "; domain=" + domain : "") +
            "; expires=Thu, 01-Jan-70 00:00:01 GMT";
    }
}
```

Now that we have the object created, we can put it to use, but we first need to create some sample data to load and play with in the HTML.

Creating and Displaying the XML

In this section, we will first create an XML structure in which to sample our `Historian` and then create an HTML file to display it all. Our XML file will contain a number of references to images that represent screens, which are grouped into navigation nodes. These screens will become what a user navigates through in the sample. Following is the sample XML data:

```xml
<?xml version="1.0" encoding="iso-8859-1"?>
<navigation>
    <screen><![CDATA[<img src="img/screen1.jpg">]]></screen>
    <screen><![CDATA[<img src="img/screen2.jpg">]]></screen>
    <screen><![CDATA[<img src="img/screen3.jpg">]]></screen>
    <screen><![CDATA[<img src="img/screen4.jpg">]]></screen>
    <screen><![CDATA[<img src="img/screen5.jpg">]]></screen>
    <screen><![CDATA[<img src="img/screen6.jpg">]]></screen>
    <screen><![CDATA[<img src="img/screen7.jpg">]]></screen>
    <screen><![CDATA[<img src="img/screen8.jpg">]]></screen>

    <screen><![CDATA[<img src="img/screen9.jpg">]]></screen>
    <screen><![CDATA[<img src="img/screen10.jpg">]]></screen>
</navigation>
```

In order to navigate from screen to screen and clear the history, we need to create an HTML page that has Next, Previous, and Clear History buttons. This page must also import our CSS and JavaScript files in order to render the screens and make the Ajax requests. The following is the HTML for the Historian HTML page:

```html
<html xmlns="http://www.w3.org/1999/xhtml">
<head>
<meta http-equiv="Content-Type" content="text/html; charset=iso-8859-1">
<title>Ajax Historian</title>
<link href="css/historian.css" rel="stylesheet" type="text/css" />
<script type="text/javascript" src="javascript/utils/Historian.js"></script>
<script type="text/javascript" src="javascript/controller/Navigation.js"></script>
<script type="text/javascript" src="javascript/model/AjaxUpdater.js"></script>
<script type="text/javascript" src="javascript/model/Ajax.js"></script>
<script type="text/javascript" src="javascript/model/HTTP.js"></script>
</head>

<body onload="javascript:AjaxUpdater.Update('GET', 'services/navigation.xml',
Navigation.loadScreen);">
<div id="navigation"></div>
<br/><br/>
```

```
<a href="javascript:Navigation.previous();">Previous</a> |
<a href="javascript:Navigation.next();">Next</a> |
<a href="javascript:Navigation.history.clear('/', 'www.yourdomain.com');
document.location = document.location;">Clear History</a>
</body>

</html>
```

As you can see from the source code for our HTML page, we are referencing an object called `Navigation`. This object will allow us to navigate from one screen to the next and reverse, plus clear the history. Now that we have all our other code in place, let's create the `Navigation` object that will pull it all together.

The Navigation Object

The example we will be creating to use the `Historian` reminds me a lot of my days working in e-learning. All the courses we built had a number of interactive screens with navigation to click from one to the next—sort of like a slideshow, but with a lot of additional functionality. These courses would also remember where you left off or bookmark the last place you were located in the course so that if you left and came back, it would take you to the bookmark. We will be creating this bookmark functionality in our sample; therefore, we will be creating a `Navigation` object to take us from one page to another. The `Navigation` object is a Singleton object that increments and decrements which screen displays from the navigation collection in the XML. In order to save the history with our `Navigation` object, we must instantiate the `Historian` object when we initialize it. Here are the `Navigation`'s `instantiation` and `initialize` methods.

```
Navigation = {};

Navigation.initialize = function()
{
    Navigation.history = new Historian("www.yourdomian.com");
    Navigation.index = (Navigation.history.collection.length == 0)
        ➥? 0 : Navigation.history.collection.length-1;
    Navigation.screenArray = new Array();
}
Navigation.initialize ();
```

In the `initialize` method, we instantiate the `Historian` object and pass it the local domain in which we want to save the cookie. I have added a sample domain; this will need to be changed to reflect the local domain of the server where you will be deploying in the sample. After we have our `Historian` object instantiated, we will get the index for the navigation array in order to display the screen that was bookmarked, if one exists. Otherwise, we will show the first in the collection by setting the value to 0. Last, we will create an array called `screenArray`. This array will be set to the collection of screens we receive in the response from the XHR, which occurs in the `loadScreen` method. The `loadScreen` method will be used throughout the rest of this object's methods to load each screen. This method is used as the `callback` method for the `AjaxUpdater` from the HTML page in the `onload` event of the body. When it is triggered and the response is `"OK"`, we simply retrieve the screens from the response and add them to our `screenArray`. After we have an array of screens, we display the index in the `screenArray` that is currently set in the `Navigation` object. By default, this index is 0, but if the `Historian` has a saved cookie of history, it is set to the last screen index that was visited by the current user. Last, we push the index to the `Historian`, which will be stored in the `collection` array and saved to the cookie if it does not already exist in the collection.

```
Navigation.loadScreen = function()
{
    if(Ajax.checkReadyState('navigation') == "OK")
    {
        Navigation.screenArray =
            ➥Ajax.getResponse().getElementsByTagName('screen');
        document.getElementById('navigation').innerHTML = Navigation.screenArray[
            ➥Navigation.index ].firstChild.data;
        Navigation.history.push(Navigation.index);
    }
}
```

In order to navigate from one screen to the next, we will create a method called **next**. This method will first make sure we are not on the last screen. If we are not, it will increment the index and fire the `loadScreen` method. If we are on the last index of the `screenArray`, we will not do anything because we would end up with null values from the array, which would break the navigation.

```
Navigation.next = function()
{
    if(Navigation.index < (Navigation.screenArray.length-1))
    {
        Navigation.index++;
        Navigation.loadScreen();
    }
}
```

In order to navigate in reverse, we simply check to make sure we are not currently at the 0 index. If not, we decrement the index and fire the `loadScreen` method. When the `loadScreen` method is fired, it has the index from the previous screen and it renders it in the page.

```
Navigation.previous = function()
{
    if(Navigation.index > 0)
    {
        Navigation.index--;
        Navigation.loadScreen();
    }
}
```

This object is pretty powerful and can fix a lot of issues related to not refreshing the browser when using Ajax. I hope that you experiment with the objects in this book and create some extremely powerful custom functionality. The next section of this chapter will cover adding drag-and-drop functionality to elements in your applications, so let's get to it.

Drag and Drop

Drag-and-drop functionality is becoming more and more popular and in the right situations it can be extremely useful. With all the new personal data storage applications that are on the Web, this functionality becomes very useful when a user wants to sort elements that contain data. For example, if you are using an application to create a list of things you have to do, you might create the list only to find out you would like to do certain things before others. This could be a real pain in the butt, or it could easily be solvable if there was a way to drag and drop the items in the order you would like, making them into a sortable list. In this section, we will be creating a sortable list of data. Let's get started by creating the object that makes it all happen.

The DragDrop Object

The `DragDrop` object is a Singleton object that allows HTML elements to have drag-and-drop functionality. This functionality allows lists to become sortable with other elements that include the same class name and parent. This means that if we have a group of elements and we would like them all to be drag and drop and sortable, we would simply call the `initialize` method of the object and pass a shared class name that all the elements would need to have in common. Here is an example of the HTML we will use for this sample:

```
<html xmlns="http://www.w3.org/1999/xhtml">
<head>
<title>Drag and Drop</title>
```

```
<link href="css/dragdrop.css" rel="stylesheet" type="text/css" />
<script type="text/javascript" src="javascript/Utilities.js"></script>
<script type="text/javascript" src="javascript/utils/DragDrop.js"></script>
</head>

<body onload="DragDrop.initialize('dItem');">

<div id="container">
    <div id="1" class="dItem">1</div>

    <div id="2" class="dItem">2</div>
    <div id="3" class="dItem">3</div>
    <div id="4" class="dItem">4</div>
    <div id="5" class="dItem">5</div>
    <div id="6" class="dItem">6</div>
    <div id="7" class="dItem">7</div>
    <div id="8" class="dItem">8</div>
    <div id="9" class="dItem">9</div>
    <div id="10" class="dItem">10</div>
</div>

</body>
</html>
```

In order to separate our `div` elements from each other visually, and add a dotted outline to the drag state of elements and a **move** cursor to the draggable elements, we will write the following CSS and save it to a file called **dragdrop.css**:

```
#container
{
    float: left;
}

#drag_dummy
{
    border: #333 1px dotted;
}

.dItem
{
    width: 400px;
    height: 20px;
    background-color: #ccc;
    border: #333 1px solid;
```

```
    margin: 2px;
    cursor: move;
}
```

In order to create the **DragDrop** object, we will start by instantiating and initializing it:

```
DragDrop = {};
```

```
DragDrop.initialize = function(className)
{
    DragDrop.className = className;
    DragDrop.currentItem = '';
    document.onmousedown = DragDrop.onmousedown;
    document.onmouseup = DragDrop.onmouseup;
}
```

This method accepts the shared class name for the drag-and-drop elements and sets it to an object variable for later reference. Then it creates a new property called **currentItem** and sets it to an empty string so that we can later set it to the element that is currently being dragged in order to reference it during a drag-and-drop occurrence. Last, we set two events to drag-and-drop events. These include the **onmousedown** and **onmouseup** events, which are set to the **onmousedown** and **onmouseup** methods in the **DragDrop** object. These two methods will fire every time there is a **mousedown** or **mouseup** event, but we will check to make sure the event is resonating from a drag element in order to keep the calls under control. The way in which we will verify that a drag item is being clicked is by taking the received event object—which is passed to our methods by default since they are fired by events—and checking whether an event object exists. After we verify that one exists, we check the target, which is the source of the event, to see whether its class name is equal to the class name that we set in the **initialize** method. If it is, we know we have a drag item that is being triggered and we move forward with the **startDrag** or **stopDrag** actions. Here is the code that handles firing the events, checking the elements, and calling the start and stop drag methods:

```
 DragDrop.onmousedown = function(evt)
{
    var evt = DragDrop.getEvent(evt);
    if(evt != null)
    {
        var t = DragDrop.getTarget(evt);
        if(t.className == DragDrop.className)
        {
            if (!t.isDragging)
            {
```

```
                    DragDrop.startDrag(t, evt.clientX, evt.clientY);
                }
            }
        }
}


DragDrop.onmouseup = function(evt)
{
    var evt = DragDrop.getEvent(evt);
    if(evt != null)
    {
        var t = DragDrop.getTarget(evt);
        if(t.className == DragDrop.className +' dragging')
        {
            DragDrop.stopDrag(t);
        }
    }
}


DragDrop.getEvent = function(evt)
{
    if(!evt)
    {
        var evt = window.event;
    }
    return evt;
}


DragDrop.getTarget = function(evt)
{
    return t = (evt.target) ? evt.target : evt.srcElement;
}
```

You are probably wondering how we fire the mousedown event. This will occur at the end of the startDrag method where we will add a listener to the document's mousemove event rather than setting it by default. Setting it by default would mean the event would be fired each time the mouse moved and while it was moving, which would be a lot of method calling.

The startDrag method accepts three parameters. The parameters are the HTML element itself, and the x and y positions of the mouse, which are gathered by the mousedown event object. The first thing we do in this method is set a few variables for later use. These properties are called orgParent, currentItem, and isDragging. orgParent is set to the parentNode of the drag element when the startDrag event is fired because we will need it in the dragTo method, and the drag item will not have the same parent at that time. The other two properties are `currentItem` and `isDragging`, which are fairly self-explanatory.

The next section of code gathers the coordinates and size of the current element and sets two properties called `dragOffsetX` and `dragOffsetY`, which will be used in the `dragTo` method to keep the element's coordinates relevant to the mouse coordinates while it is moving. The next group is a bit more interesting and creates a nice effect for the drag functionality. We will create a new element on the fly and give it an id value of `drag_dummy`. This element will take on the coordinates of the current `drag` element and eventually replace it. Before we replace it, though, we need to convert the current element to an absolute position, set its coordinates to absolute values and, as an extra effect, also set the alpha to 25% so that when the element is being dragged, it will allow us to view its position over the other elements. Adding this effect makes it seem as though there is depth to the page and makes the drag-and-drop more realistic. Now comes the replacement code, which places `drag_dummy` in place of the current drag item. The last thing we will do is add the listener for the `mousemove` event and set it to a method called `dragTo`, as was mentioned earlier. The following is the code for the `startDrag` method. It may seem like a lot at first glance, but most of it is code for gathering coordinates for the `drag_dummy` element.

```
DragDrop.startDrag = function(_this, mouseX, mouseY)
{
    this.orgParent = _this.parentNode;
    DragDrop.currentItem = _this;
    this.isDragging = true;

    // Get coordinates
    var pos = Utilities.getXY(_this);
    var x = pos.x;
    var y = pos.y;
    var w = _this.offsetWidth;
    var h = _this.offsetHeight;
    this.dragOffsetX = mouseX - x;
    this.dragOffsetY = mouseY - y;

    // Create dummy
    var dummy = Utilities.createElement("div", {id:'drag_dummy'});
    dummy.style.height = (h) + 'px';
    dummy.style.width = (w) + 'px';
    Utilities.appendChild(document.body, dummy);

    // Convert to drag class
    this.className = DragDrop.className+' dragging';
    this.style.position = 'absolute';
    this.style.left = x + 'px';
```

```
    this.style.top = y + 'px';
    this.style.width = w + 'px';
    this.style.height = h + 'px';
  Utilities.changeOpac(25, _this.id);

    // Replace with dummy
    this.parentNode.replaceChild(dummy, _this);
  document.body.appendChild(_this);

    Utilities.addListener(document, "mousemove", DragDrop.dragTo);
}
```

The `dragTo` method is triggered by the `mousemove` event, so it accepts an event object as its parameter by default. The first group of code in this method gathers the current `drag` element and gets the mouse x and y positions. Once we gather this information, we can use it moving forward. The first piece of code that will use these properties will be when we set the left and top style properties for the current element to the current mouse positions. Then we will subtract the `dragOffset` values we set in the `startDrag` method so that the element moves to the current position. Next, we will create a dummy variable that is equivalent to the `drag_dummy` element so that we can use it to place the current `drag` element later in the method. In order to place the element in a new position, we need to first figure out where the element is located and where it should be placed when it is dropped. We will do this by calling the `getNewPositionElement` method, which will iterate through the `orgParent` we set in the `startDrag` method and figure out which sibling the current element is over, based on the mouse x and y properties and their relation to the elements. After we find the correct placement, we will receive the element in that place and insert our `drag` element before it. If something happens to go wrong, we will simply append it back to the parent and not worry about the exact placement. The following is the `dragTo` method in its entirety, plus the `getNewPositionElement` method for calculating the placement:

```
DragDrop.dragTo = function(evt)
{
    this = DragDrop.currentItem;
    var evt = DragDrop.getEvent(evt);
    mouseX = evt.clientX;
    mouseY = evt.clientY;

    this.style.left = (mouseX - _this.dragOffsetX) + 'px';
    this.style.top = (mouseY - _this.dragOffsetY) + 'px';

    var dummy = Utilities.getElement('drag_dummy');
    var el = DragDrop.getNewPositionElement(_this, mouseX, mouseY);
```

```
    if(el != null)
    {
        el.parentNode.insertBefore(dummy, el);
    }
    else
    {

        this.orgParent.appendChild(dummy);
    }
}

DragDrop.getNewPositionElement = function(_this, mx, my)
{
    var target = null;
    var y = null;
    var ly = null;

    var p = _this.orgParent;
    for(var i in p.childNodes)
    {
        if(p.childNodes[i] != undefined)
        {
            if(p.childNodes[i].id != 'drag_dummy' && p.childNodes[i].id !=
              ↪undefined)
            {
                var pos = Utilities.getXY(p.childNodes[i]);
                y = pos.y;
                h = p.childNodes[i].offsetHeight;

                if(my<(y+h) && (target == null || y < ly))
                {
                    target = p.childNodes[i];
                    ly = y;
                }
            }
        }
    }
    return target;
}
```

Now that we are able to drag elements, we need a way to stop the drag. The **stopDrag** method will be used and is what we set in the beginning when we added the **mouseup** event in the **intialize** method. This method simply sets the current **drag** element's class name back to its original class name in order to return the element back to the way it started. Next we get the **drag_dummy** element and replace it with the actual element that was being dragged. This returns everything back to normalcy, with the dragged element in the new position. After the element is in place, we reset all the rest of its properties. This includes all its styles and the `isDragging` Boolean. Last, we remove the listener we implemented for the `mousemove` event, change the opacity back to 100%, and reset the `currentItem` to nothing.

```
DragDrop.stopDrag = function(_this)
{
    this.className = DragDrop.className;
    var dummy = Utilities.getElement('drag_dummy');
    dummy.parentNode.replaceChild(_this, dummy);

    this.isDragging = false;
    this.style.position = '';
    this.style.left = '';
    this.style.top = '';
    this.style.width = '';
    this.style.height = '';

    Utilities.removeListener(document, "mousemove", DragDrop.dragTo);
    Utilities.changeOpac(100, _this.id);
    DragDrop.currentItem = '';
}
```

This object may be a bit complex, but now that it has been created it can be used without ever touching the code again. But, of course, we could always add more code to create more functionality, such as adding a sort method to the object that would reset the order of the items. Although we have not integrated this object with Ajax, it can easily be done to save the positions of elements in a database for later retrieval. This is a common theme in a lot of new web applications because it lends itself well to personalizing user data as we have done in this section.

19

Usability Patterns

Up until now, all the patterns we have covered have been Ajax-enabled OOP (object-oriented programming) patterns, which occur in the background code and are never visible to the user. This chapter will differ by focusing specifically on visible design elements, the usability principles that occur in the design of an Ajax web applications interface, and the interactions that occur on the client side in the graphical user interface (GUI). The usability patterns we will be discussing are designed to provide a more intuitive user experience and eliminate all the annoying JavaScript dialogs that have existed in many applications over the years. The GUI should be free of questions and uncertainty. Most of all, though, it should definitely be free of obtrusive JavaScript dialogs by providing an extremely integrated method of error, warning, and feedback handling to the user.

As a software developer, I am well aware it is not always easy to display these errors in such an apparent interface design, but with all the capabilities that Ajax provides our applications, we should be taking on the responsibility and forging new paths in web application development, design, and interaction. There are a number of ways to integrate errors and feedback seamlessly into an application through Ajax and DHTML. Providing this feedback opens up a whole new realm of possible interactions that have not yet existed, leaving us at the forefront of something that is exciting and fun to be a part of.

A couple solutions that we will cover in more detail throughout this chapter are highlighting elements when the content or data has been updated, and displaying errors and feedback as *inline messages*. When I say inline messages, I mean a message that displays within the current page and connects messages to the elements to which they correspond. Errors and feedback should be helpful information to the user. However, abruptly throwing JavaScript alerts or confirmations at a user is not the best solution because they are usually pretty startling to a user and should be eliminated from all web applications. We are going to learn how to create graceful messages that leave users comfortable about their decisions and ultimately keep them involved and engaged in our web applications without hindering their experience and workflow. Keeping users actively involved provides life to our web applications and, if they can efficiently solve a problem with our web application, they will continue to use it. The message handling that we will be covering in this chapter could and should ultimately be applied to all forms of web applications, but they integrate most beautifully with Ajax because of JavaScript and its easy access and manipulation of the Document Object Model (DOM).

Handling Feedback, Errors, and Warnings

In Chapter 12, "Client-Side Validation," we created quite a powerful process of managing custom server-side errors based on database information with the `ErrorManager` and `UserValidator` objects. In this chapter, we will take what we learned about displaying these errors to the user and go a step further by focusing on all forms of messages that need to be presented to a user in an application. We will take a look at a few figures that show different ways of displaying messages to a user and how to keep them consistent across an Ajax application. We will also learn how to create a very simple dialog object in the section, "Designing with Code," that will have a display method for custom messages of all kinds. This object will be focused on creating visual elements with the DOM and cascading style sheets (CSS). Let's first start with a very obvious and detrimental issue that occurs with all JavaScript applications.

One of the most obvious issues with Ajax applications is the fact that they use JavaScript and, although not often, some users may actually have JavaScript disabled. If we are developing an Ajax application, we really should add a quick line of code that informs non-JavaScript users how to enable it if they would like to use the application, just in case they do not know how. It is very easy to do this with the `noscript` HTML tag. Listing 19.1 is a quick example of how we could inform non-JavaScript users of the issue.

Listing 19.1   **Displaying a Message for Non-JavaScript Users**

```
<noscript>This application requires that your browser has JavaScript
enabled.</noscript>
```

This message can be anything you decide—it can explain how to enable JavaScript, what benefits it will provide, and so on. The choice is yours, so be creative.

Originally, I was going to separate feedback and errors into two different sections of this chapter, but as I thought more about it, I realized the best responses are the ones that are handled the same way throughout an application with very subtle but obvious design differences. When I say design differences, I mean colors, font decorations, and other display differences, not the interaction model. For example, errors could have a red background or font color, whereas successful feedback messages could use green. Keeping interaction models the same is the key to obtaining consistency in an application and ultimately the user experience. Each time we introduce a new interaction, users have to take the time to learn a new concept and are taken out of their current workflow, which—even if for only a second—changes the course of their experience. This means that if we are going to make users take the time to learn a new interaction, it should be up front and extremely obvious to the point that they may not even be aware that the interaction is something creative that we customized. Also, if we keep the interaction model consistent, we allow the workflow to progress without interruption. This allows users to solve the problem that they are using our application for in the first place, in a timelier manner. Interaction models could include fading messages, highlighting form fields, and so on. Again, this is your choice, so be creative.

Figure 19.1 has a combination of quite a few forms of error handling that I have mentioned so far in this chapter. Combining error-handling methods can really help users understand exactly what it is that they need to fix in order to move forward with their workflow. How many forms of error handling are there in this one figure? Obviously, it is not as easy to know without a working sample, but this figure actually features five forms of error handling. The first two are the most obvious: The first is the actual message at the top of the page that explains the errors, and the second is the high-lighted fields in the form that correspond to the errors presented in the message. Again, it is a bit hard to notice without a working example, but the other error handlers include the cursor that appears in the first form field that has created an error, and hyperlinks on each actual error in the message at the top of the page, which when selected bring you to the form element to which it corresponds and adds the cursor to that field.

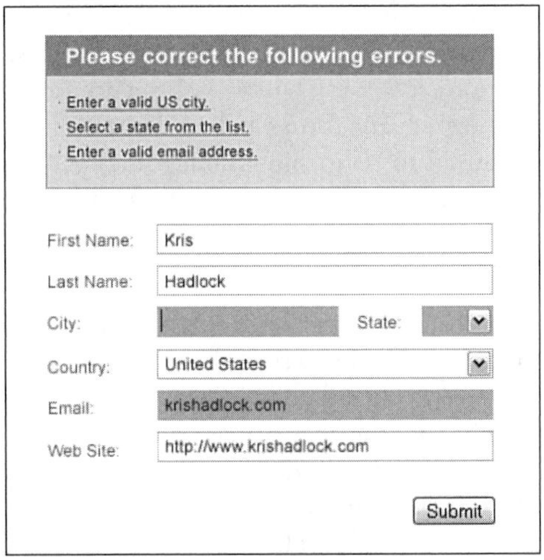

Figure 19.1   Handling errors with multiple combinations.

As Figure 19.2 shows, after the field has been updated, the strikethrough appears for the error that has been updated, and the hyperlink becomes disabled and disappears.

Figure 19.2   Adding feedback based on user error corrections.

Figure 19.3 shows an additional form of error handling that is a unique and unobtrusive way to help display errors to users. After the form has been submitted and errors occur, the form will not only highlight the incorrect form fields as our last solution did, but it will also display a "bubble" message above the first form field that caused an error and disappear along with the highlight color on the field after the error has been corrected. At this point, if there are more errors, the bubble will appear above the next error in the form and the cursor will move to that form element. To make it even more apparent, if the next form field happens not to be within visibility due to a scrollbar, the page will scroll to the location of the incorrect form field and bring it into focus.

Designing with Code

As I mentioned at the beginning of this chapter, this section will explain how to create custom messages with an object called `Dialog`. This object will display a message based on CSS classes that we connect to it and will render itself based on the properties we define in these classes. Listing 19.2 shows the `Dialog` object in full, which is simply the instantiation of the object and a method called `display`. We know what the instantiation declaration looks like at this point, so we will focus on covering the `display` method, which is the meat of this object. The `display` method takes three parameters. The first is a unique id that will represent the actual id of the `div` that is created as the dialog in the front end. The second parameter is the class name that we will use to connect the `div` to a custom CSS class that will define the properties we define. The last parameter is the message that we would like to display to the user to provide feedback, errors, or warnings.

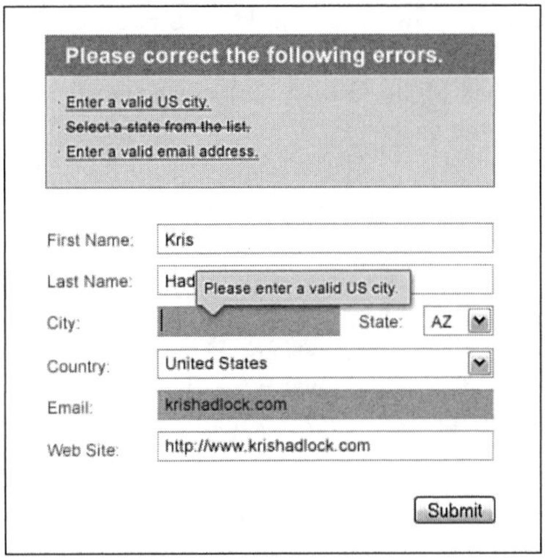

Figure 19.3   Displaying feedback directly above form elements.

After the method has been called and we have passed all the parameters, the first thing our method does is create a `div` element that will become the dialog in the front end and, ultimately, display the message to the user. After we have created the element with the `Utilities` object from Chapter 9, "Extending the Engine," we define the `elements` id and `className` properties by making them equal to the parameters we passed to the method when we fired it. In order to get the correct message to display to the user, we will use the `innerHTML` property of the `div` element to display our custom message to the user. Last, we must have a way to add the completed dialog to the page the user is currently using. We will do this by appending the element to the document body, once again with our handy `Utilities` object.

Listing 19.2   **The `Dialog` Object (`Dialog.js`)**

```
Dialog = {};

Dialog.display = function(id, c, message)
{
    var d = Utilities.createElement("div");
    d.id = id;
    d.className = c;

    d.innerHTML = message;
    Utilities.appendChild(document.body, d);
}
```

In order to use this method, we must have an HTML page to import the appropriate objects. The following code shows how to import the `Dialog` and `Utilities` objects along with a corresponding CSS file that we will create shortly, and a method call to display an error at the top of the page.

```
<html xmlns="http://www.w3.org/1999/xhtml">
<head>
<meta http-equiv="Content-Type" content="text/html; charset=iso-8859-1" />
<title>Ajax Message Dialogs</title>
<link href="css/dialog.css" rel="stylesheet" type="text/css" />
<script type="text/javascript" src="javascript/Utilities.js"></script>
<script type="text/javascript" src="javascript/utils/Dialog.js"></script>
</head>

<body onload="Dialog.display('dialog', 'error', 'Please correct the following
errors.');">
</body>
</html>
```

You probably noticed we are only creating an error message in this page and that it does not even correspond to anything. Well, you are right—this is simply an example of how to display a custom dialog, but I will also show you how to display the other two types with the following code. This code shows how to create a warning and a success feedback message.

```
Dialog.display('dialog', 'warning', ' Your form submission was successful, but you
did not enter a web site URL, click here in order to update this record.');
Dialog.display('dialog', 'success', 'Your form submission was successful!');
```

The success message works very similarly to the error message because it is straightforward, but the warning works a bit differently and takes a bit more thinking on our part. If we display a warning to users, we must provide them with a way to ignore it or act on it by updating the data based on the issue. In the sample code, I have a message that says `click here`. As an example, this could be a hyperlink that links users to a form that allows them to update the information that produced the warning, or they could choose to ignore it and move on to another area of the application.

Now that we have the method that creates the dialog and we are calling it from the application, we will have a simple message that will display to users. However, there will still not be any style to the element until we create the CSS that corresponds to the id and class name we defined. In order to define the classes that correspond with different types of messages, the application may need to display to the user that we will create a

CSS file called `dialog.css`. This file will contain four custom classes. The first will be a class that all the messages will share by corresponding to the dialog id that we passed as the first parameter to the `Dialog` object's `display` method. This class will contain the font weight and the padding for the messages, and will ensure that all our messages are consistent in this way. The code in Listing 19.3 shows this class as it is defined in the `dialog.css` file.

Listing 19.3   **The `Dialog` CSS Class** (`dialog.css`)

```
#dialog
{
    font-weight: bold;
    padding: 5px;
}
```

After we have this shared class defined, we can focus on defining the individual classes that correspond to each of the different types of messages that an application can have. Again, the different types we will be focusing on are the error, warning, and success feedback messages. In this example, we will simply change the color of the background based on the message type, but we could use many different CSS properties to make these messages distinctively different from one another. Errors will have a red background color, warnings will be orange, and success messages will be green. It doesn't get much more apparent than this, but there is always room for improvement. Listing 19.4 shows all of these classes as they are defined in the `dialog.css` file.

Listing 19.4   **Specific Classes for Each Corresponding Message Type** (`dialog.css`)

```
#dialog.error
{
    background-color: #ff0000;
}

#dialog.warning
{
    background-color: #ff9900;
}

#dialog.success
{
    background-color: #00cc33;
}
```

These classes extend the `dialog` id element class by specifically specifying the `dialog` `div` as the base class and then appending each message type as the class name for each message. These also happen to be the names that we pass to the `display` method to connect the correct class to the message. With all of this code in place, we can very easily provide feedback for any form of message with which we need to inform the user. Creating all of this code up front will actually save you a lot of grief in the long run, especially if you work on a team with members who are responsible for displaying their own feedback to the user. This way, we as the design-oriented developers do not need to be concerned with inconsistencies between each team member's messages, and I am sure they will be happy that they do not need to define their own messages as well.

V

Server–Side
Interaction

20

Understanding Ajax
Database Interaction

We have already begun to cover Ajax database interaction in previous chapters, but this chapter will takes us to a deeper understanding of the interaction model by explaining every step. Database interaction with Ajax allows developers to create interaction paradigms that can exist only with this set of technologies. The actions that occur to create database interactions with Ajax are the same as a standard interaction, but the way in which the request process occurs is quite different. The actions that exist in both interactions start with a user interaction on the front end, which fires an HTTP request to the server where a server-side language makes a query on the database. What happens in the database—for example, an insert, a delete, or a select—will all occur exactly the same as well. Again, the only difference in these two processes is the way in which they make the request. Creating connections to a database without interrupting the user experience with browser refreshes is definitely unique to Ajax and is what makes the XHR different from a standard HTTP request.

It is true that Ajax can easily be misused and often is, but it can be extremely useful in the right situations, such as when the sample application receives and/or sends emails. Imagine if you were in the middle of reading an email and your browser refreshed in order to get new messages. This would be an unusable situation because you would completely lose your place and have to reorient yourself with the interface that may have changed due to new email messages. Therefore, this is one of those situations where it would be perfect to use Ajax to make database connections. We can make requests to the server with the Data Reflection pattern we covered earlier in Chapter 17, "Data Reflection Pattern," receive updates if new messages exist, and replenish the inbox with the new data from the database. This solution also enables us to keep the other areas of our application as is or untouched while we update the necessary data inconspicuously. In other words, using the components we have built, we can replenish the data in the data grid and tree components with new messages while leaving the accordion component untouched as the user continues to read an open email message. In this chapter, we will dive into the server-side code and learn each of the steps that make a database-enabled XHR possible.

Connecting with PHP

Before we get started we will need to create the database that will be used for this example and ultimately in our final sample project. The SQL code for creating the table is shown in Listing 20.1.

Listing 20.1   **The SQL File for Creating the Email Database Table (`awad_email.sql`)**

```
CREATE TABLE 'awad_email' (
    'message' longtext NOT NULL,
    'folder' varchar(50) NOT NULL default '',
    'thread_id' int(11) NOT NULL default '0',
    'date' timestamp NOT NULL default CURRENT_TIMESTAMP on update
        ➥CURRENT_TIMESTAMP,
    'subject' varchar(100) NOT NULL default '',
    'sender' varchar(50) NOT NULL default '',
    'receiver' varchar(50) NOT NULL default '',
    'id' int(11) NOT NULL auto_increment,
    PRIMARY KEY ('id')
) ENGINE=MyISAM DEFAULT CHARSET=utf8;
```

PHP is a great language to combine with Ajax. First of all, it is open source, and second, it is very flexible and easy to learn. Because all the samples in this book have already been written, we will continue to use strict typing with PHP 5.0. Therefore, the server that the sample is running on must have PHP 5.0 or above. Let's get started by learning how to bridge the gap between the client side and back end by creating a file that simply delegates requests and returns responses as XML.

Bridging the Gap

Connecting to a database with PHP is simple after we create a file that specifically enables the connection via XHR. In the sample, I have named this file `serviceConnector.php`, but it can be named anything we want because the only requirement for this example is that it be PHP and that we request it by the appropriate name in the XHR. Listing 20.2 shows the file contents.

Listing 20.2 **The File Is the Bridge Between the Client Side and the Database**
                (`serviceConnector.php`)

```php
<?php

header("Content-Type: application/xml; charset=UTF-8");

require_once("classes/UserManager.class.php");
require_once("classes/Email.class.php");

$o = new $_GET['object']();
echo $o->$_GET['method']( $_GET['params'] );

?>
```

This listing is the key that will help us make all of our connections. The code begins
with the PHP declaration tags (as all of the PHP examples will from this point forward)
so that the server knows how to process it. The first line of code is a header, which
defines the content type of the returned data as XML. This means that any file that
requests it will receive the data back as XML. Of course, this is extremely useful when
using Ajax because we want the response to be XML in this case. The next two lines of
code are types of `include` statements unique to PHP, which require these two files to
be included in order to compile the rest of the code in the file. There is also a `require`
statement that is unique to PHP, but the `require_once` statement has additional logic
to make sure that if a required class is included twice in the same document, only one is
required. We can continue to add new PHP classes to this file if we want to call a new
object method at some later point.

After we have all our required files set up, we will instantiate a new object, which will
be defined in the query as `object`. This is an extremely powerful statement because it
allows us to instantiate objects from the client side by simply passing the correct query
variables. After we have the correct object instantiated, we can fire a method within that
object and pass parameters that we define on the client side in the XHR. After the
method has been called, we write its return value to the page so that when the server
has completed writing the file, it will return an XML file with the value that was
returned from the object. In our case, this value will be data represented by database values, or success or failure messages for database inserts or deletions, but the return value
can be anything that you can dream of returning from a server-side object. Of course,
with the great power this solution presents come great security risks. Therefore, we will
focus on creating a secure way to make these server-side requests from Ajax by password
protecting them when we reach Chapter 23, "Securing Your Application."

Making the Requests

We now understand how to bridge the gap between the front end and the database; now
we need to focus on how to make the XHR from the front side. Making the connection to the connector file we created in the last section is as easy as requesting static
XML files. It is really just a matter of understanding what parameters to pass it and how
it will return that data so you can anticipate dynamic responses. Listing 20.3 shows how
to make an XHR from our `Email` JavaScript object on the client side to our
`serviceConnector.php` file.

Listing 20.3   **Connecting to the Database to Retrieve a User's Email Folders
(Email.js)**

```
Email.display = function(username)
{
    Email.currentUser = username;
    var url = "serviceConnector.php?object=Email&method=getFolders&params="+
        ➥username;
    AjaxUpdater.Update("GET", url, TreeManager.display);
    setTimeout('Email.getMail("'+ username +':INBOX")', 500);
    Email.dataReflection("Email.display('"+ username +"')", 100000);
}
```

The `Email` object is what combines and connects all the components from the book to
the database via the Ajax engine. The first method to be called from the index PHP file
is the `display` method. This method takes a username, which is passed from the login
PHP page when a user logs in to the application. After the method has been fired, it sets
the username to an object property and proceeds to define a `url` variable to use as an
XHR. As you can see, this URL consists of the `serviceConnector.php` plus the
object, method, and additional parameters that need to be passed, which in this case is
simply the username. After the URL is defined, it is added to the `AjaxUpdater Update`
method and sent to the server via the `GET` method. The `Update` method also tells the
`Ajax` object to return the response to the `TreeManager`'s display method. If you look
closely at the URL, we are calling a PHP object called `Email` and firing a method called
`getFolders`, which gets all the folders that are necessary for creating the tree view for
the specific user we are requesting. The rest of this method consists of a `setTimeout` call
that delays another `Email` object method call to the `getMail` method. The delay is set
because each method makes an XHR. If they fire at the same time, they will cross
requests and we will end up with unexpected results. The last line is the data reflection,
which we already covered in Chapter 17. Figure 20.1 shows the email application with
all the components as they appear with data from the database.

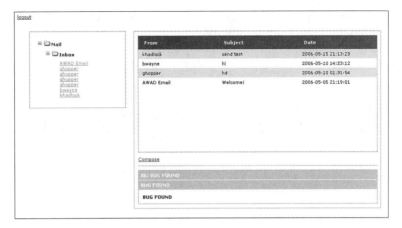

Figure 20.1   A preview of the completed email application
with all the components from the book.

The getMail and showThread methods in the Email JavaScript object are very similar
to the display method in the way that they make an XHR and delegate the response
to the appropriate components. Listing 20.4 shows the getMail method as it makes a
request to the serviceConnector.php in order to get the data that is necessary to display all of a user's mail from a specified folder.

Listing 20.4   **Connecting to the Database to Retrieve Mail (Email.js)**

```
Email.getMail = function(params)
{
    Utilities.removeChildren(Utilities.getElement('list'));
    DataGrid.initialize();

    var url = "serviceConnector.php?object=Email&method=getMail&params="+ params;
    AjaxUpdater.Update("GET", url, DataGrid.display);
}
```

As I mentioned, the getMail method makes a request to the server to get a user's mail
from a specified folder. If we take a look at the setTimeout in the display method, we
are passing the current user's username and inbox as the specific folder to retrieve mail
from. These parameters will be used in the XHR URL. Before we make the request,
there are two lines of code that are required to re-create the DataGrid component with
the new data we will be delegating to it from the server response. Within these two lines
of code, we first remove any of the previously instantiated DataGrid elements and then
initialize a new one to replenish its default values and prepare it for the new data from
the response. We use the removeChildren method from the Utilities object to

remove all the nested (children) elements in the list element, which is the element the `DataGrid` gets written to when it is created. Finally, we make the request via the `GET` method and delegate the response to the display method of the new `DataGrid`. Figure 20.2 features the `DataGrid` component with inbox data that has been saved to the server.

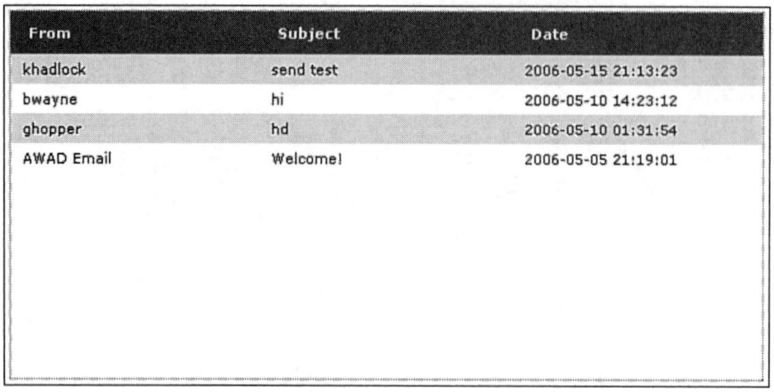

From	Subject	Date
khadlock	send test	2006-05-15 21:13:23
bwayne	hi	2006-05-10 14:23:12
ghopper	hd	2006-05-10 01:31:54
AWAD Email	Welcome!	2006-05-05 21:19:01

Figure 20.2   A populated `DataGrid` component
integrated with the application.

The `showThread` method occurs when a user selects an email from the `DataGrid` component. Listing 20.5 shows the code for this method.

Listing 20.5   **Retrieving Mail Threads from the Database (`Email.js`)**

```
Email.showThread = function(id, sender)
{
    Email.currentThread = id;
    Email.currentSender = sender;

    Utilities.removeChildren(Utilities.getElement('mail'));
    Accordion.initialize();

    var url = "serviceConnector.php?object=Email&method=getMessage&params=
        ➥"+ id +":"+ Email.currentUser;
    AjaxUpdater.Update("GET", url, Accordion.display);

    Utilities.getElement('reply').style.display = '';
    Utilities.getElement('compose').style.display = 'none';
}
```

This method takes an `id`, which is a number that represents a thread of emails, and a `sender`, which represents the username of the person who sent the email. These parameters are first used to set object properties for the `Email` object, which include the currentThread as the id parameter and the currentSender as the sender parameter. Both of these properties will be used throughout the object in various ways. Next, we remove the children of the parent HTML element that may contain previously retrieved threads. We then initialize the Accordion, and instantiate or re-instantiate any properties in the object. After we have a fresh Accordion, we make a request with the AjaxUpdater via the GET method and pass a custom url variable as we have in the previous examples. The url variable is made up of the serviceConnector.php file followed by a query string that consists of the Email object, a method called getMessage, and two parameters: the thread id and the current user. When the request is made, we delegate the response to the display method in the Accordion object and a new Accordion is displayed with the thread that was selected. This thread is representative of all the different emails that were sent back and forth between two users as a single thread. Figure 20.3 shows an example of how the Accordion looks with a threaded email.

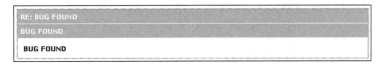

Figure 20.3   A threaded email populating the
Accordion component in the final application.

Now that we have all the methods for displaying various types of data, such as the folders, emails, and threads, we can focus on how to send a new email or a response to another user in the system. The method we will use for both of these different types of functionality is called compose. Listing 20.6 shows this method.

Listing 20.6   **Sending Mail to Other Users** (Email.js)

```
Email.sendMail = function(action, username, subject, message)
{
    var params;
    if(action == 'reply' && Email.currentThread != '')
    {
        params = username +":"+ Email.currentUser +":"+ subject +":"+ message
        ➥+":"+ Email.currentThread;
    }
    else
    {
        params = username +":"+ Email.currentUser +":"+ subject +":"+ message;
        Email.currentReceiver = '';
    }
```

Listing 20.6   **Continued**

```
    var url = "serviceConnector.php?object=Email&method=sendMail&params="+ params;
    AjaxUpdater.Update("GET", url);


    if(Email.currentUser == username && Email.currentThread != '')
    {
        setTimeout('Email.showThread("'+ Email.currentThread +'")', 500);// Reply
    }
    else if(Email.currentUser == username && Email.currentThread == '')
    {
        setTimeout('Email.getMail("'+ Email.currentUser +':INBOX")', 500);//
          ➥Compose
    }
    else
    {
        Utilities.getElement('compose').style.display = 'none';
    }
}
```

This method is a bit larger than the previous and it takes quite a few more parameters. The four parameters it takes are

- An action, which represents whether we are sending a new email or a reply
- A username, which represents the user to whom the email is being sent
- The subject for the email
- The message for the email

We start by checking to see whether the action is a reply or a new email. Depending on the result, we create a local **param** variable to a colon-delimited string, which will represent the parameters for the email. After we have the necessary parameters for the request, we will append them to a **url** variable that consists of a string. This string will call the **serviceConnector.php** file, pass the **Email** object, call a method named **sendMail**, and pass the parameters we set previously. We then fire the **Update** method for the **AjaxUpdater** object and pass the **url** parameter with the **GET** method. The difference in this call is that we do not pass a **callback** method in which to delegate the response. This is because we will simply refresh the current **Accordion** or **DataGrid** object by firing either the **showThread** or **getMail** method in the **setTimeout** method. This will create a delay in the call so that the data has been updated. Then, when the method is called, it will make another XHR for the new data, which will either replenish the **Accordion** with the reply thread or the **DataGrid** with the default inbox view. Figure 20.4 shows the Compose or Reply form as it appears in the application.

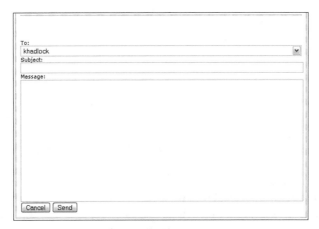

Figure 20.4   New and reply messages are
sent from this form in the application.

Making the Connection

Now that we understand how to make requests to the PHP file that will receive server-side method calls and return responses as valid XML, we can focus on the database interaction. The one object that we connect with throughout this chapter is the Email object. This file is named Email.class.php and resides in the classes folder in the application structure. This object contains a lot of functionality that I will not cover in detail because I want to provide the knowledge to understand how the database data is formatted into useable XML on the client side by the Ajax object or the objects that receive the delegated responses. Therefore, we will see all the code that is involved, but we will focus on the Ajax-oriented part of it. Let's start by requiring the necessary classes to make a database connection, declaring the Email object, and creating its constructor. Listing 20.7 shows the code to make this happen.

Listing 20.7   **Getting Started with the Email Class** (Email.class.php)

```php
<?php
require_once("classes/database/DatabaseConnector.class.php");
require_once("classes/utils/Constants.class.php");

class Email
{
    private $dbConnector;

    public function Email()
    {
        $this->dbConnector = DatabaseConnector::getInstance();
```

Listing 20.7 **Continued**

```
        $this->dbConnector->init();
    }
}
?>
```

The two classes we must require are the `DatabaseConnector` and the `Constants` class. The `DatabaseConnector` will contain all the methods for making the connection to your database as we already covered in Chapter 12, "Client-Side Validation." The `Constants` file contains all the reusable data we will need throughout the application. We will cover the `Constants` class next before moving on to the `Email` object's methods. After we declare the `Email` object, we define a property that will represent the `DatabaseConnector` object throughout the class. The constructor function takes this property and sets it to an instance of the `DatabaseConnector`, which is a Singleton object. After we have set the object to the property, we fire the `init` method within it. Let's briefly take a look at the `Constants` class to see how it will be used moving forward. Remember that the class will represent some of your server data and will have to be changed when you upload the files. Listing 20.8 shows the complete class.

Listing 20.8 **The `Constants` Object** (`Constants.class.php`)

```php
<?php
class Constants
{
    // Database connection
    static $DB_USER = "your user name";
    static $DB_PASSWORD = "your password";
    static $DB_HOST = "localhost";
    static $DB_NAME = "your database name";


    // Database Tables
    static $AWAD_EMAIL = "awad_email";
    static $AWAD_USERS = "awad_users";

    // Password
    static $PASSWORD = "TEMPPASSWORD";

    // Return Values
    static $SUCCESS = "<xml>success</xml>";
    static $FAILED = "<xml>failed</xml>";

    public function Constants() {}


}
?>
```

This class is full of static properties, which can be accessed by any object that has included it. The first set of properties we need to create depends on the server in which we are using. These properties represent the database information for our server. These will need to be changed by you in order to run the sample on your server. The next two properties are the database tables with which we will be interacting throughout the sample code. They are the **awad_email** table, which consists of all the email information that has been passed back and forth between users, and the **awad_users** table, which consists of the user data for the application. This database has been created already in Chapter 12, where we learned how to validate user information in the database via the **Ajax** object. The next property is called **password** and will be used in Chapter 23 where we learn how to secure the application with password-protected Ajax requests. The last two properties are the success and failure messages that will be returned as responses to the Ajax requests when no data is required to be sent back. For example, if a user deletes an email, we will not need to return any data as a response; instead, we will return whether or not the deletion was a success and act on the response based on the result. Now that we understand how this file will be used throughout the **Email** object, we will cover the rest of its objects. The first method we will focus on is called **sendMail** and is shown in Listing 20.9.

Listing 20.9   **Sending Mail** (**Email.class.php**)

```php
<?php
public function sendMail($params)
{
    $param = split(":", $params);
    $username = $param[0];
    $sender = $param[1];
    $subject = $param[2];
    $message = $param[3];
    $threadId = $param[4];

    $this->dbConnector->connect();
    $table = Constants::$AWAD_EMAIL;

    if($threadId == NULL)
    {
        // Get next thread id
        $query = "SELECT MAX(thread_id) FROM $table WHERE receiver='$username'";
        $result = mysql_query($query);
        $row = mysql_fetch_array ($result);
        $threadId = $row[0]+1;
        $this->dbConnector->complete($query);
    }
```

Listing 20.9   **Continued**

```
    $this->dbConnector->connect();
    $query = "INSERT INTO $table (message, folder, thread_id, subject, sender,
        ➥receiver)
VALUES ('$message', 'Inbox', '$threadId', '$subject', '$sender', '$username')";
    $this->dbConnector->complete($query);

    $this->dbConnector->connect();
    $query = "INSERT INTO $table (message, folder, thread_id, subject, sender,
        ➥receiver)
VALUES ('$message', 'Sent', '$threadId', '$subject', '$username', '$sender')";
    $this->dbConnector->complete($query);

    // TODO: need to decipher if this is true
    return Constants::$SUCCESS;
}
?>
```

This method receives the colon-delimited list of parameters that were sent from the
Email object. This parameter string is first split at the colons and then set to local
method variables. After we have the local variables, we check to see whether the thread
id is null. If so, we know that the email belongs in a new thread. If this is true, we make
a database selection to get the highest thread id and set a local variable to its value. After
we have the value, we increment the local variable and use it in the two default queries.
These queries insert the email into the receiving user's inbox and the sending user's sent
folder. After the queries have been made, we return a value stating whether or not the
insertion was a success.

The next method is used to get a user's folders for the **TreeView** component. It takes
a parameter that tells it which user to retrieve folders for. After it receives the data from
the database, it compiles an XML string that is structured as the **treeview.xml** file was
in Chapter 11, "Tree View." The structure that is created takes a fairly complicated algorithm because we want any data that belongs to specific folders to display in those folders. If we did not use this algorithm, the structure would simply represent a tree with
duplicate folders for each item, which wouldn't be very functional. The method featured
in Listing 20.10 contains comments that explain the algorithm.

Listing 20.10   **Getting a User's Folders** (Email.class.php)

```
<?php
public function getFolders($receiver)
{
    // retrieve all the current folders by userid, in treeview.xml format
    $this->dbConnector->connect();
    $table = Constants::$AWAD_EMAIL;
```

Listing 20.10   **Continued**

```php
    $query = "SELECT * FROM $table WHERE receiver='$receiver' ORDER BY folder
ASC";
    $result = mysql_query($query);
    if($result)
    {
        $response = "<?xml version=\"1.0\" encoding=\"iso-8859-1\" ?>";

        $response .= "<Mail>";
        $folder = "";
        while($row = mysql_fetch_array ($result))
        {

            // Add an item
            // Set the folder to equal the current folder
            // If the next item is the same folder, add an item
            // If not the same and the folder != '', close the prev item and
            // create a new
            // first half

            if($threadId != $row['thread_id'])
            {
                $threadId = $row['thread_id'];
                if($folder == $row['folder'])
                {
                    $folder = $row['folder'];

                    // If the next item is the same folder, add an item
                    $response .= "<a href=\"javascript:Email.showThread('".
                        ➥$threadId
                        ➥."', '". $row['sender'] ."');\">". $row['sender']
                        ➥."</a><br/>";

                }
                else
                {

                    if($folder != '')
                    {
                        // If not the same and the folder != '', close the prev
                        // item and
                        // create a new first half
                        $response .= "]]></". $folder .">";
                    }

                    $folder = $row['folder'];
```

Listing 20.10   **Continued**

```
                        // Create the first half: first thing that happens because
                        // there is
                        // not going to be a match
                        $response .= "<". $folder ." action=\"Email.getMail('".
                            ➥$row['receiver'] .":". $row['folder']
                            ➥."');\"><![CDATA[";
                        // Add an item
                        $response .= "<a href=\"javascript:Email.showThread('".
                            ➥$threadId
                            ➥."', '". $row['sender'] ."');\">". $row['sender']
                            ➥."</a><br/>";



                    }
                }
            }
            $response .= "]]></". $folder .">";
            $response .= "</Mail>";
        }
        else
        {
            return Constants::$FAILED;
        }
        $this->dbConnector->complete($query);

        return $response;

?>
```

After the XML tree structure has been created, it is returned to the
`serviceConnector.php` class. Its content type is set to XML to make it valid and
accessible through the DOM via the Ajax engine (or the method the response is delegated to), which happens to be the display method of **TreeManager** in this case. Figure
20.5 shows the tree view as it renders in the application.

Figure 20.5   The **TreeView** component renders folders
and the usernames of the senders for certain threads.

The next method we will cover is less complicated than the previous one. It is called getMail and is featured in Listing 20.11. This method receives a single parameter, which is a colon-delimited string of values in which we define this method. This means we need to know the parameters this method expects when we call it. After we split and set the local variables, we make a connection to the database and select the mail for a specific user from a specified folder and order it by thread id. After we receive the results, we create an XML string, which is structured the same as the sample for the DataGrid in Chapter 13, "Data Grid."

Listing 20.11   **Getting User Mail** (Email.class.php)

```php
<?php
public function getMail($params)
{
    $param = split(":", $params);
    $receiver = $param[0];
    $folder = $param[1];

    // all or for a particular folder by id, in datagrid.xml format
    $this->dbConnector->connect();
    $table = Constants::$AWAD_EMAIL;
    $query = "SELECT * FROM $table WHERE receiver='$receiver' AND folder='$folder'
        ➥ORDER BY thread_id DESC";

    $result = mysql_query($query);
    if($result)
    {
        $response = "<?xml version=\"1.0\" encoding=\"iso-8859-1\" ?>";
        $response .= "<data>";
        $response .= "<categories>";
        $response .= "<category>From</category>";
        $response .= "<category>Subject</category>";
        $response .= "<category>Date</category>";
        $response .= "</categories>";
        $threadId = "";
        while($row = mysql_fetch_array ($result))
        {
            if($threadId != $row['thread_id'])
            {
                $threadId = $row['thread_id'];
                $response .= "<row>";
                $response .= "<items action=\"Email.showThread('". $threadId ."',
                        ➥'". $row['sender'] ."');\" icon=\"img/mail.gif\">";
                $response .= "<item><![CDATA[". $row['sender'] ."]]></item>";

                $response .= "<item><![CDATA[". $row['subject'] ."]]></item>";
                $response .= "<item>". $row['date'] ."</item>\n";
```

Listing 20.11   **Continued**

```
                $response .= "</items>";
                $response .= "</row>";
            }
        }
        $response .= "</data>";
    }
    else
    {
        return Constants::$FAILED;
    }
    $this->dbConnector->complete($query);

    return $response;
}
?>
```

After we have created the structure as the `DataGrid` component expects it, we will
return it as the response to the XHR. When the engine receives the response, it will
then delegate it to the `DataGrid` component and display the user mail from the specified folder.

The last method in this class is called `getMessage` (Listing 20.12). Like the other
methods in this object, this method also accepts a string of colon-delimited parameters,
which are split and set to local variables. After the variables are set, a database connection
is made and we select the thread that was requested from the client side. These threads
are gathered in descending order based on their id in the database. Therefore, the
`Accordion` object will display the email threads in the order they were created.

Listing 20.12   **Retrieving User Messages (`Email.class.php`)**

```php
<?php
public function getMessage($params)
{
    // retreive a message by id, in accordion.xml format
    $param = split(":", $params);
    $threadId = $param[0];
    $receiver = $param[1];

    $this->dbConnector->connect();
    $table = Constants::$AWAD_EMAIL;
    $query = "SELECT * FROM $table WHERE receiver='$receiver' AND
        ➥thread_id='$threadId' ORDER BY id DESC";
    $result = mysql_query($query);
    if($result)
    {
```

Listing 20.12   **Continued**

```php
        $index = 0;
        $response = "<?xml version=\"1.0\" encoding=\"iso-8859-1\" ?>";
        $response .= "<accordion>";
        while($row = mysql_fetch_array ($result))
        {
            if($index  == 0)
            {
                $response .= "<panel expanded='true'>";
            }
            else
            {
                $response .= "<panel>";
            }
            $response .= "<title><![CDATA[". $row['subject'] ."]]></title>";
            $response .= "<content><![CDATA[". $row['message'] ."]]></content>";
            $response .= "</panel>";
            $index++;
        }
        $response .= "</accordion>";
    }
    else
    {
        return Constants::$FAILED;
    }
    $this->dbConnector->complete($query);

    return $response;
}
?>
```

After the XML structure is concatenated, we return it to the `serviceConnector.php`
file, which provides a valid XML file to the requesting object. As the engine does in all
the other cases, it delegates the response to another object (in this case, the `Accordion`).
The `Accordion` object receives the response through its `display` method and creates
an accordion from the response data. You can take a look back at Figure 20.3 to see an
example of the accordion as it looks with a thread of emails in the application.

This chapter has quite a bit of information in it that is completely unique to Ajax, but
if you understand the server side of things, it is not hard to pick up on the request
model we are producing in this application. When you have a solid understanding of the
logic behind these requests, you can basically accomplish anything you see today on the
Web in terms of Ajax database interactions. Who knows—maybe you'll create some of
your own standards.

21

Interacting with a Database:
The Server-Side

We have learned many aspects of Ajax interaction throughout this book. In the last chapter, we learned how to connect our sample application to a database with PHP. This chapter will explain how to connect to dynamic server-side data with ASP.NET and ColdFusion. The final sample for this book does not use these technologies, so you can skip ahead if you do not have any interest in these two approaches. We will first learn how to connect to dynamic data using ASP.NET, and then we will cover the same functionality with ColdFusion. This chapter will provide us with powerful information that can be applied to other Ajax web applications in order to connect them to dynamic server-side data.

Connecting to ASP.NET

ASP.NET is an extremely powerful programming platform. Here, we will learn how to make a connection to it with an Ajax request. The sample was created with Visual Studio, and we will simply run it in Debug mode in this example, but it can be configured to run in Windows IIS if you prefer.

The first thing that we will need to do in order to start our example is create a new C# website. After we have created our new C# website, we need to move the `Utilities`, `AjaxUpdater`, `HTTP`, and `Ajax` JavaScript files to the project directory. We will then need to import them into the `Default.aspx` file that is created in the project by default when we create the website (see Listing 21.1).

Listing 21.1   **Importing the Appropriate JavaScript Files (`Default.aspx`)**

```
<script type="text/javascript" src="javascript/Utilities.js"></script>
<script type="text/javascript" src="javascript/model/AjaxUpdater.js"></script>
<script type="text/javascript" src="javascript/model/HTTP.js"></script>
<script type="text/javascript" src="javascript/model/Ajax.js"></script>
```

After the files are imported, we will add the code in Listing 21.2 to handle the HTML that will take input from a user and make a request to the server side.

Listing 21.2   **Taking User Input (`Default.aspx`)**

```
<form id="requestForm" runat="server">
<div>Request:</div>
<div><input type="text" autocomplete="off" onkeyup="request(this.value);" /></div>

<br /><br />

<div>Response:</div>
<div id="response"></div>
</form>
```

The user will use the request input field to enter a value, which will then make a request to the server side. After the response is received, it will be displayed in the `div` with an id of `response`. The request to the server side happens in a JavaScript method, which is conveniently named `request`. Take a look at the `request` method in Listing 21.3.

Listing 21.3   **Making a Request to the Server Side (`Default.aspx`)**

```
<script type="text/javascript">
        function request(data)
        {
            AjaxUpdater.Update('GET', 'serviceConnector.aspx?request='+ data,
                ➥onResponse);
        }
</script>
```

The `request` method takes a parameter named `data`, which is the value of the input field. This value is passed to it each time the `keyup` event is fired. The method then makes an XHR via the `GET` method to a file named `serviceConnector.aspx`. The `data` parameter is appended to the URL and passed as a query value to the `request` key. Finally, a method named `onResponse` is added as the `callback` method and the request is made via the `AjaxUdpdater`'s `Update` method. The `onResponse` method will be added to this file after we know what data will be received from the response and we understand how to properly parse it. The `serviceConnector.aspx` file connects the front end to the C# code, which we will write in a moment. This C# code will receive the request and respond with a username that contain the letters that are entered into the input field. Before we create the C# code behind, let's take a look at the `serviceConnector.aspx` in Listing 21.4.

Listing 21.4   **Bridging the Gap Between the Front End and Server Side**
                (`serviceConnector.aspx`)

```
<%@ Page ContentType="text/xml" Language="C#" AutoEventWireup="true"
CodeFile="serviceConnector.aspx.cs" Inherits="serviceConnector" %>
```

This file is the link between the front-end and the back-end code. The two most important things to remember are to have only this line of code in the file (otherwise the
response will not be valid), and to make sure to add the `ContentType` property. This
property does not exist by default when the file is created and without it the response
will not be valid XML.

The way this file works is that it receives the request and passes the data to the code
behind. The *code behind*, which is the C# class that contains the code that handles the
request, is defined in the `CodeFile` property. This class will take the request, process it
through any custom methods we define, and return a response based on the logic we
define. In this case, the C# class that we create will simply receive the request, search an
array of usernames, and return a username as a string value. The username that is
returned will be formatted as XML and delivered as the response to the Ajax engine
and, ultimately, the `onResponse` callback method that we defined in the `AjaxUpdater`
request. Let's take a look at Listing 21.5 to see the C# code behind for the
`serviceConnector`, understand what classes it needs to import, and how it performs
the username searches.

Listing 21.5   **The Code Behind the `serviceConnector`**
                (`serviceConnector.aspx.cs`)

```
using System;
using System.Data;
using System.Configuration;
using System.Collections;
using System.Web;
using System.Web.Security;
using System.Web.UI;
using System.Web.UI.WebControls;
using System.Web.UI.WebControls.WebParts;
using System.Web.UI.HtmlControls;
using System.Xml;

public partial class serviceConnector : System.Web.UI.Page
{
    protected void Page_Load(object sender, EventArgs e)
    {
        this.SearchUsers();
    }
```

Listing 21.5   **Continued**

```
private void SearchUsers()
{
    string request = Request["request"].ToString();
    string usernameXml = "";
    string[] usernames = new string[3] { "Kris Hadlock", "Grace Hopper", "Pi
        ➥Sheng"
};

    foreach(string username in usernames)
    {
        if(username.ToLower().Substring(0, request.Length) ==
            ➥request.ToLower())
        {
            usernameXml += "<username>" + username + "</username>";
        }
    }

    usernameXml = "<?xml version='1.0' encoding='iso-8859-1' ?><usernames>" +
        ➥usernameXml + "</usernames>";
    XmlDocument xDoc = new XmlDocument();
    xDoc.LoadXml(usernameXml);
    xDoc.Save(Response.OutputStream);
    }
}
```

Aside from the default classes that are automatically imported via Visual Studio's new file option, we needed to import the **System.xml** class. This class will allow us to return a valid XML response to the client side. The first method fired in this class is **Page_Load**, which immediately calls the **SearchUsers** method. This is where all the action happens. The first thing we do is gather the request query that was sent. This is done by using the **request** method, targeting the **request** key, and converting it to a string. This string is set to a local string named **request** to later be used to perform the search. Next we define a **string** variable named **usernameXml** and construct an array of strings with three values named **usernames**. The three values may look familiar because they are usernames we have used in other samples throughout the book. After this array is constructed, we will iterate it and check to see whether any of the usernames begin with the request value. If they do, the names will be appended to the **usernameXml** string between username XML elements and CDATA to ensure they can be parsed properly if they contain any HTML of special characters. After we are finished iterating the **usernames** array, we will add an XML declaration to the beginning of the **usernameXml** string and nest the existing **usernameXml** string values with **usernames** elements. Although we have an XML string defined, this will not be enough to return as valid XML to the client side. This is where the **System.xml** class comes in handy. We need it to instantiate the `XmlDocument` object, call its `LoadXml` method, and pass the `usernameXml` string to it. This will provide us with a valid XML structure, which can now be returned to the client. In order to return this data, we cannot simply use a return as we do in PHP. We must fire the `XmlDocument` object's `Save` method and pass the following parameter, `Response.OutputStream`. This will output the XML data and return it as the response to the client-side callback method.

Now that we will be receiving the response on the client side, we need to create the `onReponse` method to handle it. Listing 21.6 shows how this method will receive the response, parse the data, and display the data in the `response div`.

Listing 21.6   **Handling the Response (`Default.aspx`)**

```
function onResponse()
{
        if(Ajax.checkReadyState('response') == "OK")
    {
        var usernames = Ajax.getResponse().getElementsByTagName('username');
        for(var i=0; i<usernames.length; i++)
        {
            Utilities.getElement("response").innerHTML +=
            ➥usernames[i].firstChild.data +"<br/>";
        }
    }
}
```

This method is quite simple because it follows all the responses we have created in other samples. Targeting the response and parsing the `username` data from the XML define a username variable. After we have defined the `username`, we simply write it to the response element and test our application. In order to test the application, we need to set `Debug` to `true` in the `Web.Config` file, which should be asked of us if we forget when we press the Debug button for the first time. After the application is up and running in a browser, we can test it by simply typing in the first letters in a name and seeing the response. Let's do the same thing with ColdFusion.

Connecting to ColdFusion

Server-side examples with ColdFusion are very hard to come by and I have used ColdFusion to build a number of web applications so I thought it was noteworthy for this chapter. ColdFusion is a unique language that is easy to pick up for developers who are familiar with tag-based code, such as HTML, XML, and so on. The great thing about ColdFusion is that although it is simple, it is quite powerful because it can easily be connected to databases, and it can interact directly with Flash. Nowadays, this is a bonus because Flash is becoming a powerful web application product and, of course, the reason

I am covering it is because it can easily be integrated with Ajax and ultimately our engine. This section will show you how to achieve the same results as the ASP.NET example with much less code.

The first thing we will do in order to get started is create an HTML file to import our JavaScript files and contain our display code. The `import` statements should look similar to the example in Listing 21.7.

Listing 21.7   **Importing the Appropriate JavaScript (`index.html`)**

```
<script type="text/javascript" src="javascript/Utilities.js"></script>
<script type="text/javascript" src="javascript/model/AjaxUpdater.js"></script>
<script type="text/javascript" src="javascript/model/HTTP.js"></script>
<script type="text/javascript" src="javascript/model/Ajax.js"></script>
```

After the appropriate files have been imported, we will add the JavaScript code to make the request to the server. The code looks exactly like the code in the ASP.NET example, but it is requesting a ColdFusion service connector file instead. Listing 21.8 shows this `request` method.

Listing 21.8   **Making the Request (`index.html`)**

```
<script type="text/javascript">
function request(data)
{
    AjaxUpdater.Update('GET', 'serviceConnector.cfm?request='+ data, onResponse);
}
</script>
```

As I mentioned, aside from the file it requests, the `request` method is the same as the ASP.NET example. It accepts a `data` parameter, which it appends to the URL via the query string, as a value that matches the `request` key. The other code that is placed into this file is the display code. This code is also almost identical to the ASP.NET example. Take a look at Listing 21.9 to see the code.

Listing 21.9   **Display Code for the Request and Response (`index.html`)**

```
<div>Request:</div>
<div><input type="text" onkeyup="request(this.value);" /></div>

<br /><br />

<div>Response:</div>
<div id="response"></div>
```

Now that we have the code to allow users to make requests to the server side, let's take a look at the `serviceConnector.cfm` that we created for this example. Much like the

ASP.NET sample, this code will receive a string request and search an array of `usernames` for a name that includes the string. The first thing we will do in this file is create the array of names. If this were a database example, we would simply select all the names from the database, push them into an array, and search the array for the string. Listing 21.10 shows the entire `serviceConnector.cfm` file.

Listing 21.10   **Building the Response (`serviceConnector.cfm`)**

```
<cfset userNames = ArrayNew(1)>
<cfset userNames[1] = "Kris Hadlock">
<cfset userNames[2] = "Grace Hopper">
<cfset userNames[3] = "Pi Sheng">

<cfcontent type="text/xml; charset=iso-8859-1">
<cfoutput>
    <usernames>
    <cfloop from="1" to="#ArrayLen(userNames)#" index="i">
        <cfloop from="1" to="#Len(userNames[i])#" index="j">
            <cfif #Mid(userNames[i], 1, j)# IS #URL.request#>
                <username><![CDATA[#userNames[i]#]]></username>
            </cfif>
        </cfloop>
    </cfloop>
    </usernames>
</cfoutput>
```

This file is quite small compared to the ASP.NET example, due to the fact that the language is not strictly typed and does not include any classes. As I mentioned, the first thing we do is create an array of `usernames`. This array consists of the same values that we added to the array in the ASP.NET example. After this array has been created, a very important piece of code needs to be added. The `cfcontent` tag provides us with a response of valid XML to the request. Without this line of code, the XML string structure will be just a string and therefore not valid for parsing. After we have the content type defined, we will output the XML structure as a string. This data starts with a `usernames` element and then begins to loop the array of names. In this loop, we need to nest another loop. The nested loop will iterate the actual characters within each of the array string values. In other words, it we will iterate each letter in a username. In this nested loop, we will add a flag that uses ColdFusion's `Mid` function, which is similar to the substring function in other languages. This function will be used to determine if the current set of characters is equal to the request string. If so, the username is appended to a `username` element within CDATA to ensure proper parsing. After all of the usernames are added to the XML structure, we will close the first `usernames` element and the file will be ready to be parsed by the client side.

Now that we are receiving a response on the client side, we must create a method to handle it. This method will be the `onResponse` method, which we passed as the

callback method to the **AjaxUpdater** during the request. This method can be seen in Listing 21.11.

Listing 21.11   **Handling the Response** (**index.html**)

```
function onResponse()
{
        if(Ajax.checkReadyState('response') == "OK")
    {
        var usernames = Ajax.getResponse().getElementsByTagName('username');
        for(var i=0; i<usernames.length; i++)
        {
            Utilities.getElement("response").innerHTML +=
                ➥usernames[i].firstChild.data +"<br/>";
        }
    }
}
```

This method may look familiar because it is the same one that was used to handle the response in the ASP.NET example. When the response is received, we target the array of **usernames** and set them to a **usernames** variable. This variable is then iterated and each username is added to the **response div** element.

Each of the server-side samples we have created in this book is requested the same way. The model we created will always work as long as we can respond with the appropriate data from the server-side language.

22

Advanced Ajax Database
Interaction

Now that we have covered basic database interaction with Ajax, we will learn advanced ways of creating database-driven XHRs and their responses. We will cover how to minimize the number of requests to the server by sending bulk data formatted as arrays, XML, or JSON. We will also learn how minimizing the number of requests will speed up our application, help us to create more advanced interactions with the database, and provide us with the beginnings of an API that can be accessible via HTTP in which developers can send requests, pass specific data as parameters, and either receive structured data responses from the web application or store data in the database. The second part of this chapter will cover sending custom responses as XML or JSON. Then there is a brief reminder of how to handle the response on the client side. Let's get started by taking a look at bulk updates.

Bulk Updates

Bulk updates help keep our Ajax applications running more efficiently by keeping the number of database requests down. This is because large amounts of data can be sent as an array, XML, or JSON rather than separate XHRs. This data can be deleted from, saved to, or inserted into the database as one SQL query. Imagine that we have a number of items we want to save to the database. These items could be user attributes, for example, such as names, descriptions, and so on. In most examples, requests are made with each of these attributes as separate key/value pairs. This solution works fine for simple XHRs that need to send only small amounts of data, but if we wanted to send data for multiple users, it would be much more efficient to send it as a bulk update. Let's look at three different ways that we could send bulk data to the server via an XHR.

Sending Arrays

Sending bulk updates in the form of an array follows the same pattern as the other Ajax requests that we have made throughout the book. The difference with passing arrays is that instead of sending one value per key, we will send an array (or comma-delimited list) of data per key. In the user data example, which I introduced previously, we may want to update multiple users through one request. In order to do this, we could pass keys with arrays as the key values. For example, we could pass an array of names paired with a name key or an array of descriptions paired with a description key. This part is fairly simple—the data simply needs to be pushed into an array on the client side with JavaScript, concatenated into a query string, and sent via an XHR to the server. Our first hurdle arises because a JavaScript array does not translate directly to an array in a server-side language, but this can be easily fixed. By taking what is now a comma-delimited list in our server-side language of choice, we can split the data into a new array and iterate the values in order to add, update, or remove them from the database. By approaching the request in this fashion, we can see that there are some direct correlations between a query string and a SQL query—it is simply a matter of how we are applying the query that counts. Let's use the following HTTP query as an example.

```
serviceConnector.php?object=DatabaseManager&method=parseArray&
name=Grace,Pi&description=Hopper,Sheng
```

As you can see, we have a name and a description key with corresponding values. As an example, we will act as if we are going to insert this data into a database with a method, which simply makes queries directly on our database based on the HTTP queries that were sent to it. We will first need to abstract our **serviceConnector.php** file a bit in order to simply send the HTTP query data directly to our handling method, rather than send the data as we did in the previous chapter.

```
<?php

header("Content-Type: application/xml; charset=UTF-8");

require_once("classes/UserManager.class.php");

$o = new $_GET['object']();
echo $o->$_GET['method']( $_GET );

?>
```

We are simply passing the query data as a whole rather than splitting it or sending a specific key. The following is an example of how we would write the method that will make the connection between our Ajax engine and our server-side object.

```php
<?php
class DatabaseManager
{

    public function parseArray($q)
    {
        $names = split(",", $q['name']);
        $descriptions = split(",", $q['description']);

        // Open database connection

        for($i=0; $i<count($names); $i++)
        {
            $query = "INSERT INTO myTable SET name='$names[$i]',
                ➥description='$description s[$i]'";
            // Close database connection
        }

        return "<response>". $q['name'] ." and ". $q['description'] ."
            ➥: were successfully retrieved!</response>";
    }
}
?>
```

This option is very easy to manage and, even though it is not the best solution, it can provide us with some powerful ways of manipulating bulk data.

Sending XML

Sending XML or JSON is slightly different from sending a simple array because the data can be much more complex and therefore achieve results on a larger scale. In this section, we will focus on sending XML as our request data and cover some of the possibilities that can be reached with this approach. As we have seen throughout the samples in this book, XML is a flexible language that can be used to encapsulate static or dynamic data as any custom structure that we define. This, of course, leaves a lot of room for interpretation and allows complete flexibility in our code, which enables us to exchange complex data types between different languages. This is why XML lends much more power to our requests than passing a simple array or other custom character-delimited lists. The following is an example of a simple query that can be sent from any application to pass data as XML to be used on our server side based on the object and method specified.

```
serviceConnector.php?object=DatabaseManager&method=parseXML&xml=<names>
<name>Kris Hadlock</name></names>
```

After the sample is set on your server, you can simply paste this query on the end of your URL and you will receive the response that we will now construct.

```php
<?php

class DatabaseManager
{

    public function parseXML($q)
    {
        $doc = new DOMDocument();
        $doc->loadXML($q['xml']);
        // Manipulate the database
        return "<response>". $doc->getElementsByTagName('name')->item(0)
            ➥->nodeValue .": was successfully retrieved!</response>";
    }

}

?>
```

This method will have been called based on the query that took place via the serviceConnector. In this method, I am simply showing you how to load the XML and parse the data we have sent to it. Of course, this method can be much more complex because it can receive XML, save, insert, or delete node values in the database, and so on. After the data has been used to manipulate the database, we can take the values and respond to the requestor.

Sending JSON

JSON is a great solution for JavaScript and lends a lot of power to Ajax requests, but it is not as easy to manage on the server side because we must implement or create our own parser depending on the language we choose to use. Of course, our job is made much easier if we implement one of the parsers available at http://www.json.org. If you are interested in using JSON as your data-interchange format with Ajax, I recommend taking a look at the examples found on the download sites to really get an idea of the functionality that can be accomplished.

Server-Side XML and JSON

Creating custom XML or JSON structures with a server-side language from database data and returning it as a response to an XHR is a required step for creating Ajax-enabled database integration.

XML

Although we have already briefly covered the structuring of dynamic data as an XML structure to be used as an Ajax response, in this section we will focus more on the server side of the process. Responding with valid XML requires a few easy steps that can be achieved by the following instructions.

Including an XML Declaration

In order to specify that our data structure is XML, we must add an XML declaration to the beginning of the file that we would like to return to the client side. The following code shows an example of how to add this declaration to the structure and how to also specify the format in which the XML data should be encoded by the server.

```
$declaration = "<?xml version=\"1.0\" encoding=\"iso-8859-1\" ?>";
```

Setting the Content Type to Text/XML

Setting the content type is what we have been doing in the `serviceConnector.php` file that we created in each of our server-side examples. Setting the header to this content type is the key to creating a valid XML structure that is accessible by other languages, such as JavaScript. Following is an example of the header we have been using to make our structures valid.

```
header("Content-Type: application/xml; charset=UTF-8");
```

The last thing to remember is to carefully structure the string that you want to ultimately use as the XML response with opening and closing XML tags surrounding the dynamic data. This may seem the most obvious part of the process, but is usually the most likely to be an issue.

JSON

Responding with data as a JSON structure allows us to simply convert the JSON structure into a JavaScript object on the client side. After the data has been received by the Ajax engine as a response, we can pass it to our custom parsing method. This method simply needs to use the `eval` method to convert the data into a valid JavaScript object. This leaves us with a fully functional JSON object that can be used for anything we want to achieve on the client side. If we are trying to achieve this functionality, it makes the architecture of the JSON response structure a very important piece of the process.

If we plan on sending a response back to the client as a JSON structure, we must write a custom method to concatenate the data as a JSON object that can be evaluated on the client side by JavaScript after the Ajax engine receives the response, or we can use one of the parsers available at http://www.json.org.

VI

Finishing Touches

23

Securing Your Application

Ajax database interaction is extremely powerful and provides a lot of flexibility to web applications. With Ajax database interaction we can retrieve, remove, or add any bit of data from our database via a server side language. Of course, with this great power there are also great security risks which can leave your database completely exposed from the client-side through Ajax requests. This chapter will explain what security holes are exposed in the application we created, and how to create a password system for your XHRs to avoid these security issues and secure the important data that we keep on the server.

Of course a password alone will not protect our XHRs, so we will need to add a verification process on the server side in the serviceConnector.php file from Chapter 20, "Understanding Ajax Database Interaction." This will provide us with the ability to avoid unwanted requests, if they should occur, before they even reach the PHP classes that connect to the database. This not only keeps unwanted requests out, it also keeps them a layer away from the classes that have access to critical information about our database and other proprietary information.

Security Holes

Adding database interaction to an XHR exposes security holes that can allow malicious hackers to make requests to our server side. All they would need to know is the URL of the file in which to make the request. With the new debugging tools that are available, such as the ones that were covered in Chapter 8, "Debugging," we can actually spy on requests and see the exact URL they are requesting along with the parameters that are passed. This is great for debugging, but provides anyone with the ability to easily understand the interactions that you are making with Ajax to the server by exposing your requests. This, of course, is a huge threat if you are connected to files that interact with a database or contain other important data that you do not want to share with the public. Once they had the URL they could try to inject SQL into their requests, which could allow them to retrieve information from our database, delete our database and so on. Throughout the rest of this chapter, we will focus on creating a process for password-protecting our XHRs and verifying them on the server side. The object that will create and verify these passwords is called the PasswordManager and can be seen in Listing 23.1.

Listing 23.1   **Creating and Verifying XHRs (PasswordManager.class.php)**

```php
<?

class PasswordManager
{
    private $pass;

    private function PasswordManager()

    {
        // Create a password
        $this->pass = "mypassword";
    }

    public static function getInstance()
    {
        static $instance;
        if (!is_object($instance))
        {
            $instance = new PasswordManager();
        }
        return $instance;
    }

    public function createPassword()
    {
        // Set a cookie with an encrypted version of the password for one day
        setcookie("uid", md5($this->pass), time() + 86400, "/",
        ".krishadlock.com", false);
    }

    public function verfiyPassword()
    {
        if($_COOKIE["uid"] == md5($this->pass))
        {
            return true;
        }
        else
        {
            return false;
        }
    }

}

?>
```

This object is fairly simple, but will provide us with the security that we need to make requests safely. Let's take a look at how to create the different methods in this object and use them to protect the requests that we make during runtime.

Password Protecting Ajax Requests

Password-protecting Ajax requests seems fairly simple at first. At first thought you may think that we could simply append an additional variable to the query string that represents a password and verify it on the server side. This would work fine, but on second thought anyone could easily discover the password in the URL, especially if it never changed from one request to another. We would run into the problem of people being able to see the variable being passed via the request and then they could simply impersonate our request string to gather data. In this section we will learn how to avoid this issue by creating a PHP cookie password. This way the passwords will not be exposed in the query string and will only be available on the server side. Let's see how to add a unique password, encrypt it and set it as a cookie with PHP in our new PasswordManager class.

Creating Unique Passwords

Now that we understand why it will be beneficial to use a unique PHP cookie-based password for our applications' XHRs, we will learn how to create a server-side method that creates one based on a unique password, that we choose. We already started by creating the PHP class on the server side called PasswordManager. This object will be a Singleton object so that it is accessible on an application wide level and we will always receive the same instance every time we call it, which will ensure that we receive the same data each time. In order to make this object a Singleton, we need to make the constructor function private and create a public static method called getInstance. This method will check to see whether the object has already been instantiated. If not, it will create an instance and return it; if it does exist, the method will return the previously instantiated version of the object. Listing 23.2 shows how this object uses the Singleton design pattern.

Listing 23.2   **Creating a Singleton PasswordManager Object**

```
<?

class PasswordManager
{
    private function PasswordManager() {}


    public static function getInstance()
    {
        static $instance;
```

Listing 23.2   **Continued**

```
        if (!is_object($instance))
        {
            $instance = new PasswordManager();
        }
        return $instance;
    }


}


?>
```

Now that we can access this object application wide and be certain that we are receiving the same instance of the object each time, we will add a private property to the class called $pass. Since the $pass property is private, it cannot be changed by any outside object or script, making this model even more secure. This property will be set in the constructor to a string value that represents a unique password that we choose. We will then create a method to create this unique password as a cookie. This method will be called createPassword. When the method is called, it sets a cookie with PHPs setCookie method. This method takes six parameters, a unique name for the cookie, a value, the length of time to keep it active, which we set to one day, the directory, and domain of where to save it and a Boolean that states whether or not it is a secure server, which is set to false. The name of the cookie will be called uid in this case and the value parameter is set to an encrypted version of our $pass property to be retrieved and used at a later time. To ensure that the cookie is harder to fabricate we will set the directory to a relative path and the domain to the domain that the application resides on. See Listing 23.3 for an example of the constructor where we will create the unique password string and the createPassword method, which creates the cookie.

Listing 23.3   **Creating a Password and Cookie (PasswordManager.class.php)**

```
private $pass;

private function PasswordManager()
{
    // Create a password
    $this->pass = "mypassword";
}

public function createPassword()
{
    // Set a cookie with an encrypted version of the password for one day
    setcookie("uid", md5($this->pass), time() + 86400, "/", ".krishadlock.com",
false);
}
```

Once we have a way to produce the password as a cookie we will need to create the password in the pages that are making the requests. The index.php and mail.php files are currently the files that are making requests, so we will include the PasswordManager, instantiate it and then create a cookie password from these pages. Listing 23.4 shows the code that will be added to the top of each file in order to create the password.

Listing 23.4   **Creating a Password Array (Constants.class.php)**

```
<?
    require_once("classes/security/PasswordManager.class.php");
    $pwManager = PasswordManager::getInstance();
    $pwManager->createPassword();
?>
```

With the code that we are adding to these files, a password will be created in the form of a cookie, this will allow us to later check for the password on the server side when the request is made. Now we have a unique password that is being set as a cookie, but this doesn't do any good if we do not verify the password on the server side when requests are made. Let's take a look at how we accomplish this verification and ensure that our requests are secure.

Verifying Passwords on the Server-Side

To add a final layer of security to our Ajax applications, we will verify the unique password that we have created when we send the requests to the server side. We will create a method called verifyPassword to verify that the cookie has been set from the previously visited index.php or mail.php file. If the cookie has been set, we check to see if its value is equivalent to the PasswordManagers local $pass property after it has been encrypted with the md5 method. This will help ensure that the cookie is not only present, but has not been altered or fabricated by a hacker. If the verification passes, we will return a Boolean of true, otherwise, we will return a Boolean of false. Listing 23.5 shows this method and the code we have just covered.

Listing 23.5   **Creating a Method to Verify the Password (PasswordManager.class.php)**

```
public function verfiyPassword()
{
    if($_COOKIE["uid"] == md5($this->pass))
    {
        return true;
    }
    else
    {
        return false;
    }
}
```

To put this method to use, we will add it to the serviceConnector.php file. This file will need to include the PasswordManager object in order to use the verifyPassword method. After the object has been included, we will get the instance of the PasswordManager and call the verifyPassword method. We will then check to see whether or not the verification was a success based on the Boolean that is returned from the method. If the verification is a success, we move forward by making the request and return the response from the server side method that is called, otherwise, we return a string that states "Access denied." Take a look at Listing 23.6 to see how this code is written in the serviceConnector.php file.

Listing 23.6   **Verifying the Password in the Service Connector (serviceConnector.php)**

```php
<?php

require_once("classes/security/PasswordManager.class.php");
$pwManager = PasswordManager::getInstance();

if($pwManager->verfiyPassword())
{
    header("Content-Type: application/xml; charset=UTF-8");

    require_once("classes/UserManager.class.php");
    require_once("classes/Email.class.php");

    $o = new $_GET['object']();
    echo $o->$_GET['method']( $_GET['params'] );
}
else
{
    echo "Access denied";
}


?>
```

Now that we have a secure request model setup, you can test it by copying the URL of a request and pasting it into a browser that has not had the cookie set. The response will be "Access denied" because the cookie needs to exist in order to make a request in our application and the only way that the cookie can be set is by accessing the application that uses it. I have set the cookie to expire in one day so that a user can be logged into one page and make changes via Ajax requests for a day without loosing the cookie. The only time the cookie resets is if the page is refreshed or upon the first entrance to the application. The one part that could be improved in this model is adding a way to log the user out if they make a request and the cookie is no longer available, but I am leaving that part up to you.

Although database-enabled XHRs are fairly easy to accomplish, we must keep in mind that they can be very insecure if we do not appropriately secure them. The object in this chapter is just an example of how you can secure your requests. Other methods can easily be added to the PasswordManager in order to add more encryption to the passwords and so on. Remember that with great power comes great responsibility, and it is important to secure the requests on both the client and server sides.

24

Best Practices

At this point, you know how to create an object-oriented Ajax engine, create Ajax-enabled components, and tie together all the code to create database-enabled XHRs. With this knowledge fresh in your mind, it is a good time to get an understanding of some basic best practices as to when, how, and why to use Ajax based on the examples we have covered throughout the book. Although Ajax can create great effects and amazing interactions that don't refresh the browser, this does not mean that it should be used in every situation. I strongly believe that the technology should always be chosen after a solution has been engineered. If this rule is followed, the technology chosen will most often be the best solution to the problem.

This chapter will recap the key concepts covered throughout the book and explain best practices for each. Let's get started by talking about the Ajax engine.

Using the Engine

The Ajax engine we built in Part II, "Creating and Using the JavaScript Engine," provided us with a reusable and versatile set of JavaScript objects that can be used in any Ajax-enabled project. I personally use the engine for all Ajax interactions I create because the engine provides reusable functionality that can be utilized without alterations in any project, from small websites to large-scale applications. It eliminates the need to rewrite code each time Ajax is used, which saves on development time and ultimately eliminates the need to debug this area of the application because it doesn't need to change from one application to the next.

Aside from being a flexible and reusable object, the engine and all the other components and front-end JavaScript logic are encapsulated into objects. Objects are much easier to maintain because all your code is separated and distinguishable—that is, of course, if you create meaningful object names. It also keeps all your code out of the main page, leaving only the objects to import as in other programming languages.

Design Patterns

Design patterns solve common programming problems. On the one hand, they are extremely useful and eliminate the need to produce code work-arounds. On the other hand, they are not always necessary and should not be used unless they are needed to satisfy a specific problem. The most commonly used patterns are the Singleton and the Model View Controller because they help solve structural problems that arise in almost every object-oriented web application.

Using Components

The components we built in Part III, "Creating Reusable Components," provide a few examples of how to build your own custom components and connect them with the Ajax engine and server-side data. With this knowledge, it is possible to move forward building your own custom components to be used in multiple projects and save you development time. Components provide base functionality that can be shared as open source or across multiple applications. The great thing about the components we made in this book is that the design can easily be tweaked based on the fact that the components rely solely on CSS. Relying on CSS is always a solution that will pay off because the look of a component can be completely changed based on different CSS classes and styles that we define, making them very flexible and company specific to follow branding guidelines and so on.

Static Versus Dynamic Responses

Static responses are XML or JSON files that reside on the server, which are not generated based on dynamic data from a database or third-party source. Dynamic responses are the opposite, meaning that they are based on fluid, changing data from a database, for example. Static responses are sometimes the only option you have regardless of the best solution, such as when a client does not have a database or the ability to use a server-side language on her server. In these cases, it is usually more feasible to use XML because if a client is updating the content, it is a much easier language to understand. Static XML or JSON should be used for small single websites that do not need to be updated on a regular basis. XML is also the best cross-application language such as when trying to connect with application APIs or web services.

When creating XML or JSON responses, it is always a best practice to provide the structure with informative names for elements while keeping it as abstract as possible. Keeping the structure abstract is a great way to provide a flexible and reusable response that can easily be parsed by yourself or other developers.

Dynamic responses are the best solution for web applications or even large websites in which a client wants to maintain the content, such as with a content management system.

Error and Feedback Handling

As a developer, I know the time it takes to consider every possible situation in which a message will need to be displayed to a user. Whether it is an error or a successful message that you need to display, it is time-consuming to write the code to handle each and every case. On the bright side, with the reusable JavaScript `Dialog` object from Chapter 19, "Usability Patterns," we can easily use it instead of an alert, which is what most developers use anyway because of its simplicity. The `Dialog` object is a good solution for handling all of our front-end messages because it is as simple as writing one line of code in order to use it. Another reason why this object allows us to easily follow best practices is because it keeps our messages consistent in look and feel. Keeping a consistent design for each different type of message will make your application much more intuitive.

Aside from the messages that can occur during the runtime of our applications, we must also be prepared if a user simply does not have the required technologies needed to view our application. Even more important than displaying these messages is making sure that the messages are clear and informative, or simply trying to avoid them in the first place by offering alternatives utilizing the `HTTP` object we created as an extension of the Ajax engine in Chapter 9, "Extending the Engine." If a message is unavoidable, such as when the user does not have JavaScript, be sure to provide information as to what happened and what to do in order to move forward with using our application. It is important to remember that we are building applications for the users. If they are not capable of understanding how to use our applications, all our hard work goes unused—so always remember the users and work to their advantage.

Application History

The `History` object we created in Chapter 18, "Interaction Patterns," is very useful in web applications because it can be used in a number of ways to make the user experience much more intuitive. One way in which this object makes the process more intuitive is by providing users with the most recent options they have chosen. Most users have a specific set of needs for using an application, and this object allows them to not have to make as many decisions each time they enter the application. The object we created simply saves the state of specific tasks to a client-side cookie with JavaScript, but ultimately would be much more powerful if it connected to the Ajax engine in order to send the data to the server side and store it in a user preferences or user history table in a database.

Security

When making server-side database connections with Ajax, we leave our database wide open. This is a huge problem because someone could simply make the right HTTP request to our application and wipe away data or overwrite it. This is why the security code in Chapter 23, "Securing Your Application," should be a required step in all your database-enabled Ajax web applications and should never be overlooked.

The purpose of the samples in this book is to provide reusable Ajax-enabled code that can be utilized in any web application. Object-oriented JavaScript, an Ajax engine, and all of the server-side classes are perfect examples of how to accomplish creating code for one application that can be ported to another. From all the JavaScript objects to each XML document, we have created code that is abstracted enough to lend itself to the object-oriented model.

Index

B-C